D1643919

MORALITY AND WAR

MORALITY AND WAR

CAN WAR BE JUST IN THE TWENTY-FIRST CENTURY?

DAVID FISHER

OXFORD

UNIVERSITY PRESS

172.42
FIS

OXFORD
UNIVERSITY PRESS

Great Clarendon Street, Oxford OX2 6DP

Oxford University Press is a department of the University of Oxford.
It furthers the University's objective of excellence in research, scholarship,
and education by publishing worldwide in

Oxford New York

Auckland Cape Town Dar es Salaam Hong Kong Karachi
Kuala Lumpur Madrid Melbourne Mexico City Nairobi
New Delhi Shanghai Taipei Toronto

With offices in

Argentina Austria Brazil Chile Czech Republic France Greece
Guatemala Hungary Italy Japan Poland Portugal Singapore
South Korea Switzerland Thailand Turkey Ukraine Vietnam

Oxford is a registered trade mark of Oxford University Press
in the UK and in certain other countries

Published in the United States
by Oxford University Press Inc., New York

© David Fisher 2011

The moral rights of the author David Fisher 2010 have been asserted
Database right Oxford University Press (maker)

First published 2011

British Library Cataloguing in Publication Data

Data available

Library of Congress Cataloging in Publication Data

Library of Congress Control Number: 2010937007

Typeset by SPI Publisher Services, Pondicherry, India
Printed in Great Britain
on acid-free paper by
MPG Books Group, Bodmin and King's Lynn

ISBN 978-0-19-959924-0

1 3 5 7 9 10 8 6 4 2

To Sophia

Foreword

The philosopher Immanuel Kant, in discussing the prevention of war and the preservation of peace, distinguished between the philosophers who proposed solutions to the world's problems and the bureaucrats who in practice had to deal with them. The bureaucrats, he said, should listen carefully to the philosophers, but the philosophers should respect the responsibilities of the bureaucrats.

David Fisher has the advantage of being both. He gained a double first in Mods and Greats at Oxford, perhaps the most demanding academic discipline in the United Kingdom if not the world, and there he learned the Aristotelian rigour and lucidity in argument so evident in the following pages. Had he so wished, he could have had an outstanding academic career. As it is, he has spent his life as a civil servant in the Ministry of Defence, eventually becoming senior defence adviser to the Cabinet Office and Defence Counsellor at NATO—roles in which he helped shape the complex political decisions involved in the ending of the Cold War and the Balkan crises of the 1990s. He has been a doer as well as a thinker, and that experience is reflected in every line of this book.

Fisher's thesis is as simple as it is important. There has been much discussion during the last decade about the morality of war in general and the Iraq War in particular, but it has been very largely based on conclusions that medieval theologians derived from a universally accepted moral framework that has now very largely disappeared. Today it is not enough to set out criteria of *jus ad bellum* and *jus in bello* formulated by Augustine or Aquinas and then just 'tick the boxes' for whatever war we may be contemplating or waging. Both society and warfare have changed too much. Decisions for war and peace are no longer made by princes but by democratic assemblies responsible to public opinion. Responsibility for actions within war must rest with those who carry them out, not just those who ordered them. The applicable moral criteria are not conjured up by a specific military situation: they have to be derived from universal social norms. Once, they were those of Christendom as a whole. But where can we seek them today?

That is the huge question that Fisher sets himself to answer, and he does so lucidly and comprehensively. He explores the roots of individual and social morality in order to provide the necessary framework for his specific prescriptions. In doing so he reaches back beyond the familiar doctrines of Aquinas to the almost forgotten Aristotelian concept of 'virtues' as the ground for personal and social behaviour. He emphasizes the need, in war as in peace, not simply to obey the rules, but to internalize the moral obligations from which the rules are derived. Morality, he makes clear, is not just a constraint on the conduct of war, any more than it is on social behaviour in general. It is an entire dimension of the world in which war, like any other social activity, exists.

It is perhaps no accident that David Fisher rates chief among those virtues that of 'practical wisdom'—'the habit of sound judgement about practical situations'. The bureaucrat in Fisher knows that the moral choices he may propose as a philosopher will be judged by their consequences in the real world rather than by their ethical purity. Only such a virtue can guide both soldiers and statesmen through the moral dilemmas that will beset them with every decision they have to make, and enable them, as he neatly puts it, 'to make war just, and to make only just war'.

Reading this book will do both philosophers and bureaucrats a world of good.

Michael Howard

PROFESSOR SIR MICHAEL HOWARD OM CH CBE MC is co-founder and President Emeritus of the International Institute for Strategic Studies; formerly Regius Professor of Modern History, Oxford University; Professor of Military and Naval History, Yale University; and Professor and founder of the Department of War Studies at King's College, London.

Acknowledgments

The book was written as a Ph.D. thesis undertaken in the Department of War Studies at Kings College, London, and so I should like to record my especial thanks to my supervisor, Dr Barrie Paskins. My thanks go also to Professor Mervyn Frost and my examiners, Professor Sir Lawrence Freedman and Professor Nigel Biggar, particularly the latter for his help and encouragement in turning the thesis into a book. Such was the proximate origin of the book. But it is also the product of a lifetime's reflection on the ethics of war and peace, drawing on my experience as a senior official in the UK Ministry of Defence and discussion with many friends and colleagues, not least in the amicable forum of the Council on Christian Approaches to Defence and Disarmament. I should like to record especial gratitude to Hugh Beach, Tony Colclough, Paul Cornish, Michael Howard, Keith Maslin, Frank Roberts, and Brian Wicker. I should also like to record my debt to the late Sir Michael Quinlan, who encouraged me to embark on this project and from whose help and encouragement over many years I have profited enormously. Above all, my thanks go to my wife, Sophia, for her wise and patient support of my labours.

Contents

Introduction:

A New Look at an Old Tradition

B ooks about just war have usually been written, if at all, by theologians or philosophers. I trained as a moral philosopher but have spent my career, as a senior official in the British Ministry of Defence, dealing with war. The questions on the morality of war to which I seek answers in this book are for me not just academic issues but the real-life problems with which I have wrestled in the course of my professional duty.

For most of this time, apart from sporadic bouts of concern over nuclear weapons, public discussion of morality and war has been muted. It is a surprising feature of contemporary political discourse that it has become, if not fashionable, at least respectable to discuss the morality of war. Since war can cause immense human suffering, it is hardly unexpected that this should be an area of acute moral concern. But what is surprising is that this discussion is being conducted using concepts and principles borrowed from the medieval theory of a just war. Just war concepts have become part of our vocabulary in discussing war, with even politicians, at times, employing the language of just war. We criticize politicians for taking us to war in Iraq without just cause. We berate the unjust behaviour of our soldiers on the streets of Basra in ill-treating civilian detainees.

This revival of interest in the medieval Christian just war tradition is welcome. The tradition—having flourished in the Middle Ages and reached its zenith in the sixteenth and seventeenth centuries—had been largely lost to sight until its rediscovery in the second half of the twentieth century. When I first wrote a book on just war twenty-five years ago, just war thinking was a minority interest, primarily the preserve of bishops and theologians.[1] Its use was mainly confined, as was my book, to grappling with the problems posed by the ethics of nuclear deterrence on which public debate was then raging. Just war thinking is no longer confined to the seminaries and the nuclear theologians. It is being employed widely in a predominantly secular context to discuss all kinds of war. Despite its antique origins, the just war tradition has proved a valuable tool for thinking about the morality of war in contemporary debates.

The just war tradition was never a fixed set of doctrines but rather a way of thinking about war that has evolved as war itself has changed. As we address the security concerns of the twenty-first century, further development of the tradition is now needed, if it is to continue to furnish a robust source of guidance to those facing the difficult decisions of peace and war with which we are confronted.

The first challenge to the tradition arises from the way its principles have become detached from their theological context and are now being employed in secular debate without the support of ecclesiastical authority or any wider philosophical or theological underpinning. One of the most widely read secular introductions to just war thinking is Michael Walzer's *Just and Unjust Wars* written in the 1970s, in part as a critique of the Vietnam War. Walzer describes his book as 'a moral argument with historical illustrations'.[2] Walzer admirably demonstrates the utility of just war principles in discussing historical examples, but he does not offer any systematic justification for the principles themselves. Nor is this perhaps surprising, since moral philosophers in the twentieth and twenty-first centuries have been generally rather sceptical about the possibility of providing any rational or objective grounding to morality. Decades of philosophical scepticism have gradually seeped throughout society, inducing a general diffidence about our moral beliefs and consequent reticence about the claims of morality. In international relations the prevalent school has been that of the realists for whom morality is a matter of private choice and preference. Inter-state relations are treated as an ethically free zone in which considerations of realpolitik and the pursuit of power dominate.

Moral scepticism is not the preserve of academics but has spread widely throughout society. Richard Layard, the economist and adviser to the British government, observed in an interview in 2008 that there has been 'a catastrophic failure to develop a secular morality. People find it hard to talk about moral issues.'[3] Reluctant to discuss morality, we are still less confident of our ability to teach it.

Moral scepticism presents a direct and immediate challenge to just war thinking. For, if we are moral sceptics elsewhere in our thinking, how can we be moral rationalists when it comes to thinking about war? If there is no secure rational basis for moral principles, in general, then we may doubt there is such a basis for the just war principles, in particular. But why then do we need to obey them? The just war principles seem to be left floating free, unsupported by wider philosophical argument, the product of a local (Western) tradition, lacking wider, still less universal, appeal. As a result, the just war enterprise begins to look fragile: 'a flawed and problematic survivor from earlier times', in the words of one commentator.[4] It also becomes vulnerable to unscrupulous political or military leaders who seek to pick and choose the principles that suit them and discard those that do not.

This is not just a theoretical challenge to just war thinking but an intensely practical challenge for our military. We expect our soldiers to behave morally, but, as a Head of the British Army has recently complained, when they are recruited into the Army today, they may have received no moral teaching from their family or the wider community.[5] This is not a problem that can be solved by teaching recruits once they have signed up. For, quite apart from the difficulty of knowing what they should be taught in the absence of any consensus on morality within society, it is impractical to suppose that the military could operate ethically within a wider moral vacuum, without support and guidance from the society from which they are drawn and whose interests they are called upon to serve.

If the just war tradition is to provide the robust guidance that we require, our first task is to respond to the challenge set by moral scepticism. We need to furnish a rational basis for our moral thinking both in general and, in particular, in relation to the difficult issues of war and peace. To be able to write a book about morality and war, it is necessary first to secure the foundations of morality.

The next challenge is to ensure that just war teaching reaches out to provide guidance to all those who may be involved in decisions on peace and war. We need to broaden the audience at which just war teaching is aimed. For the medieval just war theorists, the teaching was aimed primarily at the princes and rulers who took the fateful decisions on war and peace. When just war thinking was revived to assist the debate on nuclear deterrence during the 1960s to 1980s, the target audience was again primarily the political and military leaders who took the decisions on nuclear deterrence. This was not unreasonable, since the operation of nuclear deterrence, while it affected the lives of millions, was, unusually in the annals of warfare, conducted by an extremely small elite.

With the ending of the Cold War and the rediscovery of the utility of conventional force, war has once more become the occupation, as well as the preoccupation, of many. It is a feature of the way conventional wars are fought today that responsibility is being devolved to ever lower levels. Strategists talk of a 'Three Block War' in which operations can shift within the same space and timescale from war-fighting through peace support to humanitarian missions. Those taking key decisions of life and death in such variegated warfare may be junior personnel, like the so-called strategic corporal. Decisions taken at the tactical level can have profound strategic significance. The strategic objectives of a humanitarian mission can be undermined by the unethical behaviour of a few soldiers on the ground, as we have seen in Iraq. We need not just politicians and generals but our ordinary service people to become adept in just war doctrine. Just war teaching needs to provide guidance to all those involved in war, from the highest to the lowest level. We should require that our political and military leaders are schooled in just war doctrine, whose counsels should ring out in their Cabinet war rooms. The wisdom of the just war tradition needs not only to be expounded in the officers' classroom but also to be embedded in the daily practice and experience of the barracks and battlefield.

This leads to the third, closely related, challenge. This is how to ensure that our politicians and soldiers are not only familiar with just war teaching but behave justly. Just war doctrine, as it emerged from the pens of the lawyers and juridically minded theologians of the sixteenth and seventeenth centuries, was conceived as a set of rules to be followed. A moral rule book is necessary for the ethical behaviour of those involved with war. But rules alone are not sufficient to ensure that the right decisions are taken before, during, and after war.

All those involved in decisions about peace and war—from the politicians, generals, and civil servants at the highest level down to the ordinary soldiers, sailors, and airmen and women—need to have been trained to confront the moral challenges they face with the appropriate beliefs, desires, and feelings and to have acquired a habit of sound reasoning in practical matters. They need to have been schooled in the virtues so that ethical conduct becomes for them second nature, as deeply engrained as habits of thought and action as may be the drills with which the soldiers wield their weapons. Only thus will there be any prospect that the right decisions will be taken in the heat and passion of war. The virtues—lost in recent just war teaching—need to be rediscovered and reintegrated within the just war tradition, as they had been in the thirteenth-century teachings of Aquinas. Practical wisdom is no longer, as Aquinas taught, the prerequisite of princes and generals. It is required, along with the other virtues, of all those involved—at all levels—in the conduct of war.

In order to address these three interrelated challenges to the just war tradition, I seek in Part One of this book to develop an ethical framework that brings together conceptual insights from a number of different and, indeed, rival current schools of ethics. On the one hand are the moral absolutists and virtue ethicists, who agree among themselves that what matters are the interior qualities of our moral actions but disagree as to whether the key moral features are the rules under which the actions fall or the virtues displayed in the actions. As against both of these are the consequentialists, who hold that it is mistaken so to extol the personal integrity of the agent and that all that matters—or all that really matters—are the consequences of actions. I argue that each of these theories is partly right but each is profoundly wrong. Adherents of the theories are right in perceiving that intentions, rules, consequences, or virtues are important to our moral lives. But they are wrong in failing to recognize that all these features are important and instead supposing that their own preferred ethical feature is all that matters, or at least what matters most, in our moral decisions. Virtuous consequentialism—as I call this ethical framework—insists rather that the complexity and challenge of our moral lives, in both the private and public realms, can be properly addressed and our ethical beliefs soundly grounded only if we give appropriate weight to all facets of moral agency. This includes both the internal qualities and external consequences of our actions, as well as the principles that guide those actions and the virtues needed to enact the principles in our daily lives.

Part One aims to establish a robust ethical framework to support and reinforce the just war principles and to provide guidance in their application and implementation. Just war teaching, as developed in Part One, is then put to work in Part Two to address a number of current security challenges.

One challenge I do not address is that posed by nuclear deterrence. This is not because I do not recognize the immense ethical difficulties presented by nuclear deterrence. But I have written about these elsewhere and I wish in this book to broaden the just war debate away from the nuclear field, to which much of the argument in recent years has been devoted.[6] With the end of the Cold War, the salience of nuclear deterrence in Western security policies has also much declined, while that of conventional warfare has increased. Many of the most pressing contemporary ethical issues arise from the bewildering variety of conventional conflicts currently being waged.

In considering the changing nature of war, I question the current fashion for talking about the 'new wars' that have replaced the old model of industrial inter-state war. War is a protean monster that regularly changes its nature. We need to avoid the pitfall of planning for the next war on the basis of the last. But it is as mistaken to suppose that the latest protean mutation of war is the form war will henceforth take, as it was for those traditionalists who supposed that the paradigm of industrial inter-state war, for which they had trained, would itself dominate for ever. Many of the so-called new wars also bear uncanny resemblance to old wars. If we always redescribe the challenges we face as if they were entirely novel, we risk failing to learn lessons from our past. We risk making a similar mistake to that of the American military planners who shredded their manuals on counter-insurgency operations as they left Vietnam, only to have to rein-vent them—painfully and belatedly—to guide current counter-insurgency operations in Iraq and Afghanistan. The just war tradition is a historical tradition. The practical wisdom needed to discern how just war principles are to be applied to resolve particular security dilemmas may require the judicious exercise of historical insight.

Following the attacks on New York and Washington on 11 September 2001, we now face the threat posed by al-Qaeda and other terrorist groups, operating with global networks and potentially armed with weapons of mass destruction. To counter these 'new' threats US policy-makers and com-mentators have argued that extreme times justify extreme measures. These include new methods of interrogation to uncover terrorist plots and pre-emptive military action to forestall them. Just war thinking would license neither the new US doctrine of pre-emption nor the new interrogation techniques for terrorist suspects held in Guantanamo Bay or elsewhere. The methods employed, while hailed as 'new', look, in any case, very like the old interrogation in-depth techniques employed briefly in Northern Ireland and banned by the British government in 1972.

Lack of historical insight, including a curious amnesia over the difficulties attendant upon previous imperial occupations of Iraq, was one of the many failings of the coalition forces in the Second Gulf War. The inception, conduct, and conclusion of the war are examined, in comparison with the First Gulf War, and both wars are assessed against the just war criteria. I conclude that the Second Gulf War was as unjust as the First Gulf War was just. From this conclusion it does not, however, follow that coalition forces should be now precipitately withdrawn, with as careless a disregard for consequences as was shown when they invaded. But, while the Second Gulf War is condemned as unjust, I argue that just war teaching would permit, and may even require, humanitarian intervention where the threat to the lives of innocents is sufficiently grave. The case for humanitarian intervention is reforged in the light of our experiences of intervening unjustly in Iraq.

With the ending of the strategic certainties and moral clarity of the Cold-War period, we have entered a challenging period of confusion and change. Wars are now undertaken more from choice than the necessity of territorial defence. The need for moral clarity over when, where, and how to start, conduct, and conclude war has never been greater. The challenge for politicians, the military, and ourselves as citizens is to make war just and to make only just war. The book concludes that the just war tradition, as developed, provides not only a robust but an indispensable guide for addressing the security challenges of the twenty-first century.

PART ONE

Morality

ONE

War without Morality

The realist case

This book is about war and morality. But there are powerful arguments for saying that war and morality have—and should have—nothing to do with each other. As Theodore Draper remarked in the debate on nuclear weapons: 'If we should bite off our tongues before uttering one word in this discussion that word is "morality".'[1]

This view is known as realism. In its most extensive form its proponents believe that relations between states, in general, and warlike relations, in particular, are governed not by morality but by realpolitik: a 'policy of placing the material greatness and success of one's own nation before all other considerations'.[2]

There are two main variants of the realist argument on war: all-out realism, which maintains that moral considerations are irrelevant to all considerations of war—before, during, and after; and a more modest claim that, while moral considerations may affect the decision to go to war, once the decision is made, morality is irrelevant. Military necessity—whatever is necessary to achieve victory—then takes over.

Thucydides' realism

A powerful exposition of all-out realism is given by Thucydides in his history of the Peloponnesian War between Athens and Sparta. The war lasted twenty-seven years from 431 to 404 BC. It ended with the crushing defeat of Athens and Athenian democracy. Thucydides expounds the realist view with brutal clarity in the Melian Dialogue in book 5 of his history.

Fifteen years into the war, in 416 BC, Athens, still confident of eventual success, is seeking to consolidate its maritime supremacy by bringing under its control any islands in the eastern Mediterranean not yet within its empire. One such island is Melos, a former colony of Sparta, which declines Athens' invitation to become its subject. Athens despatches a military force to coerce its subjugation. Before embarking on military action, the Athenian generals—Cleomedes and Tisias—invite the Melians to take part in a 'dialogue'.

The Athenians set the terms for the dialogue by saying that they will use no fine words to justify their action on moral grounds. They want rather a 'practical discussion' with the Melians, noting that: 'When these matters are discussed by practical people, the standard of justice depends on the equality of power to compel and in fact the strong do what they have the power to do and the weak accept what they have to accept.'[3] The discussion is not to be about morality but about the exercise of power.

The Melians have no choice but to accept the terms set for the dialogue and put up a brave defence of their position. They ask why they cannot become neutrals rather than subjects. The Athenians brush this request aside, arguing that it would be interpreted by others as a sign of Athenian weakness. The Melians then plead for the Athenians to spare them, arguing that the gods will favour the cause of Melos, while their relative weakness in power will be compensated by the arrival of Spartan assistance.

The Athenians caution the Melians not to count on the Spartans, who are unlikely to risk running up against Athenian maritime supremacy to come to their aid. As for the gods:

> Our opinion of the gods and our knowledge of men lead us to conclude that it is a general and necessary law of nature to rule wherever one can. This is not a law that we made ourselves, nor were we the first to act upon it when it was made. We found it already in existence, and we shall leave it to exist forever among those who come after us.[4]

The Athenians invite the Melians to accept the very reasonable terms on offer—'an alliance on a tribute-paying basis and liberty to enjoy your own property.'[5] The Athenians offer a few final words of advice: 'This is the safe rule—to stand up to one's equals, to behave with deference towards one's superiors and to treat one's inferiors with moderation.'[6]

The Melians decline this advice, and Athens lays siege to their city. As the Athenians had forecast, Sparta fails to come to the aid of the Melians.

Nonetheless, at first, the Melians have some military successes. But the tide is turned against them by internal treachery within their ranks. The Melians are obliged to surrender to the Athenians, 'who put to death all the men of military age whom they took and sold the women and children into slavery. Melos itself they took over for themselves sending out later a colony of 500 men.'[7]

The Melian Dialogue is often presented by commentators as if it represented an entirely aberrant view on the part of the Athenians. It is held to exemplify—fifteen years into the war—'the general deterioration in character throughout the Greek world'[8] that earlier in his history Thucydides had noted was brought about by war, 'the harsh teacher'.[9] Indeed, so shocked by the Athenian sentiments was the ancient commentator, Dionysius, that he was convinced the dialogue was a work of fiction. The Athenians would not have spoken thus. 'Such words would be appropriate to an oriental monarch addressing Greeks.'[10] Michael Walzer similarly claims that the Athenian generals at Melos, 'speak as generals have rarely done in military history'.[11]

In fact, the sentiments expressed in the dialogue are not at all aberrant but are echoed in similar words by politicians and generals throughout Thucydides' history. A few examples will illustrate this.

At the start of Book 1 Thucydides gives a brief account of the growth of states from the earliest times to substantiate his claim that the Peloponnesian War was the greatest known to date.[12] His account takes it as axiomatic that the growth and development of relations between states is governed by the pursuit of power—*arche*. For example, Crete's maritime empire under King Minos was achieved since 'the weaker because of the general desire to make profits were content to put up with being governed by the stronger'.[13]

In 432 BC the Spartans held a council to decide whether or not to go to war with Athens. Athenian delegates were invited to attend. These delegates, speaking before the onset of war and its harsh discipline, provide a robust defence of Athenian imperialism, in words reminiscent of the Melian Dialogue. They explain why they cannot give up their empire:

> Three very powerful motives prevent us from doing so—security, honour and self-interest. And we were not the first to act in this way. Far from it. It has always been a rule that the weak should be subject to the strong...Considerations of morality have never yet turned people aside from opportunities of aggrandisement offered by superior strength.[14]

At the end of the first year of the war, Pericles, the Athenian leader, delivered a funeral oration to honour those who had died in the war. Rather than praising the dead, he famously delivered an encomium of Athenian democracy, 'an education to Greece'.[15] He concluded by inviting his fellow Athenians to 'fix your eyes everyday on the power of Athens and become her lovers'.[16] Even for the great Pericles power is the supreme motive.

Nor is this sentiment confined to Athenians. At the Congress of Gela called in 424 BC by some of the Sicilian states to consider whether to accept Athenian offers of alliance, Hermocrates of Syracuse advises them not to do so. But he frankly concedes Athens' right to seek to expand its power: 'For men in general it is always just as natural to take control where there is no resistance as to stand out against aggression.'[17]

Finally, in 413 BC after the defeat of the Athenian expeditionary force that had been sent to conquer Sicily, the Athenian general Nicias urges the demoralized Athenian troops on to one final effort. He says they should not fear divine retribution for their aggression; for in this they were simply 'doing what men do'.[18]

Judged by what other generals and politicians in his history say, Thucydides would not have regarded the realist sentiments expressed by the Athenians at Melos as, in any way, aberrant. For such realism pervades his whole account of the war. Nor does Thucydides ever offer any explicit condemnation of the Athenian actions nor of the harshness of the sentence carried out at Melos. Nonetheless, we can perhaps deduce that Thucydides would not have approved of the sentence from the parallels between what he records happening at Melos and what had happened—or not happened—eleven years earlier at Mytilene.

In 428 BC Mytilene led a revolt of cities on the island of Lesbos against Athens. This rebellion was not quelled until the following year and rattled the Athenians, not least since Mytilene had been an ally of Athens. A decree was passed in the assembly of the Athenian people condemning all the men to death and the women and children to slavery: the same sentence as at Melos. But the next day the Athenians felt uneasy at the harshness of this sentence and the debate was reopened in the assembly.

Cleon argues that the penalty should stick. To change their minds would be seen as a sign of weakness and the death penalty was necessary to deter other allies from revolt. 'The only alternative is to surrender your empire, so that you can afford to go in for philanthropy.'[19]

In his response, Diodotus resists arguing on moral grounds: 'This is not a law-court, where we have to consider what is fit and just; it is a political assembly, and the question is how Mytilene can be most useful to Athens.'[20]

He rejects Cleon's arguments for deterrence, noting that the death penalty attached to many lesser crimes fails to dissuade would-be criminals, since they always think they can get away with it. Such a harsh penalty would encourage rebels to hold out to the end, since they had nothing to lose. Only the guilty should be punished. Punishing the innocent democrats, as well as the guilty oligarchs, could provoke more rebellions by alienating the democrats in other states who would normally support Athens. Acting with moderation is the most effective way to preserve the empire.

By a narrow vote Diodotus wins the day and a trireme is immediately despatched to countermand the sentence previously issued. It arrives just as the sentence is being read out: 'So narrow had been the escape of Mytilene.'[21]

What is striking about the Athenians' debate on the fate of Mytilene is the lack of any moral arguments against the sentence. It is not a debate between morality and realism. It is rather a debate between two realists about how best to maintain Athenian power. The view that prevails over the fate of Mytilene—but not of Melos—is that the exercise of power without excess is the best way to preserve the empire. We are reminded of the Athenians' advice to the Melians that 'the safe rule' is 'to treat one's inferiors with moderation'. It was this advice that the Athenians at Melos failed to follow.

Thucydides' charge against the Athenians at Melos is not that they acted immorally but that they were bad realists. They did not act in the best interests of Athenian imperialism. That is precisely the charge that Thucydides levelled against all the Athenian leaders who succeeded Pericles after his death from the plague in 429 BC. Pericles had urged the city of Athens to prosecute the wars cautiously. Victory would be won by Athens:

> if she avoided trying to add to empire during the course of the war, and if she did nothing to risk the safety of the city itself. But his successors did the exact opposite, and in other matters which had apparently no connexion with the war private ambition and private profit led to policies which were bad for the Athenians themselves and their allies.[22]

The chief of these errors, in Thucydides' view, was the decision in 415 BC to embark upon a major war of aggression against Sicily with the war against Sparta not yet concluded: precisely the war on two fronts against which

Pericles had warned. The Sicilian expedition—significantly recorded by Thucydides immediately after his account of the events at Melos—ended in 413 BC with the ignominious defeat of the Athenian expeditionary force in the bloodstained waters of the River Assinarus.

Thucydides' realism is consistent throughout his history. It is a thorough-going realism applying not just to all stages of war but to international relations generally. Morality is a matter for personal relations between individuals, like the individual souls that Thucydides records visiting sick friends and relatives smitten with the plague, even at the near-certain risk of catching and dying from it themselves.[23] But in international relations, where power is unequally distributed, morality has no purchase. States pursue their own national interests and the strong rule wherever they can. This is not a doctrine that Might is Right. It is rather the view that Right is irrelevant. Might just is what everywhere prevails.

This doctrine is not an antique theory of little interest for the modern era. Realism is alive and flourishing today.

Thucydides' world view was introduced into the modern era by Hobbes, who in 1651 translated Thucydides' *History of the Peloponnesian War*. Hobbes's thinking was deeply influenced by Thucydides. He pictures international relations in starkly Thucydidean terms:

> But though there had never been any time wherein particular men were in a condition of warre one against another; yet in all times Kings, and Persons of Soveraigne authority, because of their Independency, are in continual jealou-sies, and in the state and posture of Gladiators; having their weapons pointing, and their eyes fixed on one another; that is, their forts, Garrisons and Guns, upon the frontiers of their kingdoms; and continual Spyes upon their neigh-bours; which is a posture of warre.[24]

This Hobbesian view of international affairs as a state of lawless anarchy because of the lack of any supranational authority has had much appeal to modern realists.

Modern realism

Modern realism developed, in the immediate aftermath of the Second World War, as a reaction to what George Kennan called 'the legalistic-moralistic approach to international problems', an approach that realists believed had contributed to the failure of the League of Nations to prevent the growth of Nazi power in the 1930s.[25] To avoid the mistakes of the past, a tougher-minded approach was required for the post-war period. This should be based, as Hans Morgenthau—the founding father of the new movement—proclaimed, on a clear recognition that 'statesmen think and act in terms of interest defined as power'.[26] What drives all men is 'an ineradicable lust for power'.[27] The realm of politics is the realm of power. The autonomy of politics should be preserved from subversion by other modes of thought, such as morality. Morality was a luxury in which statesmen could not afford to indulge. Individuals could proclaim '*Fiat Justitia, pereat mundus*' (let justice be done, though the world perish), but no statesman should put at risk the survival of his state for the sake of justice.[28]

As the icy chill of the Cold War froze into apparent perpetual immobility, the rivalry between East and West, the resulting stand-off between the two power blocs, underpinned by mutual nuclear deterrence, seemed to confirm everything the realists had been saying. Realism quickly became the dominant school in international relations, despite the judicious scepticism expressed by critics from the so-called English school such as Hedley Bull.[29] The dominance of realism has persisted, although, as with other schools of thought, rival factions within the school have developed over the years and events such as the ending of the Cold War have provoked serious questioning.

Power has remained for all variants of realism the constant, as the key explanatory variable for understanding the behaviour of states. But for the so-called structural realists, led by Kenneth Waltz, power is to be regarded less as an end in itself and more as a means to the survival of a state. Moreover, what drives the system is not so much—as Morgenthau thought—the power lusts of individual men, as the anarchic structure of the overall international system. So, for Waltz, 'there is a constant possibility of war in a world in which there are two or more states each seeking to promote a set of interests and having no agency above them upon which they can rely for protection'.[30]

The obvious remedy to such anarchy would be to establish a supra-national agency. But neo-realists are as disdainful as their classical realist forebears of the feasibility or desirability of world government. For Waltz the solution rests rather in the establishment of a stable balance of power.

The mere balancing of power is, however, too pusillanimous a solution for those who call themselves 'offensive realists'. For John Mearsheimer, writing—significantly—after the collapse of the Soviet Union, 'The best guarantee of survival is to be a hegemon, since no other state can seriously threaten such a mighty power'.[31] The role of individuals diminishes still further. States are to be viewed like 'black boxes or billiard balls'. It 'does not matter for the theory whether Germany in 1905 was led by Bismark, Kaiser Wilhelm or Adolf Hitler or whether Germany was democratic or autocratic. What matters . . . is how much political power Germany possessed at the time.'[32]

The new realists are a tough-minded breed who tell us how the world is, not how we might wish it to be. We are firmly back in a Thucydidean view of the world, the world of the Melian Dialogue.

Realism offers a powerful antidote to the woolly idealism of the interwar years. As a description of how states often behave, the realist account appears depressingly accurate. The twentieth century furnished only too many examples of strong states attacking and subjugating weaker ones: from Hitler's attacks on Czechoslovakia (1938) and Poland (1939) to the Soviet Union's attacks on Hungary (1956) and Czechoslovakia (1968) to Saddam Hussein's invasion of his weaker neighbour Kuwait in 1990. Nor is the pursuit of power—arche, as Thucydides would say—confined to the villains of history—the tyrants and dictators. British colonial expansion in India and Africa in the eighteenth and nineteenth centuries also illustrated Thucydides' 'general and necessary law of nature to rule wherever one can'.

There is sympathy for the realist view of the world among the British media and political class. It was striking that when a Labour Foreign Secretary, Robin Cook, announced in July 1997 the introduction of an 'ethical foreign policy', this provoked near universal mirthful condemnation in the British media, as if the last thing we would want to do in dealing with foreigners was to be ethical. The motivation for this response was, no doubt, complex. A significant factor may simply have been the media's perception that, once politicians start to talk of morality, banana skins aplenty usually await them, as John Major had found to his cost after launching his 'Back to Basics' moral campaign not long before. But there also appeared to be an implicit presumption that in international relations realpolitik presides and that any attempt by a politician to pretend otherwise was bound to involve hypocrisy, and to be likely to end in failure. The delicious irony was noted that Cook had launched his policy from the Locarno Suite in the Foreign

Office, the very room in which the ill-fated era of collective security had been inaugurated with the signature of the Lucarno Treaty in December 1925. In contrast to such misplaced idealism, *Getting Our Way* was the title of a recent book and TV series by the former British Ambassador, Sir Christopher Meyer, which purported to reveal what international relations were really like and to tell 'the Inside Story of British Diplomacy'.[33]

The realist analysis—in both its Thucydidean and modern forms—has much to commend it. But as an explanatory account for all international behaviour the theory faces a number of difficulties.

First, it is a simplistic, uni-dimensional theory. It uses just one variable—power—to describe and explain the complex and rich field of international relations. It is as if an artist were to essay to paint a colourful carnival scene in Venice with just one colour. States seek to maximize their power but not always. In the interwar years the USA could have played a major role in international affairs but chose not to. States pursue many other ends, such as economic welfare. Moreover, even when states pursue power, other considerations may override this. Defence spending may be curtailed to permit increased expenditure on health or education.

Second, realism, particularly in its structuralist versions, offers too mechanical an explanation of international behaviour. Balances of power are not automatically maintained by the workings of an impersonal international system. They are rather the product of individual decisions by individual people over time. Their maintenance requires the constant care and attention of policy-makers. States are not black boxes or billiard balls. Germany's relative power position may have been important, as Mearsheimer claims, but it is absurd to suggest that, in explaining international events, such as the origins of the Second World War, we can ignore Hitler, his Nazi ideology, or the uncompromising totalitarian nature of his regime.

Moreover, while realism may accurately describe some periods of history, it is less applicable to others. Modern realism was born out of reflection on the interwar years and sustained by contemplation of the growth of the Cold War thereafter. It is less readily applicable to the complex multi-polar world that has emerged from the demise of the Cold War. The suspicion is that here, as elsewhere, analysts may be solving the problem of the previous war, rather than addressing what may happen next.

This seems supported by the way the predictive power of the theory has—as many commentators have noted—been challenged by the collapse of the Soviet regime.[34] It may seem harsh to criticize realists for failing to predict what liberals also failed to foresee. But the criticism sticks more against realists because they did not merely fail to predict the collapse but led us to expect something very different. Waltz, writing in 1988—only a year before the Soviet Union began to implode—proclaimed that the Cold War was 'firmly rooted in the structures of post-war international politics and will last as long as that structure endures'.[35] According to the theory, such a bipolar power balance was stable and enduring and, if change were to occur, this was expected to be through war. The theory was taken by surprise by the peaceful revolution that actually happened. It was the very optimism of the rebirth of Central Europe following the collapse of the Berlin Wall that challenged the pervasive pessimism of realism.

Realism is too impoverished a theory to explain the rich diversity of international life in its totality. But its expurgation of morality from the realm of international affairs may still be justified. Let us consider next why realists think morality irrelevant to international affairs. A number of reasons are advanced.

First, the moral neutrality of the international realm is proclaimed as just a fact. That is how the world is when we remove our rose-tinted spectacles. Politicians, like a British Foreign Secretary, may cloak their motives in moral language, but this is just a charade. As Mearsheimer puts it: 'The pronouncements of the policy elites are heavily flavoured with optimism and moralism. Behind closed doors, however, the elites who make national policy speak mostly the language of power.'[36]

Moreover, if and when morality intrudes into the autonomous realm of politics, it can be positively harmful. Moralists are presented with two horns of an unenviable dilemma: morality is either irrelevant or counter-product-ive. As an example of the latter, Morgenthau quotes the way Britain and France nearly went to war with Russia in 1939 because of their concern that Russia's attack on Finland was in breach of the rules of the League of Nations. Fortunately, Sweden declined to allow British and French forces to pass through its territory. 'If this refusal by Sweden had not saved them, France and Britain would shortly have found themselves at war with the Soviet Union and Germany at the same time.'[37]

The next argument for the lack of purchase of morality in the inter-national realm is that 'moral rules operate within the consciences of individual men'.[38] States are different. They are not individuals. States have responsi-bilities and duties that individuals do not. Individuals can pursue justice even though the heavens fall, but a state, which has a duty to survive, cannot.

States are, furthermore, a precondition of morality. The internal order and external security provided by the state are what make it possible for us to live our lives as ethical agents. States make morality possible. Morality does not, therefore, apply to states. Just so had Stalin remarked in 1927: 'We can and must build socialism in the Soviet Union. But in order to do so we first of all have to exist.'[39]

Finally, it is argued that morality holds between approximate equals, not between states with massively disparate powers. This was the argument of the Athenians at Melos. As Thucydides records their words: 'Into the discussion of human affairs the question of justice only enters where there is equal power to enforce it.'[40] The realm of morality is between individuals who are approximate equals in power. It does not apply between macro- and micro-states.

Let us consider each of these arguments in turn.

First, is it a fact that states never act from moral considerations? The realist rightly underlines the importance of the pursuit of power in international relations. The realist correctly observes that politicians may use the language of morality to cloak their true motives. The language of realpolitik is often heard behind the closed doors of the corridors of power. But it is an exaggeration to suggest that states never act sincerely from considerations of morality or law. Slavery was abolished in the British Empire in 1833 in response to a moral campaign. Pursuit of power may be a key motivator, but, as Hedley Bull judiciously observed, most states obey most rules of international law most of the time.[41]

Indeed, in a democracy a government that goes to war in defiance of morality may lose the consent and support of the people. Democratic armed forces may require assurance that the actions they are being asked to undertake by governments comply with morality and international law. This was evidenced in March 2003 by the request of the British Chief of Defence Staff prior to the engagement of British troops in Iraq for the Attorney General's formal assurance that their actions would comply with international law. Such an assurance was given but far from universally accepted. The consequent persistent doubts over the legality and morality of the military action played a significant part in undermining popular support for the war.

States sometimes act from moral considerations, and governments may face popular condemnation when they do not do so. It is not true that morality is irrelevant. But this still leaves the second half of the dilemma: if morality applies, it may be positively harmful. Whether or not that is so depends on the nature of the moral considerations adduced. The example quoted by Morgenthau of the British and French decision to declare war on Russia in response to its invasion of Finland sets up a simplistic opposition between an unworldly morality and the worldly-wise realist. But the pursuit of national interest is not necessarily immoral nor is it necessarily unrealistic to be moral. Realists talk very little about morality except to dismiss its claims. But what they do say often appears to presume a crude and simplistic notion of the nature of moral reasoning. It will be the aim of this book to establish a framework for moral reasoning, based on the just war tradition, that is imbued with rather more practical wisdom than that of the realist caricature, and that can offer robust guidance both to policy-makers and ordinary service people in considering questions of war and peace.

As for the argument that morality applies to individuals not to states, it is true that states are not individuals. But they are collections of individuals. States are traditionally conceived as the union of political communities and governments. Hedley Bull defines states as 'independent political communities each of which possesses a government and asserts sovereignty in relation to a particular portion of the earth's surface and a particular segment of the human population'.[42] Political communities are made up of individuals, as are the governments who act as their agents in international affairs. If morality applies to individuals, it is difficult to see why it would not apply to the individuals who comprise the state.

States have responsibilities and duties that individuals do not. We, for example, cede to government a monopoly over the use of force and entrust it with the responsibility for providing for our defence and security. But it does not follow from this that states, and the individuals who make them up, are exempted from the claims of morality when they act as states. As individuals, we may have particular responsibilities stemming from the roles or offices we fulfil, such as a mother or a policeman. But these do not, in any way, exempt us from following the general moral code. Just so, the individuals who act on our behalf in international affairs may have public duties to perform. But they are still ethical agents subject to the same moral rules, facing similar ethical dilemmas and employing the same moral reasoning as the rest of us. As we shall explore further in Chapter 7, morality extends as a seamless web from the private into the public realm.

It is argued that states are a precondition of morality. That may be true in a sense, since, as Hobbes noted, states provide a remedy against anarchy. But it is difficult to see why that should exempt states from the claims of morality. We could equally argue that families make morality possible, since without their support during infancy we would never emerge as adult ethical agents. But no one would suggest that this exempts families from morality.

It is, in any case, an exaggeration to say that states make morality possible. It could be claimed rather more plausibly that it is morality that makes states possible. If a political community did not have some shared values, the formation and maintenance of a state would be a very fraught operation. It is, therefore, rather more plausible to suppose that states come into being not simply because of a negative fear of anarchy but also because of a positive desire for community: a shared interest in living together reflected, *inter alia*, in economic, cultural, religious, and social ties and underlain by common moral values. As Michael Walzer observed: 'Not army camps alone, as David Hume wrote, but temples, storehouses, irrigation works and burial grounds are the true mothers of cities.'[43]

Finally, let us examine Thucydides' argument that morality has a purchase between approximate equals only where there is some prospect of enforcing the moral code. This was the claim made by the Athenian generals as they looked down with disdain on the petty power of the Melians.

The Athenians are right to point out that the enforcement of morality may be difficult, or even impossible, where there are gross disparities of power, as in the international arena. Such difficulties can, however, be reduced by changing the international institutional framework. Gross inequalities of power can be neutralized and power balanced by the formation of alliances, as realists delight to tell us. There are also international institutions, like the International Criminal Court, whose role and powers of enforcement could be strengthened, however less delightful that might be for most realists. The difficulties of enforcement are not immutable.

Moreover, even if—as seems likely without a radical restructuring of international relations not currently in prospect—enforcement difficulties will remain, that does not mean that morality has no purchase. Thucydides may have believed this to be so. But, if so, we surely want to protest that Thucydides was wrong. Even if morality cannot be enforced, this does not mean that it no longer applies. The mistake the Athenians made at Melos was not that they were bad realists. They were bad people. They made a moral mistake. They may have exceeded the Melians in power. They may, therefore, have been able to get away with what they did. But they should not have executed all the Melian men and enslaved the women and children, regardless of individual guilt or innocence. What they did at Mytilene, where only the guilty were punished, was right. What they did at Melos was simply wrong.

War is hell

So much for all-out realism. Let us now consider partial realism. The most famous—or infamous—exponent of this doctrine was General Sherman, the victorious Unionist commander of the American Civil War, whose name is for ever associated with the chilling slogan that 'War is hell'.

Atlanta was an important base for the Confederate Army, at the junction of four railways, and, as Sherman noted, 'a fortified town, with magazines, arsenals, foundries and public stores'.[44] After a difficult campaign he finally succeeded in capturing it on 1 September 1864. Shortly afterwards he ordered the forcible evacuation of the city by its inhabitants—by then mainly women and children. On 15 November he burnt down almost the entire city so that it could never again serve as a supply depot for Confederate forces. He then marched on Savannah, with his troops foraging at will and wreaking widespread destruction of civilian property. The trail of devastation was designed in Sherman's words to let the people of Georgia 'see what war meant'.[45]

These actions provoked howls of outrage, not least from the Confederate commander, General Hood. In a letter to Sherman he described the forced evacuation of Atlanta as transcending, 'in studied and ingenious cruelty, all acts ever before brought to my attention in the dark history of war'.[46] In his response, Sherman rounded on Hood, arguing that the blame rested squarely with 'you who, in the midst of peace and prosperity, have plunged a nation into war—dark and cruel war'.[47] Two days later, Sherman responded similarly to the pleas of the Mayor of Atlanta protesting at the 'appalling and heart-rending' consequences of the proposed evacuation.[48] Sherman defended his actions on the grounds that 'war is cruelty and you cannot refine it'. Blame should not be hurled at him who 'had no hand in making this war'. Rather 'those who brought war into our country deserve all the curses and maledictions a people can pour out'. Protesting against the cruelties of war was fruitless: 'You might as well appeal against the thunderstorms as against these terrible hardships of war. They are inevitable.'[49]

Unlike the all-out realist, Sherman is not arguing that moral considerations have nothing to do with war—before, during, and after. On the
contrary, he regards the decision to start the war by the Confederate states
as immoral—'deserving all the curses and maledictions a people can pour
out'—and the North's decision to resist this as morally justified. What he is
claiming is that, once unleashed, war has a momentum and logic of its own,
to which the constraints of morality are irrelevant: 'War is cruelty and you
cannot refine it.' His realism is partial, since he concedes morality applies up
to and including the decision to go to war. It is only thereafter that moral
considerations are swept aside until victory is secured.

War is like a force of nature—a thunderstorm or a forest fire that, once lit,
will rage on with its own energy and violence. Our only priority is to quell
it and to do whatever is necessary to achieve this. The evacuation and
burning of Atlanta may have been distasteful but, in Sherman's view, were
necessary steps towards defeating the Confederate forces. They were necessary not just because of their immediate military utility: they avoided the
need to waste precious troops on garrison duties; and removed Atlanta as a
potential supply base for Confederate troops. But they were also necessary
to send a clear message to the people of the South that the people of the
North 'were in earnest' and so—like the devastating march through Georgia—to bring home to the people the costs of the war they were supporting.[50] By bringing war directly to the people, Sherman presaged modern
industrial war and justly earned Basil Liddell Hart's accolade for him as 'the
prototype of the most modern age'.[51]

For the partial realist it is a foolish mistake to allow moral qualms to
oppose what needs to be done to secure victory and so delay the restoration
of peace. When war starts, morality ends. A general must then do whatever
a general needs to do to secure victory as quickly as possible.

General Sherman's partial realism has often been echoed by politicians
and generals through the ages justifying the unpalatable actions they have
taken during war on grounds of military necessity. The more they are
convinced, like Sherman, of the justice of their cause, so more readily
they may be persuaded to do whatever is necessary to secure victory. Just
so, the need to defeat the monstrous tyranny of Nazism was deemed to
justify the British bombing of German cities that commenced after the
German attack on Coventry in November 1940 and continued through
to the destruction of Dresden in the spring of 1945. 'The bombers alone',
Churchill declared, 'provide the means of victory'.[52]

This argument has even attracted so robust a defender of the claims of morality in war as Michael Walzer. Walzer argued that there may be situations of 'supreme emergency' when the moral rules have to be suspended, a view he summarized as: 'do justice unless the heavens are (really) about to fall.'[53] In his view such a supreme emergency faced Churchill in 1940–2 when the British stood alone against Hitler, although not thereafter, once the USA and Russia had joined in. The bombing of Dresden in 1945 remains condemned. Supreme emergency also faced the West during the prolonged Cold-War stand-off with the Soviet Union. For Walzer, supreme emergency justifies immoral actions, like area bombing or nuclear deterrence.[54]

Partial realism is a more attractive and plausible doctrine than all-out realism, not least because of its more limited scope. It concedes that morality applies to most international relations. It also concedes that it applies—and applies most forcefully—to the fateful decision whether or not to go to war. But, once war has begun, we are then plunged into the realm of military necessity where morality is, at best, irrelevant and, at worst, may be positively counter-productive.

The partial realist relies heavily to develop this argument on the metaphor of war as a natural force that is beyond our control. But this metaphor should not be pressed too far. War is not literally a natural force like a thunderstorm or forest fire. It is rather a complex activity engaged in over time by a large number of human beings who make a multiplicity of decisions and carry out a wide variety of intentional actions. It would seem entirely arbitrary to maintain that only some intentional actions (those leading up to war) are subject to moral appraisal, while others (those undertaken during war) are somehow exempt from moral scrutiny. Indeed, such an arbitrary distinction would seem to subvert the very nature of morality, which governs all human intentional activity.

Nor is it true that war cannot be refined and that the sufferings of war are all equally inevitable. War can be conducted in ways that bring more or less suffering. The decision whether or not to go to war is not the only decision to which morality applies. Morality also applies to the way the war is conducted, and to the way it is brought to an end, where decisions of equal moment to the welfare of human beings may be taken. Moreover, we may make different judgements about the decision to go to war, how the war is conducted, and how the war is concluded. A just war can be fought unjustly. An unjust war can produce good generals like Rommel.

Nor is it self-evident that, if moral considerations are brought to bear, this would inevitably be counter-productive by undermining the military strategy for winning the war. Indeed, as we shall explore in later chapters, with the wars of choice in which we are now engaged, ethical restraint may be necessary to the strategic success of military campaigns. The protection of civilians is a key to winning counter-insurgency operations, while the unethical behaviour of a few soldiers can undermine the humanitarian objectives of a military mission. It is worth noting that Liddell Hart's approval of Sherman's policy of bringing war home to civilians led logically to Hart's subsequent advocacy in the interwar years of city bombing as the way to win wars. But it is far from clear that city bombing in the Second World War achieved this objective. It is arguable that, just like the effect of the Blitz on the people of London, the bombing of German cities hardened the German people's will to resist. Moreover, even if the bombing had broken civilian morale, it was always unclear how this was supposed to induce the political changes required to end the fighting in a totalitarian society from which all political opposition had been banned. Moral qualms may not run counter to military need. The arguments of military necessity require careful scrutiny.

Conclusion

Realism seeks to exclude morality from certain areas of human activity. All-out realism excludes morality from all international relations, including war. Partial realism excludes morality from the conduct of wars.

It is, however, the nature of moral reasoning, as traditionally conceived, that it applies universally, to all intentional human action and activity. Morality is not a private affair between individuals. It applies as much to our public as to our private actions. It applies in our domestic and in our international dealings. Nor does morality end when war begins. There are no moral free zones before, during, or after war; not even—*pace* Michael Walzer—during moments of supreme emergency. Morality is not some optional extra that can be brought in or out—or switched on or off—as it suits us. For it would then be too easy for us to argue for the exceptions that would act in our favour. If morality applies at all, it applies to all our actions.

But in our postmodern liberal society, could we ever agree what that morality should be? To that challenge I turn in the next chapter.

TWO

'Whose Justice? Which Rationality?'[1]

The moral sceptic's case

Realists contend that morality and war have nothing to do with each other. Their view stems, in part, as we have just explored, from a positive belief that that is how the world is. The pursuit of power—not morality—is what impels statesmen to act in the international realm. But the view is also based on a negative view about the limits of morality. This is not a view the realists invented for themselves. It is rather a view that they inherited from the broader intellectual climate of Western society in the twentieth and twenty-first centuries. For it is a widespread presumption of our postmodern society that morality is primarily a private affair between consenting adults. Like religious belief, morality is a matter for our private choices and personal preferences. The prospects for achieving consensus on any kind of publicly agreed morality that could constrain the behaviour of governments, in general, and the warlike behaviour of states, in particular, would appear remote.

Liberal doubts

This view reflects, in part, an impeccable liberal sentiment that we should eschew the cultural imperialism and 'the blanket colonial certainty' of the past.[2] Missionaries may have followed armed forces in the nineteenth century. But in the twenty-first century their roles should be kept entirely separate and distinct. We should not seek to impose our views on others but should rather tolerate and, indeed, welcome a diversity of values, a variety of 'experiments in living'.[3] As the founder of modern liberalism, John Stuart Mill, proclaimed in his great clarion call to the modern age: 'The only purpose for which power can be rightfully exercised over any member of a civilised community, against his will, is to prevent harm to others. His own good, either physical or moral, is not sufficient warrant.'[4] The role of government is to provide and maintain a safe and secure framework within which citizens can freely conduct their own lives; choose their own values; and pursue their own visions of the good life.

Liberal philosophers, such as Michael Walzer and Isaiah Berlin, proclaimed that there was a rich and diverse plurality of such visions of the good life; and no compelling ground for choosing between them. According to Walzer, 'people conceive and create goods'.[5] There is no single overriding standard of justice. Every social good or set of social goods furnishes its own standard for determining what counts as just. The rich diversity of goods is an attractive feature of the liberal vision. What gives pause is the presumed extent of our unconstrained freedom to choose among goods. For Walzer, even the Indian caste system represents a legitimate choice for its participants. For the system provides for the just distribution of goods according to the shared understandings of its Hindu members. So long as those shared understandings persist, there is no external criterion of justice against which the distribution can be criticized.[6] The spheres of justice are plural and autonomous.

For Berlin it is both impractical and a conceptual confusion to suppose that there is a single determinate answer to the perennial question 'How should I live?' Berlin maintained that the primary cause of the great wars and carnage of the twentieth century had been the denial of pluralism in favour of a misplaced ideological and moral certainty. Berlin, therefore, argued for a minimalist 'negative' concept of liberty, as non–interference with others, rejecting any 'positive' concept of liberty. For he was fearful that a positive vision of liberty would let in those who think they have solved the 'cosmic jigsaw puzzle', those who think there is a single answer, a 'final solution' to the question 'How should I live?'[7]

> One belief, more than any other, is responsible for the slaughter of individuals on the altar of the great historical ideals . . . This is the belief that somewhere, in the past or in the future . . . there is a final solution.[8]
> For if one really believes that such a solution is possible, then surely no cost would be too high to obtain it . . . To make such an omelette, there is surely no

limit to the number of eggs that should be broken—that was the faith of
Lenin, of Trotsky, of Marx, for all I know of Pol Pot.[9]

Just as the political realists, as we traced in the previous chapter, had
blamed morality for the failure of the democracies to stand up to the
dictators, so now liberal philosophers were blaming moral and ideological
conviction for the excesses of the dictators. In the face of such criticism, the
only appropriate response appeared to be the adoption of the urbane
scepticism and indulgent tolerance of diversity that Berlin extolled. So, as
British society in the late twentieth and twenty-first centuries became—
through prolonged immigration—more and more mixed, such liberal sentiments have formed the basis for a peculiarly British version of multiculturalism. We not only tolerate and welcome a widespread diversity of views
and values but also pride ourselves on what Timothy Garton Ash memor-
ably called 'the very undemanding vagueness, the duffle-coat bagginess of
Britishness'.[10] As another observer of British society commented: 'Our
central value is that we tolerate the values of others.'[11]

How to choose between values?

Moreover, what crucially underlies this liberal embrace of a multiplicity of
values is the perceived difficulty, if not impossibility, of choosing between
values. If the state is to promote and, in turn, to be judged by a particular set
of values, which values should these be? 'Whose Justice? Which Rationality?'—to echo the hauntingly sceptical title of Alasdair MacIntyre's savage
critique of modern moral philosophy. To these questions philosophers in
the twentieth and twenty-first centuries have had few convincing answers.

In the UK, the twentieth century had started with the confident optimism
of the intuitionists for whom ethical properties were objective non-natural
properties discovered by intuition. They claimed to be able to perceive or
'intuit' what was the right thing to do, although the basis for this ability was
left mysterious. It was striking how for the intuitionists what held supreme
value were, according to G. E. Moore, 'personal relations and aesthetic
enjoyments'.[12] In thus confining morality to the private rather than the public
spheres, the intuitionists set the tone for much of the twentieth century. But
their Edwardian self-confidence about the objectivity of morality did not
survive the carnage of the trenches in the First World War.

From the 1920s onwards moral scepticism prevailed. This was fuelled initially by the logical positivists who dismissed moral statements as meaningless.[13] Such statements failed the test of the verificationist principle that divided the realm of meaningful discourse into either logical tautologies ('A bachelor is an unmarried man') or statements based on empirical observation. Ethical statements were neither tautologies nor based on empirical observation. They were best construed as not statements at all but rather the expressions of feelings, like 'Hurrah!' This view was subsequently developed and refined by the emotivist school led by Charles Stevenson.[14] Following the Second World War the non-cognitive nature of moral discourse continued in fashion, with Professor Hare advocating a prescriptivist analysis of ethical statements as disguised imperatives.[15]

As the twentieth century advanced, the verificationist principle—which it was noted appeared to fail its own test—fell out of favour. Many of the details of these linguistic analyses were jettisoned. But the difficulty of providing any rational foundation to ethics continued to be regarded by most philosophers as an insurmountable challenge. This was supported by the perceived wide diversity of ethical views between different cultures. Bernard Williams, one of the most influential British moral philosophers of the second half of the twentieth century, even lamented the gulf between ourselves and Aristotle: 'In some part, Aristotle's account of the virtues, with regard to courage, for instance, or self-control seems very recognisable; in other respects it belongs to another world.'[16]

At a logical level, it was argued that there was an unbridgeable gap between factual and ethical statements, summarized in the Humean slogan that one cannot infer an 'ought' from an 'is'.[17] At the level of human nature, post-Darwinian evolutionary theory—according to Williams— underlined the profound lack of harmony between human capacities and needs. Unlike Aristotle's vision of the man of virtue living in harmony with nature, modern man is perceived to be a sorry creature, an 'ill-assorted *bricolage* of powers and instincts'.[18]

Williams, accordingly, concluded: 'The project of giving to ethical life an objective and determinate grounding in considerations about human nature is not in my view very likely to succeed.'[19] At the start of the millennium, Simon Blackburn summarized the Humean perspective in his judicious introduction to ethical thought, *Being Good*: 'When it comes to ethics we are in the domain of preference and choice. And here, reason is silent.'[20]

A slide towards relativism

Fuelled by such philosophical scepticism, the view has become widespread throughout modern Western culture that morality is a matter for private choice and personal preference. Those holding this view may not necessarily regard themselves as relativists—for whom there are only the different values of different cultures. They may accept that there are some cross-cultural common values, moral principles reiterated in different times and places. That is an important concession. But such principles tend to be very narrowly construed, including, for example, a prohibition on murder but excluding the virtues that are deemed too culturally dependent. Most of morality remains beyond their purview. More importantly, if we are still left without any objective or rational basis for our moral values, indeed, if even the 'moral minimum' is to be regarded, in Walzer's phrase, as 'a jerry-built and ramshackle affair', then the foundations of morality continue to look shaky and insecure.[21]

If—as the philosophical sceptics have taught us—moral statements lack factual or objective grounding, rational argument over ethical issues becomes difficult, if not impossible. We are afforded no means of resolving ethical disputes between, or even within, cultures other than personal choice or preference. Nor are we equipped with any means to assign priorities to our ethical choices. If there is no objectively valid moral view but only personal choices, different moral outlooks between, and even within, cultures would appear to be equally valid. It may then become difficult to resist a slide towards a wider relativism. The combination of liberal toleration of values and philosophical scepticism about the basis for those values leads to a radical form of multiculturalism that not merely tolerates a diversity of values but is unable to discern any rational basis for distinguishing between them where they differ.

Such moral scepticism has pervaded a broad and increasing span of our intellectual life, including economics, political theory, and international relations, as well as our moral thinking, education, and philosophy.

Economists, for example, as Richard Layard has recently reminded us, have concentrated their attention on measurable statistics, such as growth in gross domestic product, and eschewed any interest in values, like happiness, which they have been taught by philosophers to regard as, at

best, lacking any objective grounding and, at worst, meaningless concepts.[22] One of the founders of the movement to expunge ethics from
economics was Lionel (later Lord) Robbins, who, heavily influenced by the
logical positivists, argued in the 1930s that, if we disagree about morality,
'there is no room for argument'. Accordingly: 'It does not seem possible to
associate the two studies (ethics and economics) in any form but mere
juxtaposition. Economics deals with ascertainable facts; ethics with valu-
ation and obligation.'[23]

Economists, in their turn, counselled politicians to pursue measurable
goods, such as maximizing gross domestic product, as a proxy for happiness,
failing to notice that as people become wealthier they do not necessarily
become any happier. Indeed, according to the Gallup and other polls cited
by Layard, in modern Britain and elsewhere in the Western world, citizens
have become much materially better off since 1950 but their happiness has
not increased.[24]

In political philosophy, even an avowed non-sceptic such as John Rawls
took it as axiomatic that morality was a matter of private preferences, on
which public consensus was unlikely, so seeking instead to forge consensus
around his political principles of justice.[25] For a sceptic such as Richard
Rorty, there is no right or wrong but only whatever views people happen
contingently to hold: 'A liberal society is one which is content to call "true"
(or "right" or "just") whatever the outcome of undistorted communication
happens to be; whatever view wins in a free and open encounter.'[26] The
citizens of Rorty's liberal Utopia must become 'liberal ironists . . . people
who combine commitment with a sense of the contingency of their commitment'.[27] Since we are only too conscious of our fallibility, we should
hold our views only contingently, ready to exchange them, like hats, as the
prevailing mood shifts.

The prevalence of moral scepticism has had a profound effect on moral
education. It has undermined confidence in our ability to answer the
question 'Why should I be moral?', while the decline in religious belief
has reduced the attraction of an appeal to authority to found moral claims.
As a result, we have ceased to believe there is such a concept as moral
wisdom. We no longer seek ethical counsel from the wise. We are diffident
about our ability to teach morality. Morality may still be taught in churches,
but fewer and fewer people now attend churches. There has, however, been
no compensating growth of a secular morality; still less is there any agreement on how such secular morality should be taught. Lord Layard, as we

noted in the Introduction, has recently lamented that there has been 'a catastrophic failure to develop a secular morality. People find it difficult to discuss moral issues.'[28]

This collapse in moral education has had grave practical consequences, including for those recruited to the armed services. This has led a Head of the British Army recently to bemoan:

> In past generations it was assumed that young men and women coming into the armed forces would have absorbed an understanding of the values and standards required by the military from their family or from the wider community. Such a presumption today cannot be made.[29]

Against this background, it is hardly cause for surprise that moral scepticism also took hold in international political theory. If there is no rational basis for morality, the moral view we adopt is just a matter of our choices, influenced by our cultural tradition and national upbringing. There is, therefore, no objective basis for declaring one war to be just and condemning another as unjust. Each nation will naturally declare its actions to be just and those of its opponents unjust. There is no rational basis for resolving such disputes. The realm of international relations is a moral-free zone.

What is perhaps surprising is that relativist sentiments even appeared to infect the US Catholic Church. In its 1983 Pastoral Letter on nuclear deterrence, the US National Conference of Catholic Bishops introduced a new moral category for appraising warfare, which they called 'comparative justice'. They explained their thinking thus:

> In a world of sovereign states recognizing neither a common moral authority nor a central political authority, comparative justice stresses that no state should act on the basis that it has 'absolute justice' on its side. Every party to a conflict should acknowledge the limits of its 'just cause' and the consequent requirement to use only limited means in pursuit of its objective. Far from legitimizing a crusade mentality, comparative justice is designed to *relativize* absolute claims and to restrain the use of force even in a 'justified' conflict.[30]

The Bishops were, no doubt, wise to counsel a degree of scepticism in our appraisal of the claims of political leaders. But, with even the Catholic Church—elsewhere resolutely absolutist in its moral views—apparently conceding a role for relativist thinking, the task of furnishing a robust framework for the ethical appraisal of war would appear daunting indeed.

The argument against moral scepticism

So let us consider each strand of the argument for moral scepticism, starting with the liberal case for toleration of a multiplicity of views.

Mill claimed that the only purpose for which the state can interfere in the lives of its citizens, against their will, is to prevent harm to others. Some modification of this principle is needed to recognize that the state may, on occasion, legislate to prevent a citizen harming herself—for example, through use of dangerous drugs or failure to wear a seat belt. But the basic principle remains that the state should not intervene coercively except to prevent a greater harm to its citizens.

The most persuasive argument in support of this principle is that, when the state interferes in the lives of its citizens, particularly when it employs the coercive arm of the legal system to do so, harm inevitably follows. This occurs most obviously when a citizen is incarcerated. But it can occur in other ways too. This is illustrated by what happened to Alan Turing, the eminent mathematician and Second World War code-breaker. Turing was driven to suicide in 1954 following the judicially imposed medical treatment he was obliged to undergo to suppress his homosexual tendencies. Even the threat of legal sanctions can cause misery to those who, fearful of such sanctions, feel obliged to suppress their sexual impulses. The threat or imposition of harm by the state on one of its citizens can be justified only if a greater harm is thereby prevented. Mill's judgement on this assuredly remains valid. His precept, suitably modified, continues to offer crucial guidance in setting limits to the coercive activities of the state.[31] We should tolerate a multiplicity of views and not seek to coerce others to accept our views and values.

Mill's argument for setting limits to the coercive activities of the state was not, however, an argument for divorcing politics from values but rather insistence that the activities of the state should be guided by utilitarian values, aimed at minimizing harm to its citizens. We shall consider the merits of this approach further in the next chapter. Within the constraints thus set, he argued that people should be free to pursue a variety of what he termed 'experiments in living'. He believed this would provide the best framework for humans to flourish and, in particular, for intellectual creativity, originality, and genius to thrive. A parallel may be suggested with the open and critical discourse of science.

Mill's insight into the intellectual stimulation provided by diversity is important. But it does not follow from this that all values are equal. Nor was this the view of Mill, who famously held: 'It is better to be a human dissatisfied than a pig satisfied, better to be Socrates dissatisfied than a fool satisfied.'[32] There are, however, 'other instruments to persuade people to their good than whips and scourges'.[33]

Science encourages a variety of views and an open and critical discourse, without coercion to adopt a particular view. But science does not thereby deem all views to be of equal worth. On the contrary, science rigorously and ruthlessly weeds out views not supported by the facts, as it tests and retests the hypotheses it frames to advance our understanding of the workings of nature. An open and self-critical society, adopting best practice from scientific method, would not be one in which all values are regarded as of equal merit. Science is, on the contrary, meritocratic and elitist in its pursuit of truth.

Moreover, the contingency of our beliefs and consequent indulgent toleration of diverse views, which Rorty supposed a key feature of liberal society, has been challenged in recent years by the emergence of a new, ideologically based, terrorist threat to liberal society itself. This threat was dramatically exemplified in the attacks in New York and Washington on 11 September 2001 and the subsequent bombings in Bali, Madrid, and London. The threat is posed by extremist Islamist suicide bombers, some—as we have discovered in the UK—born and brought up within our society, whose values are radically discordant with and subversive of the society in which we live. Silence or a tolerant shrug of the shoulders at the rich diversity of values does not seem an appropriate response when faced with such discordant views. For, as Michael Sandel, a political philosopher critical of the liberal flight from values, has judiciously observed: 'Fundamentalists rush in where liberals fear to tread.'[34]

If we are to defend liberal society from terrorism, we need not only to take appropriate action to reduce the physical threat to the lives of our citizens. We also need to be able to confront and challenge in argument the rival values and ideology from which the violence springs. We need to be able to explain and defend the liberal vision of the good life and the values that underpin liberal society, including not only the protection of the innocent from violent attacks but also the importance we attach to democracy, freedom of speech, and the rule of law. The UK government's counter-terrorism strategy, accordingly, now seeks not just to *pursue* terrorists, to *protect* the public from terrorist attacks, and to *prepare* for the consequences of such attacks but also to *prevent* terrorism, including by 'engaging in the battle of ideas—challenging the ideologies that extremists believe can justify the use of violence'.[35]

In this new battle of ideas and ideologies in which we are engaged, moral neutrality appears a less attractive and, indeed, potentially dangerous option. As Roger Scruton argues in his analysis of the challenges facing contemporary international society, *The West and the Rest*: 'The enemy is of two kinds: the tyrant dictator and the religious fanatic whom the tyrant protects . . . to act against the second requires a credible alternative to the absolutes with which he conjures. It requires us not merely to believe in something, but to study how to put our beliefs into effect.'[36]

If we are engaged in such a battle of ideas, on what basis can we establish and promote our values? We need next to consider the moral philosophers' arguments for ethical scepticism.

These arguments were based, in part, on a linguistic analysis of ethical statements. This purported to show ethical statements not to be statements at all but expressions of feeling or emotion ('Hurrah!') or disguised imperatives ('Don't break your promises!'). Such linguistic analysis—now mercifully largely fallen out of fashion—always faced two key objections. The first was that, even if linguistic analysis showed that ordinary language incorporated a particular world view, it hardly showed this world view to be true. The second objection was that the analysis was, in any case, far from establishing the validity of its proffered linguistic insights.

Nor was this surprising, since the theories were based on a somewhat improbable claim. This was the curious notion that an American or British professor sitting in isolation in his ivory tower somehow knew what the rest of humanity meant when they used words in a way that they themselves did not. So, when people used sentences to make ethical statements that they believed to be capable of truth or falsity (for example, the true judgement that 'Stalin was a cruel tyrant'), they were somehow not really doing this but engaged in a totally different endeavour—issuing orders or evincing emotive grunts. Given the inherent implausibility of such claims, what is surprising is that theories, such as emotivism and prescriptivism, lasted for as long as they did.

A much more challenging argument for ethical scepticism is that from ethical diversity. This is the argument vigorously propounded by Gilbert Harman in his defence of moral relativism. Harman argues that there are profound moral differences not only between societies but within societies that can lead to intractable moral disagreements, such as the debates within contemporary US society on abortion or euthanasia. He concludes that the most plausible explanation for the diversity of views is that there is no single objectively valid ethical viewpoint: 'It is hard to see how to account for all moral disagreements in terms of differences in situations or beliefs about non-moral facts. Many moral disagreements seem to rest instead on basic differences in moral outlook.'[37] Bernard Williams, as we noted earlier, observed a deep ethical gulf even between ourselves and Aristotle.

Ethical diversity is a fact. But moral sceptics exaggerate its extent. We can also be struck by the broad measure of cross-cultural agreement on core moral values, which is more extensive than some moral minimalists have been prepared to concede. Mary Midgely noted: 'Whatever doubts there may be about minor moral questions and whatever respect each culture may owe to its neighbours, there are some things that should not be done to anybody anywhere.'[38]

This convergence of ethical judgement makes possible international consensus on documents, such as the UN Universal Declaration of Human Rights, as well as the international codes and laws governing the conduct of war. These embody substantive judgements, whatever may be their shortcomings, particularly as regards lack of enforcement mechanisms. Moreover, while we may be appalled by the discordant values held by an Islamist suicide bomber, brought up within our society but rejecting its principles, his disregard of the injunction against killing the innocent is far from mainstream Islamic thought. Mainstream Islamic teaching prohibits the shedding of innocent blood. This testifies—as do the many other shared key moral values, including those relating to the conduct of war—to the common cultural heritage of the Islamic and Christian faiths.[39]

Similarly with Aristotle's discussion of the virtues, we may be startled by the arrogance and deluded self-sufficiency of his 'man of great soul'. This is the man who, conscious of his own greatness, 'claims, and is entitled to claim, high consideration from his fellows'; and 'is ashamed to receive benefits, because it is a mark of a superior to confer benefits, of an inferior to receive them'.[40] We may find this concept alien and be reluctant to follow Aristotle's classification of 'greatness of soul' as a virtue. Our reluctance may, however, in part, reflect a misunderstanding that 'greatness of soul' is a common virtue. It is not. It is rather an exceptional virtue attributed only to exceptional men or women, those who are truly great statesmen. We may seldom, if ever, encounter such greatness, but, if we do, our view may change. So Leo Strauss confided to a friend in 1946. Although he had previously viewed Aristotle's concept of greatness of soul or *megalopsychia* as incomprehensible, he now approved of it: 'A man like Churchill proves the possibility of *megalopsychia* exists today *exactly* as it did in the fifth century BC.'[41] Even Aristotle's greatness of soul may not be quite as alien a concept as we supposed. Moreover, whatever may be our differences from Aristotle, of far more significance is the extent to which, despite the lapse of 2,500 years, when we read Aristotle or Plato we are living in the same moral world and grappling with the same moral challenges. Crucially, we share with them a similar view on the nature and importance of the cardinal virtues of courage, justice, temperance, and practical wisdom.

It is noteworthy that the examples Harman cites of ethical issues that provoke intractable moral disagreements within society are issues such as abortion or euthanasia.[42] These are, however, genuinely difficult cases where the disagreement may, in part, arise from genuine uncertainty over the boundaries of our concepts. It is a key question in the debate on abortion whether or not we are to count foetuses within the womb as persons, and hence with the moral rights of persons, a question to which there may be no simple ready-made answer. This may require a decision on where the precise boundaries of the concept lie. That such boundary issues provoke lively debate is hardly surprising. But it goes no way to establish that there is no common core of shared values on which we can readily agree with our fellow human beings.

Harman's argument is an instance of a manœuvre that moral sceptics employ more generally in a variety of domains of discourse. This might be called the fallacy of difficult cases. The manœuvre involves two steps: first, exaggerating the extent of the difficulty in difficult cases; and then claiming the difficulties are universal. So, it is argued that, because in some cases it is difficult to discern between the competing claims for justice of two warring belligerents, the concept of just cause lacks general robust application. Indeed, such reasoning may, in part, explain the proposal we have just noted of the US Catholic Bishops to introduce a concept of 'comparative justice'.

It is, however, fallacious to suppose that, because some cases may be difficult to decide, all cases must be similarly or even harder to resolve, as if the claims to the justice of their cause of Hitler and Churchill were equally disputatious. Just so, is it fallacious to infer from the fact that there are some mathematical theorems that are un-provable that all mathematical theorems are un-provable. Moral reasoning is difficult, and some cases may be particularly hard to resolve, not least where we are operating at the boundaries of our concepts. But from this it does not follow that all moral decisions are equally difficult, still less that they are all rationally un-decidable. For in our ordinary moral lives we can and do make moral decisions; and we can and do offer valid reasons for so doing. We are able to agree upon an extensive core of shared moral values.

Relativism may be appropriate for our aesthetic or culinary tastes but not for our core moral values. You like Picasso, I like Monet. We welcome curry as an Indian contribution to the diversity of our cuisine, but do not deem *suttee* or the Indian caste system to be an acceptable social practice. Nazism remains evil, however it may be locally fashioned and refined.

Indeed, it is the relativist's apparent readiness to deny key moral judgements that the rest of us hold true that is his undoing. This is starkly illustrated by the intellectual contortions through which Harman goes in dealing with the moral judgement that Hitler was morally wrong to kill the Jews. Harman denies that any ethical statement is objectively true or false. Such terms apply, if at all, only relative to a particular ethical framework. Tough-minded relativist that he is, Harman does not shrink from concluding that we cannot condemn Hitler for attempting to exterminate the Jews, which—from within his own ideological/ethical framework—may have appeared justified. He concludes: 'The critic will not be able to say, for example, "It was morally wrong of Hitler to have acted in that way" if the critic is a moral relativist who supposes that Hitler did not have a compelling objective reason to refrain from acting as he did.'[43]

In science where a theory entails a manifestly false conclusion this is regarded as grounds for rejecting the theory. If—as Harman maintains—relativism entails such a manifestly false conclusion, this should be regarded as undermining relativism. Just so, Thomas Mann, surveying in 1947 the evil excesses of the Nazis from which Europe was just emerging, concluded of Nietzsche's moral scepticism: 'How bound in time, how theoretical too, how inexperienced does Nietzsche's romanticizing about wickedness appear...today! We have learnt to know it in all its miserableness.'[44]

Relativism is ultimately a self-defeating doctrine. A political relativist such as Richard Rorty counsels that in a liberal society 'whatever view wins in a free and open encounter' is right. But it is open to question whether Rorty was really prepared to accept this, even if the view that prevailed was that of right wing neo-conservatism, to which, as a left-wing political activist,

Rorty elsewhere in his writings was bitterly opposed.[45] The two sides of Rorty's character—anti-realist political philosopher and left wing political activist—sit uneasily together.

The challenge for the relativist is that if—as he proclaims—anything goes, then anything really does go. He cannot then pick or choose between what goes. If there is no objective basis for our ethical judgements, they are all equally valid or invalid. The views of Socrates are no more (or less) valid than those of Hitler or Stalin. We have no grounds on which to condemn the millions sent to starvation and death in the Soviet gulags or Nazi extermination camps; or, more recently, those macheted to death in the Rwandan genocide. But such ethical promiscuity is surely not what liberal theorists, such as Rorty, or the political realists in international relations, really espouse. They recognize and share with the rest of humanity the moral judgement that condemns such mass killing of innocents.

Isaiah Berlin is right to provoke our suspicion of any politician who purports to offer a 'final solution' to the human condition, given the complexity and unpredictability of the human condition. But, as an argument for divorcing politics from values, the argument works only if allied with a relativist assumption that there is no rational basis for choosing between values. For, if there is such a basis, the correct response to what was wrong with Hitler's or Stalin's vision is not that they sought to promote values but rather that the particular values that underlay their visions— whether the scant regard for human life or the pseudo-science from which Aryan racial supremacy was derived—were deeply flawed. It was not the promotion of values *tout court* but the promotion of those particular values that had such disastrous consequences. Just as from the fact that a schoolboy makes an egregious mathematical howler it does not follow that all mathematics is invalid, so is it equally mistaken to infer that all ethics is flawed because some tyrants have chosen perverse moral systems.

Conclusion

So the sceptical arguments of those modern philosophers who led political theorists, such as the realists, astray into relativism, in the end, falter. Moreover, in the grand sweep of philosophical endeavour, the moral scepticism of twentieth-century Anglo-Saxon philosophy has been a very short aberration from a tradition, stretching back over the centuries through

Aquinas to Aristotle and beyond, that had a very different view of morality. In that tradition—in which, as we shall explore in the next chapter, there has been a recent revival of philosophical interest—morality was conceived as pre-eminently an area for rational discourse; and ethics as a moral science. There is no perceived unbridgeable gap between facts and values; values are rather conceived as the precepts, practices, and dispositions of character we need to nurture if we are to flourish as human beings.

But is that Aristotelian tradition any longer available to us in the twenty-first century? The sceptics' arguments may founder, but we have yet to show that morality can be rationally grounded. Is it possible to provide a rational justification for morality that will guide not just our private but our public lives? To this key challenge of moral philosophy we now turn.

THREE

Virtues and Consequences

It is not a trivial question: what we are talking about is how one should live
one's life.

Plato, *Republic* 352d

Introduction

In posing the question how one should live one's life, Socrates was not
asking how one ought to live in a special moral sense of 'ought'. For there
was no such concept of moral obligation in Greek culture. The demand was
rather for guidance on what it is necessary to do in order to achieve *eudaemonia*, to have a fulfilled life, to flourish as a human being. The surprising answer
that Socrates, Plato, and Aristotle gave to this question was that it was
necessary to be moral, to practise virtue.

This answer is surprising to the modern ear for two reasons. First, the Greek
word we have translated as a 'fulfilled' or 'flourishing life'—*eudaemonia*—is
often translated as 'happiness', which, in modern parlance, means not just a
satisfying life but also carries with it implications of pleasant sensations and
experiences. It may seem odd, indeed, to suppose that morality would
represent a good strategy to achieve happiness in that sense.[1] We think rather
of falling in love or winning the lottery as being keys to such happiness.
Second, while morality may perhaps be a more plausible candidate to contribute to a fulfilled life, even that claim would seem open to challenge. For,
as we explored in the previous chapter, we have been taught by modern
philosophy that there is a sharp dichotomy between facts and values. There is
thus no reason to expect any consonance between what morality requires and
our natural desires; no reason why morality should conduce to a flourishing
life.

But, however surprising their answer may be, the Greek philosophers believed that morality was necessary for a fulfilled life and that this provided us with a reason to act morally. The challenge I wish to address in this chapter is whether in the twenty-first century it is possible to provide a rational justification for morality as a guide to our public and private actions.

Consequentialism

One modern attempt to make morality a rational activity is utilitarianism, the best-known variant of the form of ethical reasoning known as consequentialism. The nineteenth-century reformers Jeremy Bentham and John Stuart Mill rejected what they perceived to be the prevailing Victorian view of morality as a system of unquestionable moral principles and inscrutable fiats. Instead, they sought to provide a rational framework for discussing moral issues by arguing that what counted as a right action should be determined by reference to its consequences and, in particular, to its contribution to the promotion of human happiness. Since its foundation in the nineteenth century, the popularity of utilitarianism has waxed and waned. But, even during its relative decline in the twentieth century, it has remained an honourable exception to the general trend of philosophy in that century to seek to restrict morality to the private sphere. For utilitarianism has always been intensely concerned with morality in the public, as well as private, realms.

Utilitarianism offers a way to make morality a rational activity by assigning a clear role to reason. This is to calculate the consequences of actions and determine among the various outcomes which are most likely to promote human happiness. Utilitarianism has had a proud record as an agent of social reform, providing an effective practical guide in public policy-making. Starting with Bentham's zeal to reform the eighteenth- and nineteenth-century legal system, many of the great social reform movements of the nineteenth and twentieth centuries were guided by consequentialist reasoning.

So, for example, in the UK such reasoning underpinned the great sweep of reforms to the criminal law introduced during the 1960s. Suicide was decriminalized because more harm than good was achieved by treating as criminal an act that harmed no one but the agent (1961). Capital punishment was abolished because no one could satisfactorily show that the evident harm caused was outweighed by the beneficent deterrent effect, which could be achieved just as readily by imprisonment (1965). Homosexuality was legalized between consenting adults because such behaviour, however distasteful to some, had no harmful consequences (July 1967). Finally, abortion was legalized where the harmful consequences of proceeding with the pregnancy outweighed the disadvantages of its termination, whether through the risk to the physical or mental health of the mother, or because of the risk that the child, if born, would be seriously handicapped (October 1967). Consequentialism's promotion of social reform has continued into the twenty-first century, with the prominent British social reformer Lord Layard employing unashamedly utilitarian arguments to justify the case for better treatment for those suffering from mental health problems. A rallying cry of his successful campaign was 'Bully for Bentham'.[2]

Despite its proud record of social reform, consequentialism has been under sustained attack in recent years from both deontologists/moral absolutists, who hold that fundamental to morality are absolute moral rules; and from the recently revived school of virtue ethics, for whom virtues are the key to moral behaviour. In the face of such attacks, consequentialists have tended to bunker down, give no quarter and fight off all intruders.[3] In turn, the deontologists and virtue ethicists have heaped further contumely upon consequentialism, a doctrine they regard as not just profoundly erroneous but pernicious. Indeed, since Elizabeth Anscombe first introduced the term 'consequentialism' in her scathing critique of modern moral philosophy, it has become almost a term of abuse.[4] For Anscombe, consequentialism was necessarily 'a shallow philosophy'.[5] Peter Geach roundly declared that consequentialist calculations—which he argued could lead to an endless chain of consequences—were 'absurd': 'I therefore reject consequentialism root and branch'.[6] John Finnis similarly described consequentialist calculations as 'senseless', since they require us to compare goods that are, in his view, incommensurable.[7]

An unbridgeable gulf has thus appeared to open up between consequentialists, on the one hand, and deontologists and virtue ethicists, on the other, with each side slinging insults at the other and neither appearing willing to amend his or her position to accommodate the arguments of an opponent.

In this chapter I propose to argue that there is no such unbridgeable gap and that the consequentialist, the virtue ethicist, and the deontologist can each learn from the other. Far from rejecting all the arguments of his opponents, the consequentialist should be prepared to revise and amend his doctrine to accommodate the genuine concerns of his opponents; and that, if he does so, it may be possible to end up with a form of moral reasoning that can draw strength from all the traditions. I shall call this 'virtuous consequentialism'.

To determine whether such an accommodation is possible we need first to consider some of the main objections levelled against consequentialism.

Objections to consequentialism

Consequentialism is sometimes presented with such all-embracing object-ives that its very ambition can seem overweening. Bentham's initial popular injunction was that we should pursue 'the greatest happiness of the greatest number'. He subsequently modified this to the more judicious formulation 'the greatest happiness of all those whose interest is in question', making clear that his concern was with the greatest total sum of happiness.[8] But, even so, it still sounds an ambitious target, suggesting, as Geach complained, a grandiose calculation of endless causal chains that may appear beyond human capacity. Bentham also thought happiness could be reduced to pleasure, which is unduly restrictive, since we pursue many other ends than pleasure.

Utilitarians sometimes speak as if the principle of utility provided a guide to all our actions, a panacea for reaching any decision on any subject. But that seems an implausible claim. A man who proposed to his girlfriend on the grounds that their marriage would, on balance, increase overall happi-ness would be lucky to get away with a slapped face! Utilitarian calculation is hardly appropriate to explain love or friendship.

If consequentialism is not to fall at the first hurdle, we need to be careful to avoid expressing it in over-ambitious terms. Consequentialism can, however, be reformulated in a more modest way. This would be to offer advice to those pondering what is the right thing to do: that they should choose that course of action the consequences of which are judged likely to contribute more to the welfare or reduction of suffering of those whose interests are involved than those of the available alternatives.

Such a more modest formulation of the principle helps address Geach's complaint that consequentialist reasoning inevitably involves endless chains of consequences. For in this more modest formulation there is no reason why it should do so. We can and do apply sensible cut-off points to avoid such pitfalls, restricting the consequences to be considered to those that are reasonably foreseeable. Finnis's complaint about the incommensurability of values can also be challenged. For, in our everyday practical reasoning, of which moral reasoning is but part, we frequently and successfully weigh up and evaluate the different consequences of our actions and, in doing so, necessarily rank and choose between our values. If we could not do this, it is difficult to see how we could ever come to practical conclusions about what we should do, even in such mundane matters as choosing to visit a sick relative in hospital rather than going to the cinema. Still less could we reach decisions of greater moment, such as choosing to evacuate a football stadium to protect the spectators from a terrorist bomb, even though this interrupted the skilled performance on the pitch.[9] A list of incommensurable values would also offer little guidance to the policy-maker. For it is frequently necessary to rank values in the complex formulation of public policy—for example, in determining the allocation of scarce resources between competing demands. The task is often difficult, even daunting, but it is not impossible.

Let us now consider some of the criticisms that present more fundamental challenges.

First, the deontologists complain that consequentialism belittles and ignores the moral rules and principles that they believe are fundamental to morality, rules that, in their view, are absolute and admit of no exception. Geach explains:

> And legalism will further hold that if in working out the description of an action we reach certain descriptions, e.g. that it is an act of blasphemy, or killing the innocent, or perversion of just judgment, or perjury, or adultery; then we need consider no further: this is already the cut-off point and the act is ruled out.[10]

An act that is forbidden by one of the 'bedrock' rules of morality is forbidden, regardless of its consequences.[11] Indeed, in such cases it is inappropriate to have any further regard to the consequences. The consequentialist who insists that consequences should always be taken into account is led to propound implausible and counter-intuitive moral judgements, including the licensed killing of the innocent.

I shall consider the claims of moral absolutism in more detail in chapter 5. But at this stage it is important to note that there are strengths and weaknesses on each side of this debate.

The consequentialist is right to point to the way moral principles can conflict and that there may, on occasion, be cases where sticking to the rules may bring about very much greater harm than breaching them and that, when that happens, it would be rational to break the rule. An example is that of a householder sheltering Anne Frank and her family in her attic. A Nazi storm trooper knocks on the door and enquires if there any Jews inside. Most would agree that in such circumstances it would be permissible to lie in order to save many lives.

The consequentialist is also right to note that our moral lives are more complex than the deontologist assumes and that many crucial moral decisions may not be covered by moral rules. Examples might be the choice of a career or how to spend an inheritance; or, in the public sphere, what social or environmental policy to adopt. A decision whether or not to go to war would also fall into this class. For, although there are principles to guide and structure our reasoning about warfare, issues of such moment are hardly likely to be decidable by simple application of a rule, without a great deal of further profound deliberation.

The consequentialist is, however, wrong to suggest that moral principles are, as Smart describes them, mere 'rules of thumb' to be discarded whenever our calculations show there might be even a slight balance of advantage in doing so.[12] The rule utilitarian may face difficulties, as does the deontologist, because of his failure to offer guidance when rules conflict or no rules apply. But he is right to object to such downgrading of the importance of moral principles. This grossly oversimplifies the complexity and difficulty of moral decision-making. Moral principles incorporate the accumulated experience and wisdom of ages. An agent, faced with a difficult ethical dilemma, unsure how to act and with little time to calculate consequences, may sorely need the guidance of moral principles, whose wisdom he would be ill advised to ignore. There is a very strong presumption in favour of the rules, any breach of which is likely to cause harm. Any breach would require the most profound justification and be sanctioned only *in extremis* if there is clear evidence that very much greater harm would thereby be avoided. Moral principles play a key role in guiding our decision-making. The consequentialist should accord great importance to moral principles. *The first adjustment to consequentialism is that it needs to be principled consequentialism.*

The next charge against consequentialism is that it offers an outsider's view of ethics. All that matters are the consequences of actions, and no special status or role is accorded the agent. This can lead to absurd conclusions. One such is Smart's suggestion that, in a universe consisting of only one sentient being who falsely believes there are others undergoing exquisite torment, it would be preferable that he should take delight in their sufferings rather than sorrow over them. For, as Smart says: 'After all, he is happy, and since there is no other sentient being what harm can he do?'[13] The answer is the harm that the deluded sadist does to himself which Smart can only ignore because he neglects the key role of the agent and the importance we accord to the interior quality of the action, as well as its external effects.

This is well illustrated by Peter Strawson's example:

> If someone treads on my hand accidentally, while trying to help me, the pain may be no less acute than if he treads on it in contemptuous disregard of my existence or with a malevolent wish to injure me. But I shall generally feel in the second case a kind and degree of resentment that I should not feel in the first.[14]

In assessing the moral qualities of an action, it is not just the external consequences that count. The mental states of the agent are also crucial. For, as human beings—as intentional agents—we are concerned not just with what happens to us. It matters intensely to us how others view us, what beliefs, feelings, and intentions they have towards us. It equally matters to others what are our mental states towards them. Acts with the same effects (a crushed hand) can be judged differently depending on the mental states of the agent. An act with good effects may not be judged good if undertaken with a wrong intention. A prince who invades his neighbour's territory and, in so doing, overthrows a brutal and oppressive regime is not deemed to have acted justly, despite the beneficial outcome, if his motive was not to liberate the people but to seize control of his neighbour's gold mines.

In determining the moral quality of an act we need to attend not just to its effects but to the role and status of the agent. *Any balanced ethical judgement needs to address both the internal and external aspects of action: the mental states of the agent and the consequences of his agency.*

The next charge against consequentialism is that it misdescribes and oversimplifies the nature of moral reasoning.

For the consequentialist, the act of moral reasoning is construed as if it were a simple calculation of consequences, with the course of action to be chosen that whose consequences are more beneficial than those of the alternatives. But this makes moral choice appear simpler than it is. It hardly corresponds to the bewildering complexity and sheer difficulty of our moral life. It is very hard to be good. The difficulties we face are not just—as the consequentialist would concede—in the complexity or uncertainty of the calculation of consequences. Our moral mistakes may be multifarious. Consequentialism, just like deontology, makes the decision process appear too easy.

Modern man, without any schooling or training in moral conduct, is supposed to be able to confront the most complex and challenging moral dilemmas and behave correctly. He is able instantly to discern the right thing to do, whether, for the deontologist, by seeing which moral principle to apply; or, for the consequentialist, by undertaking a rapid, yet accurate, calculation of consequences. If only it were so easy! In reality, our moral life is more demanding. Consider three examples.

In a recent court martial case in 2007 eight US marines were charged with murdering Iraqi civilians in Haditha, a city in the western Iraqi province of Al Anbar.[15] This followed an incident on 19 November 2005 when twenty-four Iraqis, including women and children, were killed, after an attack by terrorists with an improvised explosive device that killed a US Marine Lance Corporal and wounded two other Marines. Quite what happened in this case has not yet been fully established. But it was alleged during the court martial that the soldiers had gone on a rampage seeking revenge on those they held responsible for the murder of a well-liked comrade. Rage and anger at their comrade's death were a major motive for their actions. Anger may often be an important motive on the battlefield. Just so, three millennia earlier, the rage of Achilles at the death of his comrade Patroclus impelled his return to the battlefield and mass slaughter of Trojans, including the slaying and profane mutilation of Hector's body.

The second example is in Afghanistan. A British soldier spots a woman behaving suspiciously on the edge of a crowded marketplace. Is she an innocent shopper or a Taliban suicide bomber? He has seconds to decide whether or not to shoot, with the lives of many innocents hanging on the outcome of his deliberation.

The third example is of a happily married senior executive who drinks too much at a Christmas office party and ends up in bed with an attractive junior trainee. Inflamed by alcohol and lust, he gave no thought at the time to the ethics of his conduct, although next morning regrets bitterly what he has done.

What these examples underline is that moral decisions do not always—or even usually—present themselves to us neatly labelled as such. Recognizing that our choices may have ethical implications may be a crucial first step to making the right moral judgement. The angry soldiers in the first example may not have appreciated in the heat of the moment the full moral significance of what they were doing. Fuelled by rage at their comrade's death, they acted without thinking, attacking with the frenzy of berserk Norse warriors.

These examples also show the importance of the emotions we feel; and that what passions we feel and how we have been taught to control them may contribute crucially to the quality of the moral judgements we make. They show how unlikely it would be that we would make the right choice if we had to make complex calculations of consequences on each and every occasion. Indeed, the second example shows how critical moral decisions may need to be taken in seconds, with no time for complex calculation of consequences. The final example shows the importance to our moral life of the habits of character we have acquired as a result of which we may succumb to or be able to resist the excesses of alcohol and of lust. A man practised in the virtue of temperance would know how to resist such temptations.

It was a fallacy of most twentieth-century ethical theories to suppose that a person confronts each moral dilemma as *homo episodicus*: fresh-eyed, empty-headed, a man with no past or future, only the present, untrained, and equipped with, at most, a powerful calculator. The prospects of such a person choosing the right course of action in the heat and passion of the moment and amid the many tempting paths to error would be remote indeed.

We need rather to recognize that we confront each moral dilemma as *homo durabilis*: a man with a past and a future, whose present choices may, in part, be determined by those he made in the past, which helped make him the sort of person he is now, and which may also crucially affect how he acts in the future. Indeed, if he is to have any hope of choosing rightly, he will need all the help he can get and to have undergone a great deal of moral education and training, so that he confronts the difficult moment of choice with appropriate thoughts, feelings, and desires.

Virtues

Considerations such as these have rightly reawakened interest in the teachings of Aristotle, who underlined the importance of a sound moral education and training to help us acquire the appropriate states of character—the appropriate virtues—to enable us to make the right choice, unswayed by passion or emotion, when faced with difficult moral decisions.[16] The variety of virtues, ranging from self-regarding virtues, such as temperance and prudence, to other-regarding virtues, such as generosity and justice, also reminds us, in a way that a uni-dimensional consequentialism can overlook, of the richness of our moral life and the multiplicity of dispositions and skills that are needed if we are to make ethically correct choices.

These are important and profound insights that any adequate restatement of consequentialism would need to incorporate. *Virtues are crucial to our moral life.* But the virtues on their own may not always provide all the guidance we require when we are faced with difficult ethical choices. We are told that the right thing to do is—depending on the circumstances—whatever is just or courageous or temperate (or whatever other virtue might apply). If we ask how we are to discern such actions, we are told they are what a just or courageous or temperate person would do. So how do we find a just or courageous or temperate person to guide us? If we are told it is whoever performs just or courageous or temperate actions, we seem to have been led around in a circle.

The circle is not as unhelpful as it may appear, since virtue terms are 'thick' ethical concepts that describe particular ways of behaving and so do provide guidance. A Greek soldier, who broke the line in battle and fled, knew well that his action was not what a courageous man would do. But, as we shall explore further in Chapter 6, we may be faced with situations where we are not sure what virtue is required; or where the virtues appear to conflict and point in different directions; or where none of the established virtues provides clear guidance. How do we then decide what to do? Aristotle recognized the difficult choices with which we could be faced and counselled that the man of virtue would then need to exercise practical wisdom to determine the right thing to do. He defines practical wisdom as 'correct deliberation about what serves an end'[17] and 'the ability to reach sound conclusions about . . . what conduces to the good life as a whole'.[18]

So, to help determine the right thing to do in situations of moral perplexity, we may, according to Aristotle, need to reflect on how our actions will conduce to human flourishing. This, in turn, will require attending not just to the nature of the action but also to its consequences. Virtue ethics may thus need help from consequentialism, just as consequentialism does from virtue ethics. But, even if consequentialism is amended and supplemented in the ways we have suggested, are we yet in a position to answer the question that we posed at the outset of this chapter: Why should I be moral? Why should I act justly?

Why should I be just?

This question has perplexed philosophers almost since philosophy began. This was the challenge thrown down by Thrasymachus in book 1 of Plato's *Republic* and taken up by Glaucon and Adeimantus at the start of book 2. The *Republic* was Plato's attempt to answer the challenge.

The question 'why should I be just?' has been central to philosophy for over two thousand years. But, for most of the twentieth century, as we explored in the previous chapter, most philosophers declined to answer it. They declined to do so for a variety of reasons, of which the most challenging is that the question, while important, is just too difficult to answer. This was the view, widely shared by other philosophers, expressed by Bernard Williams: 'The project of giving to ethical life an objective and determinate grounding in considerations about human nature is not in my view very likely to succeed.'[19]

There was also a concern expressed by deontologists and some virtue ethicists that the question was inappropriate. We should do what is right because it is right, for its own sake, not for some other reason. We should not seek to ask why we should be moral. To do so is to misunderstand the nature of morality. As Archbishop Whately of Dublin put it: 'Honesty is the best policy; but he who is governed by that maxim is not an honest man.'[20]

So the question that Plato placed at the centre of philosophy was for different and, sometimes, conflicting reasons judged to be unanswerable. A key area of human life—morality—becomes an irrational activity for which no reasons can be given. Do we have to accept this gloomy conclusion?

The claim of the deontologist or virtue ethicist that we should do what is right for its own sake embodies an important insight into the nature of moral motivation. But that insight needs to be tempered to avoid the implication that our objective is only to enhance our own moral integrity rather than concern for others. The insight would also not necessarily preclude seeking a deeper grounding for morality. After all, Aristotle—who is often cited in support of this view and who certainly stressed that virtue needs to be pursued for its own sake[21]—also maintained that virtuous conduct consti- tuted the good for man, essential to our flourishing as human beings.[22] A brave soldier displays courage in the heat of battle because that is the honourable thing to do and does not seek for further reasons.[23] But, if the path of virtue is unclear, if moral rules conflict, or if the man of virtue is asked to explain why he has chosen a life of virtue, then a deeper explan- ation of how such actions contribute to human welfare may still be in order. There is no necessary inconsistency in both recognizing the special nature of moral motivation and seeking a rational justification for morality.

Even if there is no such inconsistency, we still face the objection from those who accept that the question is appropriate and important but think it is just not possible to answer it. So is it possible to explain why we should be just?

One answer is that acting morally is in our own interest, if not in the immediate, short term, then at least in our longer-term, enlightened self- interest. The advantage of this appeal to self-interest is that it is a motivation that everyone can safely be assumed to have. This justification does not depend on the contingency of altruistic feelings that may or may not be present.

This is the argument that Glaucon eloquently expounded in Plato's *Republic*:

> Our natural instinct is to inflict wrong or injury and to avoid suffering it, but the disadvantages of suffering it exceed the advantages of inflicting it; after a taste of both, therefore, men decide that, as they can't have the ha'pence without the kicks, they had better make a compact with each other and avoid both. They accordingly proceed to make laws and mutual agreements, and what the law lays down they call lawful and right. This is the origin and nature of justice.[24]

To achieve the greater benefit of never being harmed by others, we forgo the lesser benefit of sometimes harming them. We may be tempted to steal others' goods, but we do not want our own property stolen. So we abstain from theft to assure the security of our own property. This exchange is necessary, because we are approximate equals in power. If we were not equals—or if we were equipped with magical powers, like Gyges with his magical bezel ring by turning which he could make himself invisible—we could get away with harming others with impunity and so would have less reason to accept the constraints of morality. Men are, however, by and large and for the most part, as Aristotle would say, approximate equals, and so they have reason to act morally. We can thus provide grounds for acting justly.

Since Glaucon first expounded the theory that morality is founded on mutual advantage, it has attracted many supporters.[25] The agreement underlying morality may be regarded as informal or, as with the social-contract theorists, it may be treated as a more formal, if still idealized, agreement. A distinguished modern exponent of the social contract was John Rawls, who sought to show that his principles of justice as fairness would be the rational choice for determining the distribution of social goods within society of men in a state of nature, unaware of the position each would occupy in society, and acting only to further their own interest.[26]

The claim that moral rules work to our mutual advantage has substance. It works well with self-regarding virtues, such as temperance. Moderation in satisfying her physical appetites can be readily judged to conduce to the well-being of an agent who practises it. It also seems not unreasonable to suppose that some of the most basic moral constraints, such as the prohibitions on murder, theft, and rape, are mutually advantageous. But there are three fundamental problems with this approach.

First, while the approach works up to a point, it soon runs out of explanatory power. For it fails to explain all our moral actions, including, crucially, those that are held up as models of moral behaviour. One such paragon is the Good Samaritan, who went to the aid of the stricken stranger on the road to Jericho. Of the Good Samaritan, we are told: 'when he saw him, he was moved to pity.'[27] He acted from compassion for the stranger, not because he calculated that it would be in his interest to offer aid. Still less is it apparent how parents who, at great personal cost, devote their lives to caring for a severely disabled child—for example, a child afflicted with cerebral palsy—can deem that their action will be to their advantage.

Second, social-contract theorists face notorious difficulties in explaining how moral rules adopted to constrain behaviour within a society can be extended to cover behaviour between societies and so be extended internationally.[28] The assumption on which such theories are based of an approximate equality of powers seems difficult to apply in an international arena where superpowers jostle uneasily with powerless microstates.

Moreover, underlying both these doubts is the concern that we noted earlier of Archbishop Whately that the notion that morality pays, even if true, does not capture the motivation that we feel appropriate for moral action.

Should we then jettison altogether the idea that acting morally can be to our mutual advantage? That would be mistaken. The insight is valid as far as it goes. But it does not go far enough. What else then do we need?

One option would be simply to add to our assumption that a person acts from self-interest, the recognition that she can sometimes, as a contingent fact, also act altruistically. Such was the view that Philippa Foot once put forward, famously observing that 'the people of Leningrad were not struck by the thought that only the contingent fact that other citizens shared their loyalty and devotion to the city stood between them and the Germans during the terrible years of the siege'.[29] Her observation on the motives of the brave denizens of Leningrad is well made. But the mere addition of the contingent possibility of altruism to a human's presumed selfish egoism still seems to furnish too fragile a basis for morality.

What we need rather to do is question the assumed nature of a human being on which all these arguments are based. Since the Enlightenment, the paradigm that we have unquestioningly adopted is that a human is, *au fond*, an isolated, atomistic individual each selfishly pursuing his or her own interest. If such is human nature, then the only grounding for morality might, indeed, appear to be a kind of reciprocal tit-for-tat, like the mutual grooming for fleas of chimpanzees.[30] If man is pictured as such a selfish egoist, then we have already conceded too much to Thrasymachus, so that his challenge may, indeed, be unanswerable. But that paradigm is not the only one available and would seem based on a partial and flawed view of human nature. As Alasdair MacIntyre noted: 'What for the kind of ancient and medieval moral enquiry and practice which Thomism embodied was the exceptional condition of the deprived and isolated individual became for modernity the condition of the human being as such.'[31] An older and wiser view was that of Aristotle, for whom 'the human being is by nature a political animal'.[32] Indeed, Aristotle countered: 'It is rather peculiar to think of the happy person as a solitary person: for the human being is a social creature and naturally disposed to live with others.'[33]

Man is an animal that lives in a *polis* or community, an animal that flourishes in and through the life of a community. A being that lacks such communal concerns would not be human but, like the Cyclops, anthropomorphic in form but subhuman and monstrous in nature. As Homer relates of the Cyclops: 'They have no assemblies that make decisions, nor do they have binding conventions. But they inhabit the summit of lofty mountains . . . and they have no concern for one another.'[34]

Humans, by contrast, live a communal life. That life, as MacIntyre reminds us, begins with us as vulnerable, dependent babies and may end for us in decrepit senility once more reduced to dependent vulnerability. In between, others may have depended on us and to them we may have freely given our services in a complex web of relationships of uncalculated giving and receiving: uncalculated because 'what I am called upon to give may be disproportionate to what I have received and . . . those to whom I am called upon to give may well be those from whom I have received nothing'.[35]

If we are political animals, animals drawing life in and through a community, and animals mutually dependent each upon the other, then what counts for us as human flourishing will be very different from that envisaged by the selfish egoist of the post-Enlightenment paradigm. Human flourishing would not be the passive enjoyment of pleasure or satisfaction of desires sometimes imagined by utilitarians. It would be rather the complex of actions and activities that go towards our living well together in communities, where importance is accorded not just to the external effects of agency but to its internal qualities, to how we view and are viewed by those with whose lives ours are intertwined. Recognition of our communitarian nature also helps explain how it may be rational for us to cede individual rights for the sake of the common good—for example, through redistributive income tax policies. For the rational egoist, by contrast, individual rights may always appear over-riding.

Having shifted our paradigm of human nature, we can see more clearly how it may be possible to answer the question why I should be just. Moral constraints, reinforced by the precepts and practice of virtue, are essential to our flourishing together as humans. Indeed, for us to flourish as humans is to live well in a community, with the good of others as important, if not more important, to us as our own good and, in an important sense, becoming our own good. The good of others may, equally as our own, furnish reasons for our action. In acting morally we may, as the social contract and other theorists supposed, be pursuing our own good. But that good is not conceived as a narrowly egoistic good but is transformed into a good that also comprehends the good of others.

This complex interplay of motives can be illustrated by family life, an example suggested by Herbert McCabe:

> Running a family cannot be done unless it is possible to rely on the justice of others and unless others can rely on your inclination to act justly—including faithfulness to vows to provide stability over time and over varying circumstances essential to raising a family. A family will tend to fall apart if people involved are simply at the mercy of their passion, acting upon every passing sexual attraction—if they lack the virtue of temperance, the project of a family is doomed. Courage is required in adversity . . . and, above all, there is required the moral/intellectual virtue of good sense, knowing what to do in order to realise the goods of family life in these particular circumstances.[36]

The virtues are needed for the successful management of a family. Acting virtuously within a family is mutually advantageous. But that is only part of the answer. For it does not explain the unconditional love that a mother may give to her child, even a child who is severely disabled and who may never be able to return the kindness. Family life illustrates the way the good of others can become our own good, with moral rules and virtuous action promoting both our own good and the good of others, with the distinction between the two becoming increasingly difficult and artificial to draw. The consequences of agency to which we need to attend are not to be narrowly construed as in the post-Enlightenment model as those promoting our own self-interest. They need rather to reflect our communitarian nature, with the goods of others furnishing reasons for acting quite as much as our own. So interpreted, the beneficial consequences of virtue may be as much for others as for ourselves.

This recognition of our communitarian nature also provides the final crucial bridge enabling virtue ethics and consequentialism to be reconciled. For one of the reasons virtue ethicists have been loath to acknowledge the key role that consequences play in our assessment of moral action is their concern that, if we act virtuously only because of the beneficial consequences to us—because morality pays—this subverts the true nature of morality. Such a view reflects an understanding of consequences based on the post-Enlightenment paradigm of human agency, with consequences interpreted narrowly as those promoting our own self-interest. If we broaden our concept of human flourishing to reflect our communitarian nature, the good of others may furnish reasons for acting quite as much as our own. The virtue ethicist is right to reject the contention that morality pays. But, in rejecting such a view of morality, as too narrowly conceived, we should not conclude that all consequences should be ignored. Consequences are a key part of our moral assessment, but the consequences should reflect the good of others and not just our own.

Responding to Thrasymachus' challenge

So are we now in a position to respond to Thrasymachus' challenge and furnish reasons why he should behave justly? Acting morally is necessary for human flourishing, to enable us to live together well in communities. But could Thrasymachus not agree that virtues are necessary, in general, to the good life and yet still argue that, in his particular case, they were not needed? He could still add the profits of his injustice to the benefits he receives from others' justice. He could be like Bernard William's successful villain, 'who is horrible enough and not miserable at all but, by any ethological standard of the bright eye and the gleaming coat, dangerously flourishing'.[37]

But could he? It is important to note the extent of Thrasymachus' claim. He is not just arguing that there may be a particular individual case where acting unjustly may contribute better to his flourishing, a possibility we would concede. He is rather arguing that for him and others like him—the rich and powerful—a *practice* of injustice would contribute to his well-being more than that of justice. That is more difficult for him to justify. He might get away with lying and cheating on one occasion. But, if he makes a practice of this, it will risk undermining his relationship with others in the community—family, friends, and others with whom his life is intertwined. He risks ending up an isolated, lonely individual. He may need reminding that man is not the solitary and independent egoist he may have assumed, that his good is bound up with the good of others.

Aristotle cautions us to judge someone happy 'not just for any length of time but for his complete life'.[38] That life, as we have seen, may include at the beginning and end, and at any time in between, periods when we are dependent and vulnerable. Thrasymachus may flourish for a while, and may flourish in his bushy-tailed prime, but what happens to him when he is old and vulnerably dependent on others? What help can he expect from those with whom his relationship has been poisoned by his lying and cheating? If Aristotle is right that we are by nature 'political animals,' who live and flourish only in and through communities, it is less easy to suppose that Thrasymachus could flourish—could live well in a community—and do so over a lifetime if he adopts such an egocentric practice of injustice.

Moreover, since our characters are moulded and shaped by our individual acts, as are our relations with others from whom we may be divorced by a single selfish act, Thrasymachus would be wise to pause before committing even a single act of injustice. For it is through our individual acts that we become the people we are. If he becomes an unjust man, he risks being cut off from ties of friendship and family. He risks his life becoming subhuman, like that of a monstrous cave-dwelling Cyclops.

So perhaps the challenge set by Thrasymachus can be met. We have reason to act justly because only thus will we be able to live well together in communities, so fulfilling our social needs and nature. Morality is justified because it furnishes the rules and guidelines we need to enable us to live together well in communities and so flourish as human beings.

Moral rules, including the precepts of virtue, are justified by their beneficial consequences. But we do not normally need to deploy a complex calculation of consequences to justify individual acts. Once it is clear that an act falls under a moral rule or virtuous precept, that may provide sufficient justification for the action. The Good Samaritan acts from charity in direct response to the urgent needs of the stricken stranger. The brave soldier acts as he does once he sees what courage requires him to do.

But the moral rules and requirements of virtue may not always so clearly point the way. Calculation of consequences at a more fundamental level may still be required to determine the right thing to do on individual occasions where it is uncertain whether and what rule or virtue applies to the situation or where the virtues or principles may appear in conflict. When faced with such ethical dilemmas, as well as attending to the internal quality of the action, we may need to calculate consequences to determine which of the actions available to us would better promote welfare or reduce suffering.

In so doing, the requirement to reduce suffering—to respond, for example, to the cries of the stricken stranger on the road to Jericho—may often provide the more immediate and practical guidance. But the negative injunction to reduce suffering does not always over-ride the positive. If that were so, we would be obliged always to give in to the demands of a bully threatening violence in order to avoid suffering. A democracy might then find it difficult to resist the claims of a dictator. But, as we shall explore in the next chapter, it may be permissible for a democracy to use force to defend its way of life against the aggression of a dictator. A democracy is not always obliged to cede to a dictator's demands to avoid the suffering that war brings.

The requirement to promote welfare or reduce suffering helps guide our actions when ethical conflicts or dilemmas arise. But following this guidance does not necessarily yield easy or simple solutions. Drawing what support we can from moral principles and our virtuous training, we still need to apply careful practical judgement in determining the right thing to do. In so doing, we will be exercising a virtue that itself needs to be acquired, practised, and internalized, the virtue of 'practical wisdom'. This is the virtue that Aristotle insists is needed to guide and inform all moral conduct. We shall consider this virtue further in Chapter 6, when we address in more detail the role that the virtues play in our moral lives.

Moral rules and virtuous conduct are needed to enable us to live well together in communities. Morality is necessary for the good life. But it is not, as Stoic philosophers supposed, sufficient. There is room for our private choices and preferences over the kind of lives that we lead, the occupations, pastimes, and pleasures we pursue. But, without the guidance and constraints of morality, communal life becomes difficult, if not impossible.

It is, moreover, a key feature of morality that it extends its claims progressively further out through ever-widening concentric circles of the communities to which we belong. We start our lives and first learn moral rules and virtuous behaviour within a family. But the claims of morality soon extend outwards from the family to: a school, a village, a regiment, a town, our country, and so outwards to the international realm. We learn that morality governs our behaviour as individuals even towards distant strangers. Morality also governs the relations between the political communities or states to which we belong.

This extension of the claims of morality does not mean that we have exactly the same responsibilities everywhere. The utilitarian claim that each person counts for one and no one more than one is an oversimplification. This can lead to the 'blandly generalized benevolence' criticized by Alasdair MacIntyre since it is directed towards an abstract Other rather than the particular others with whom we share common goods and participate in a network of relationships.[39] A mother has particular responsibilities to her own children she does not have to others. A soldier feels a sense of loyalty to the comrades whom he knows well in his own platoon or regiment that he may not feel to others. It is not inappropriate for loyalty to be geographically confined. The intense loyalty that a soldier feels towards his immediate comrades he could not feel towards people he has never met or known. But, as we shall explore in Chapter 6, loyalty that becomes too narrowly based and that, at the extreme, even encourages soldiers to break the law to cover up the crimes of their comrades turns a virtue into a vice.

A mother may have particular responsibilities to her own children. But the obligation not to kill innocents applies equally to other children as to her own. Such moral rules apply equally, everywhere. We also respond to urgent pleas for help, regardless of location or relationship. The Good Samaritan went to the aid of a stricken stranger on the road to Jericho, offering help to a neighbour whose status was defined by need rather than physical proximity. A mother will rush to save her child that has fallen down a well. But she will equally respond to pleas for help from a child, not her own, that has fallen down a well within her village. If travelling abroad, she will respond to the cries for help of an unknown child, stuck in a well shaft in a distant land. For, as Aristotle judiciously noted: 'One may also observe in one's travels to distant countries the feelings of recognition and affiliation that link every human being to every other human being.'[40]

Conclusion: Virtuous Consequentialism

The gulf between virtue ethics and deontology, on the one hand, and consequentialism, on the other, is not unbridgeable in the way sometimes supposed. Each party can, and needs to, learn from the other. It is only by doing so that we can furnish a convincing answer to the question why should I be moral. It is a mistake to stress just one aspect of our moral lives, to the neglect of others—whether these are rules, intentions, virtues, or consequences. Morality is a multidimensional activity. Both in appraising the actions of others and in ourselves deciding how to act, we need to consider all these features. To account satisfactorily for the full complexity and richness of our moral lives, as well as to provide the guidance needed to respond to the difficult ethical challenges we face, requires attending, and according proper weight, to all these aspects of our moral agency.

The approach of what I have called 'virtuous consequentialism' seeks to draw strength from each of these traditions. It is very different from consequentialism as traditionally conceived. It accords proper weight to moral principles that enshrine the moral wisdom of our forebears and play a key role in guiding our actions. It recognizes the importance of both the internal quality and the external effects of moral agency, so eschewing an uncomfortable outsider's view of ethics. Above all, it seeks to learn from the teachings of Aristotle and Aquinas on the nature of man to help furnish a broader and more generous vision of what constitutes human flourishing and hence what consequences are to be attended to in making moral judgements. To live well is to live well together in a community, not as passive recipients of pleasure but as active contributors to the common welfare, where our flourishing depends not just on what happens to us but on what we do and how we view and are viewed by others, with whose lives ours are intertwined. In that enlarged vision of human happiness, the good of others may furnish us reason for action as much as our own.

Virtue ethics rightly stresses the range of skills that contribute to human flourishing and the importance of moral training and education in those skills to help us address the difficult challenges of the moral life. If we are to stand any chance of acting rightly in the heat and passion of the moment, we need schooling in the virtues, so that we develop states of character that enable us to discern and to choose what is right, undeflected by passions or emotions. Virtues are crucial to our moral life.

But consequences, while only a part, are still an important part of our moral evaluation. We justify the virtuous life because of its beneficial consequences. The moral rules and precepts of virtue are justified because they contribute to human welfare and the reduction of suffering. We may also need calculation of consequences—considering which action will better promote human welfare or avoid suffering—to help us determine the right thing to do where it is uncertain whether or what moral rules or virtues apply or where the rules or virtues may be in conflict.

Virtuous consequentialism, accordingly, insists that the complexity and challenge of our moral lives can be properly addressed only if we give appropriate weight to all facets of moral agency: to both the internal qualities and external consequences of our actions, as well as to the principles that guide those actions and the virtues needed to enact the principles in our daily lives.

Now that we have established a framework for evaluating our moral actions, the next challenge is to consider how this might be applied to the central question with which this book is concerned—the morality of war. We shall first examine the body of teachings known as the just war tradition.

FOUR
The Just War Tradition

The historical tradition

Just war teaching is not based on a fixed body of doctrine but is rather a tradition that has evolved over the centuries and is still evolving in response to the changing circumstances and nature of war, with different commentators emphasizing different aspects. But within this shifting tradition there is a reasonably settled core of principles, built up and crafted over the centuries, which are designed to provide guidance to our thinking about war.

The tradition can be traced back to St Augustine, who in the fifth century AD wrestled with the perennial question of whether a Christian may engage in war without sin. From the earliest days of the Church there had been those who taught that the answer to this question was unequivocally in the negative: war was always wrong and to be avoided. Such a pacifist response had an appealing moral clarity but was not always easy to reconcile with the harsh realities of daily life, where force might sometimes be necessary to allow right to prevail—for example, to protect the innocent from assault. So, as Christians assumed greater positions of responsibility within the Roman state, including undertaking the civic burdens of military service, there was a need to explore ways of reconciling the requirements of statecraft with the constraints of morality.

In seeking to respond to this challenge, Augustine drew not just on Christian teaching but also on Roman law and the wisdom of classical philosophers, such as Cicero. St Augustine concluded that a Christian could engage in war, but only if the war was just: 'As a rule just wars are defined as those which avenge injuries, if some nation or state against whom one is waging war has neglected to punish a wrong committed by its citizens, or to return something that was wrongly taken.'[1]

The tradition evolved further as a result of church-led peace movements in the eleventh to thirteenth centuries that sought to restrict the ravages of war by limiting the days on which war could be fought (the Truce of God) and the classes of people against whom war could be waged (the Peace of God). The Peace of God sought protection for people such as churchmen and peasants tilling the soil. The Truce of God was honoured more in the breach than the observance, with even the Fourth Crusade launching its attack on Constantinople on the Holy Thursday before Easter in 1204. But the Peace of God movement had significant influence on just war teaching. It was reinforced from the chivalric tradition, from where came the explicit prohibition on attacking women and children, whom the courtly knight deemed it un-chivalric to assault.[2]

In the thirteenth century, Aquinas, combining elements from the medieval tradition with the teachings of Aristotle, began to shape just war teaching into recognizable modern form. Aquinas laid down: 'For a war to be just three things are required: the authority of the prince . . . a just cause . . . and a right intention.'[3] The tradition was brought to fruition in the sixteenth and seventeenth centuries by the Spanish jurists Vitoria and Suarez and the Dutch lawyer and theologian Hugo Grotius. The crucial contribution made by Vitoria was to extend the tradition from a set of guidelines for Christian princes on how to conduct war within Christian Europe to universal principles, established by natural law, applicable to anyone, anywhere, and anytime. On that basis, Vitoria developed a devastating critique of the behaviour of the Christian conquistadors in the wars they had recently waged against the Incas and Aztecs of Southern and Central America: wars of conquest roundly condemned by Vitoria as unjust.[4]

The tradition was then largely neglected in the succeeding centuries, with the emphasis shifting to fashioning practical legal rules—'the laws and customs of war'—that should govern the conduct of war, including the treatment of prisoners, as set out in the Hague (1899 and 1907) and Geneva Conventions (1864 with revisions in 1906, 1929, 1949, and 1977). Just war teaching was rediscovered in the second half of the twentieth century, initially by the American theologians Father John Ford and Paul Ramsey. It was developed further on both sides of the Atlantic, primarily to furnish an ethical framework for the debate then raging over the morality of nuclear weapons.[5] With the ending of the Cold War, the nuclear debate has subsided, but interest in the tradition continues, with even politicians adopting some of the language, if not the substance, of just war teaching. The US named their 1989 military intervention in Panama Operation 'Just Cause', thereby seeking to foreclose debate on the issue!

The tradition has a Christian origin but was developed in opposition to theories of war undertaken for the sake of religion. Crusades and holy wars are firmly rejected. The teaching is based on natural law and intended to appeal to men of reason anywhere.

It is sometimes claimed that the tradition is founded on a presumption against war.[6] That is so in the sense that the tradition has always insisted that the onus of proof should rest on those seeking to disturb the tranquillity of the world by resorting to war. But from the earliest days the tradition also acknowledged that such a burden of proof may sometimes be satisfied and that war may sometimes be morally permissible. Indeed, as we shall explore further in Chapter 11, it may even, on occasion, be a moral duty. St Augustine observed: 'It is the wrongdoing of the opposing party which compels the wise man to war.'[7] War is recognized as a legitimate instrument of statecraft. What has, however, always pervaded the tradition has been an acute and vivid awareness of the horror and pity of war. For St Augustine, the wise man should 'lament that he is subject to the necessity to wage war'.[8] For Christine de Pisan, writing at the turn of the fourteenth and fifteenth centuries, war is an 'accursed thyng and not due'.[9]

So, while acknowledging that war may sometimes be necessary to protect human welfare, the tradition recognizes that war causes immense human suffering and seeks to limit that suffering by restricting the occasions on which war may be begun and the manner in which it is conducted. It prescribes a number of tests that have to be met before war can be under-taken—the *jus ad bellum* principles—and further tests to be met if a war is to be conducted justly—the principles of *jus in bello*. Each of these tests has to be passed if a war is to be just. The principles are set out below.

The just war principles

Jus ad bellum

It is permissible to embark on a war if and only if:

- it is authorized by a *competent authority*;
- it is for a *just cause*;

- it is with *right intention*;
- it is a *last resort*;
- the harm judged likely to result from the war is not disproportionate to the good to be achieved, taking into account the probability of success (the principle of *proportion*).

Jus in bello

In the conduct of the war, the following further principles must be complied with:

- the harm judged likely to result from a particular military action should not be disproportionate to the good to be achieved by that action;
- non-combatants should not be deliberately attacked.

A final further condition has recently been suggested of *jus post bellum* to ensure that wars not only begin and are conducted justly but also end justly in the establishment of a just peace.

Let us consider each of these conditions in turn.

Jus ad bellum

Competent authority

Aquinas explained the requirement of competent authority thus:

> A private individual may not declare war: for he can have recourse to the judgment of a superior to safeguard his rights. Nor has he the right to mobilize the people which is necessary in war. But since responsibility for public affairs is entrusted to the rulers, it is they who are charged with the defence of the city, realm or province subject to them.[10]

So, private wars—a curse of the Middle Ages—are ruled out. War has to be authorized by a legitimate government.

For modern commentators the medieval interpretation of competent authority may seem at once too restrictive—since there may be occasions when a just rebellion may be undertaken against an oppressive state—but also too permissive, with the suggestion that in the modern era only the United Nations should be able to authorize war.

Given the immense destructiveness of modern wars, there are good reasons for no longer trusting states to be the sole source of authority for wars. The authorization of the United Nations is desirable and would be sufficient to meet the requirement of competent authority. But the question is whether it is always a necessary condition. That is more difficult to decide because the UN is itself an imperfect instrument, fashioned and wielded by humans who may not always be impelled to behave by the highest ethical motives. A compelling recent example was the NATO military action in 1999 to protect the Kosovar Albanians from Serbian ethnic cleansing. This action enjoyed a wide measure of international support. But UN authorization was not sought from the Security Council because it was feared that Russia or China, each acting from its own national self-interest, would veto the motion. To insist on UN authorization on every occasion may, therefore, be too demanding.

What this suggests is that, in determining competent authority, there may be a graduating scale, with the score to be applied depending on both the degree of international consensus and the gravity and urgency of the crisis to be averted. The best indication of international consensus—and the goal always to be aimed at—is unequivocal authorization by the United Nations, as was achieved for the military intervention in Korea in 1950 and the 1991 coalition operations to expel Saddam Hussein from Kuwait. But the NATO operation against Serbia would also score high, since, despite lack of explicit UN authorization, there was substantial international support for the operation, while the crisis to be averted—the threat to the lives of thousands of Kosovar Albanians—was grave and immediate. On the other hand, as we shall explore in Chapter 10, the coalition operations against Saddam Hussein in 2003 would score low on the graduating scale, since there was no imminent grave threat or humanitarian catastrophe to be averted and international opinion was deeply divided on the rightness of military action at that time.

Just cause

When the just war tradition was revived in the second half of the twentieth century, some commentators argued that the condition of just cause was of more formal than substantive value. This, in part, reflected the problem that had much concerned jurists during the Middle Ages of what was called 'simultaneous ostensible justice': if each side claimed to have justice on its side, how was one to determine where justice lay.[11] This is a difficult issue. Even in the Second World War, allied soldiers—fighting what they thought was self-evidently a just war—were surprised to discover that the Germans they were opposing thought they had right on their side.[12] Moreover, with moral scepticism and relativism widely prevalent, it was perhaps to be expected that the problem of discerning where justice lay was deemed by many to be insuperable.

Such relativism is, as we argued in Chapter 2, unfounded. Nonetheless, given the complexity and fallibility of the human condition, each side may have some right and some wrong on its side. The classical just war theorists stressed, however, that a war in which right was *equally* divided between the participants would not be a just war and should not be fought. Vitoria roundly declares: 'If it is agreed that both parties have right and justice on their side, they cannot lawfully fight each other, either offensively or defensively.'[13] The just war theorists held that in a just war only one side could have a just cause. Where there is some right or wrong on each side, the challenge is to assess where the overall balance of justice lies. This may, in practice, be difficult, and sometimes very difficult to discern. But it would be to commit the fallacy of difficult cases, as we noted in Chapter 2, to infer from this that all cases are equally difficult or even undecidable. In the Second World War example just quoted, the German soldiers who thought they had a just cause in fighting for the monstrous tyranny of Nazism were simply and straightforwardly mistaken.

So, what constitutes a just cause? War is a matter of great moment and cannot be embarked on for inadequate reasons. According to Vitoria, difference of religion cannot be a cause of war nor can enlargement of empire, still less the personal glory or convenience of the prince. Rather, 'the sole and only just cause for waging war is when harm has been inflicted'.[14] These words of Vitoria are often quoted in support of the view that only wars in self-defence constitute just wars. Vitoria's concept of the harm that could be legitimately countered was, however, wider and more altruistic than this. He maintained that, 'in lawful defence of the innocent from unjust death, even without the pope's authority, the Spaniards may prohibit the barbarians from practising any nefarious custom or rite'.[15] Grotius broadened the concept of just cause further to permit action to counter 'injuries which . . . grossly violate the laws of nature or of nations in regard to any person whatsoever'.[16]

This broad definition of just cause became progressively narrowed in the centuries following the 1648 Treaty of Westphalia. This treaty heralded the inception of the modern era of horizontally organized states recognizing no superior authority, whether of church or emperor. The rights of states predominated, and only military action in defence of states was deemed licit. A self-defence paradigm prevailed and reached its apogee in the 1945 UN Charter. After two devastating global wars resulting from the intervention of great states in the affairs of lesser states (Austria Hungary in the affairs of Serbia, and Germany in those of Czechoslovakia and Poland), the UN Charter prohibited the threat or use of force in international relations. Only two exceptions are allowed. Article 51 recognizes 'the inherent right of individual and collective self-defence if an armed attack occurs'; and chapter VII permits military action authorized by the Security Council in response to 'any threat to the peace, breach of the peace or act of aggression'. As the Cold War settled over Europe, with an ever present fear that any conventional conflict could escalate to the nuclear level, a restrictive interpretation of just cause to self-defence became the norm among just war commentators. I shall consider in later chapters whether some relaxation of this interpretation may now be justified to reflect the changed nature of war and the different security challenges that have arisen following the ending of the Cold War. But even self-defence as a just cause for war has recently come under attack.

It has been claimed, for example, by David Rodin, that the alleged analogy between the right to self-defence in individual cases of domestic violence and in war breaks down because we accord to soldiers fighting in war rights that are not recognized in the domestic case.[17] Combatants are permitted to shoot soldiers who are asleep or withdrawing. Someone resisting an individual attack should withdraw if he is able to, whereas soldiers have no such duty to withdraw. States are entitled to defend against a 'bloodless invasion' where no violence to individuals may be at stake. There is, moreover, what Rodin regards as a decisive objection stemming from the different moral treatment we accord each case. In war there is what Walzer has called a 'moral equality of soldiers', with soldiers on each side in a war licensed to attack the other.[18] No such moral equivalence holds between the attacker and defender in individual cases of self-defence.

Rodin correctly notes the difference in treatment between acts of violence in war and individual self-defence, but he is wrong to attribute this to a disparity in the ethical basis of the cases. For the difference derives rather from the different nature of the threat posed in domestic and international violence.[19] For the domestic threat is typically from an isolated, single act of violence, whereas in war the threat extends over time and space and involves a number of people. There may also be no remedy available against the threat other than to act in one's own defence. Consistent with the right of self-defence, more force may be licensed in war than in the domestic situation. We are permitted to attack a sleeping soldier because when he awakes he may resume his attack on us. Soldiers are not obliged to withdraw because, unlike the domestic case, there is no alternative authority available, such as the police, to whose protection they can look. Our right to defend against a bloodless invasion may be regarded as analogous to a householder's right to defend her property against an attack, although in both cases the amount of resistance thereby licensed will be constrained by the requirements that only proportionate and necessary force may be applied. This may reduce or even remove the right of self-defence if its exercise may cause more harm than it prevents.

Rodin regards the moral equality of soldiers as the most compelling objection against the self-defence analogy. But he also claims—somewhat inconsistently—that this moral equality does not exist. For he argues: 'Soldiers fighting an unjust war have no permission to kill.'[20] The denial of moral equality undermines his objection to the self-defence analogy. It is also a dangerous move. For, if every action of any soldier fighting in an unjust cause were illicit, there would be no incentive on the soldiers to moderate their actions. Yet we regard such restraint as crucial to the just conduct of war. That is why we commend the actions of the German generals who refused to obey the most outrageous of Hitler's orders. Rommel is praised for burning the order from Hitler on 28 October 1942 that all enemy soldiers encountered behind enemy lines were to be killed at once.[21] We admire the chivalry of Montgomery, who, on the conclusion of the battle of El Alamein on 4 November 1942, invited the captured Commander of the Afrika Korps, General von Thoma, to dine with him at his headquarters.[22] We consider, with good reason, there to be a moral parity between soldiers fighting on each side and accord to each of them a right to use force. There is, however, no such moral parity between the politicians, together with their military and civilian advisers, who take the decision to resort to war without just cause and those taking the decision to defend their country against such aggression. The former have no right to use force, whereas the latter do. It is this moral disparity that parallels that between the individual who decides to mount an unjust attack and the person who decides to defend herself against one in the domestic case.

Right intention

It is not enough that there should be a just cause; the military action must also be undertaken for the sake of the just cause. The just war tradition was forged from the experiences of statecraft over the centuries and takes an intensely realistic view of human nature. It seeks to preclude the temptation for a politician to proclaim a just cause, while, in fact, acting with other intentions. Such duplicity vitiates the moral quality of the action, which depends not just on the external but also on the internal aspects of agency. The necessity of a right intention is underlined by Aquinas: 'For,' as he wryly observes, 'it can happen that even if a war is declared by a legitimate authority and for a just cause, that war may be rendered unlawful by a wicked intent'.[23]

This does not mean that a mixture of motives is always precluded. What are ruled out are wicked intentions, such as greed or cruelty. But humans typically act from a variety of motives. What counts is the dominant intention, which needs to be determined by the just cause. Other secondary intentions, provided they are at least morally neutral, need not invalidate the right intention. The fact that Iraq's strategically important oil deposits may have been a factor in the coalition's response to Saddam's invasion of Kuwait in 1990 does not invalidate the legitimacy of the action, provided the predominant intention was, as the allies claimed, the need to defend Kuwait against the unprovoked aggression from which it had suffered.

Right intention is sometimes treated within the tradition as a kind of general pacific benevolence, a longing for peace and justice. There is, however, merit in defining right intention precisely by reference to the just cause. Just cause and right intention mutually reinforce each other. A just cause will not legitimate military action unless the action is undertaken for the sake of the just cause—that is, with right intention. Political leaders are also constrained from expanding or changing their proclaimed objectives for military action by what is specified in the just cause. Right intention is the intention to rectify the wrong specified in the just cause. Right intentions, thus narrowly construed, still lead to peace. For it is by such corrective action that peace is re-established. Peace is deemed by the tradition to be man's natural state, which is threatened by wrongful aggression. By rectifying such wrongs peace is restored. It is in this sense that, as Augustine says, 'we wage war in order to achieve peace'.[24]

Last resort

The requirement that war should be undertaken only as a last resort recognizes the immense suffering that war may cause. It is not, however, a temporal condition, requiring that all other means must have first been tried and failed before force can be resorted to. Such delay could be a recipe for military disaster. Indeed, the early application of force may in some cases enable much less force to be used and the objective to be secured with less harm caused. The requirement is rather that war should be—not temporally but logically—last, only to be preferred if other options are deemed unlikely to succeed. It thus parallels the requirement within the domestic self-defence case that force should be used only if it is necessary.

Nor is it a presumption of the just war tradition that other options are always preferable to war. There was a widely held view for much of the twentieth century that sanctions were always to be preferred to war, as if sanctions, unlike war, imposed no harm. But, as our experience of sanctions in the latter part of the twentieth and early twenty-first centuries testified, sanctions may take a long time, if ever, to be effective. This was illustrated by the protracted sanctions imposed on Rhodesia after its unilateral declaration of independence in 1965. Sanctions may also cause considerable suffering of innocent civilians, as the economic sanctions imposed on Iraq after the First Gulf War testified. Advocates of sanctions seldom satisfactorily explained how the suffering was to be translated into effective political action to change a regime's policy, particularly when that regime was led, as in Iraq, by a tyrant unresponsive to democratic pressures. General and economic sanctions are designed to achieve their effect by inflicting considerable suffering on the ordinary population. They have, therefore, a similar moral dubiety, as judged by the principles both of proportion and of non-combatant immunity, as has the medieval practice of inducing a besieged population to surrender through starvation; or the imposition of a general naval blockade, such as that enforced in the First World War by the UK against Germany, with great cost to the civilian population.

Proportion I

It is a key feature of just war teaching that a cause, however just, does not license war unless one reasonably expects that the harm caused by the war will not outweigh the good to be achieved, as specified in the just cause. As Vitoria judiciously observes: 'Care must be taken to ensure that the evil

effects of war do not outweigh the possible benefits sought by waging it.'[25]
The requirement that there should be a reasonable prospect of military
success is usually treated within the tradition as a further separate condition.
It is, however, logically best treated as part of this first application of the
principle of proportion. For, in assessing whether more good than harm will
result from war, one must inevitably take into account the probability of
each occurring, so that one can assess the overall expected benefit or
disbenefit that will accrue from war.

The requirement of proportion has been much criticized by recent
commentators, because of the perceived difficulty, indeed impossibility, of
predicting the consequences of dynamic and protracted events such as war.
The difficulties of assessing the Second World War are well brought out by
Rodin:

> The Nazi regime was brutal and aggressive: it systematically murdered ap-
> proximately 6 million innocent people, and subjected many more to a regime
> of extraordinary moral repugnance. But the war itself cost somewhere in the
> region of 55 million lives. In addition it made 40 million people homeless,
> caused incalculable destruction to the world's cultural and material wealth,
> and had the after-effect of initiating the Soviet Union's brutal half century of
> dominion over Eastern Europe. This was a horrific price for stopping Nazi
> Germany.[26]

So it was. But, unlike Rodin, the judgement of most commentators is that it
was a price worth paying to protect the world not just from the evils the
Nazis perpetrated—which Rodin mentions—but rather more from the evils
he fails to mention, which they would have undertaken had they been
allowed to complete their domination of the world, evils that would have
included the final extinction of the Jewish race. To ignore what would have
happened if Nazi aggression had been allowed to triumph is to commit what
has been called Parmenides' Fallacy: assessing a state of affairs by measuring
it against past states that are no longer available as options rather than
comparing it with other possible futures.[27] The correct comparison to be
made is not between the world as it was before and after the war, but rather
between a world in which Nazi aggression was unchecked and our world in
which Nazi ambitions were constrained.

Rodin's argument is not just to question the particular consequentialist
judgement that the sacrifices made in the Second World War were worth
paying to defeat Nazism. He also questions our more general ability to make

such judgements at all. Consequentialism, he suggests, frequently provides a disappointing guide to assessing whether a war is right: 'The principal reason for this is that the scope of this question is simply too broad to be amenable to the kind of cost/benefit analysis that consequentialism proposes.'[28]

We can concede that the assessment of consequences, which the first application of the principle of proportion requires, is immensely difficult and daunting. It should be undertaken with due humility and in full recognition of those difficulties. But it is mistaken to argue that the politicians who take decisions on war and peace should be excused from assessing the consequences of their actions because of the practical difficulties involved. Some politicians might welcome such exemption. But this is not a view that those concerned with the morality of war should support. Indeed, the moral criticism usually levelled at politicians is not that they attempted to assess the consequences of what they were doing but rather that they neglected to do so or did so only inadequately. Such, for example, is the charge levelled against the US and British governments for failing adequately to assess the *post bellum* consequences of the military action to oust Saddam Hussein in 2003. We shall examine this charge further in Chapter 10.

In assessing the balance of good and harm, an important constraint is that the politician is not free to specify whatever goods he likes. Rather, what can be included is specified by the just cause. Moreover, the requirement to ensure that the harm caused is not disproportionate to the good achieved does not only apply just before war is undertaken but needs to be reassessed as the war progresses. This reassessment covers both the good to be achieved, as set out in the just cause, and the harm caused by its achievement, both elements of which need to be kept under review as circumstances change and new facts emerge. Once the wrong specified in the just cause has been rectified the war should be terminated. Expansion of the war aims is precluded unless, as it is accepted may sometimes happen, important facts emerge that justify some modification of the just cause—for example, the discovery of Hitler's genocidal plans against the Jews. New facts may also emerge about the damage caused by war, so changing the overall balance of good over ill.

The need for a continual reassessment helps alleviate the difficulty of the initial calculation, since consequences unforeseen before the war may become only too apparent as the war progresses. Failure to conduct such a reappraisal was one of the criticisms levelled against the political and military leaders in the First World War, who failed adequately to reassess the balance of advantage and readjust their strategy and tactics accordingly as the grisly attrition of the trenches grew apace.

Difficult and daunting as the task may be, calculation of consequences is an essential part of the just war appraisal, just as it is an essential component of our ordinary moral reasoning.

Jus in bello

Proportion II

Careful appraisal of the consequences of action is required by the just war tradition not just before but during the war in relation to each military action undertaken. The principle of proportion is applied: before and during the war to ensure the overall costs of war are not disproportionate to the benefits to be secured; and during the war to ensure that the good achieved by a particular military action or actions outweighs any harm caused.

The principle of proportion is applied at four different, albeit closely interrelated and overlapping, levels, involving four sets of agents: the political, strategic, theatre, and tactical levels.[29] The first level is the *political* level, at which the decision whether or not to go to war is taken and the political objectives for military action are set. These objectives are then translated at the *strategic* level into the military formations and actions—the military strategy—required to achieve the political objectives. It is the task of the *theatre* commander to coordinate all the military actions and activities within a geographical area so that they contribute to achieving the strategic objectives. The final level is the *tactical* level, where individual battles and military engagements take place, ranging from great battles such as Trafalgar to a brief skirmish in a Basra alley.

Decisions at the political/strategic level are crucial to the assessment of whether or not it is just to go to war—the *jus ad bellum*. Both prior to and during the war the political leaders, supported by their military and civilian advisers, are required at both the political and strategic levels continually to assess that the good expected to be achieved by the war, as specified in the just cause, will not be outweighed by the harm caused and that there is an overall beneficial balance of consequences stemming from the war.

In the conduct of the war, the political and military leaders are also required to make an appraisal to assess the consequences of military actions undertaken at the theatre level of operation against the objectives of those actions. Actions undertaken at the theatre level—that links the strategic and tactical levels—can directly influence the strategic outcome of war. An example would be the 1944 D-Day landing in Normandy, where the casualties expected to be incurred had to be weighed against the contribution of the action to winning the war and so protecting Europe from the Nazi tyrant. This was a decision not just for the military commanders but for the War Cabinet itself.

During the war, it is also necessary to make an assessment at the tactical level before any individual military action is undertaken, to ensure that casualties incurred are not disproportionate to the objective to be secured by that action—for example, the capture of the town of Caen during the Normandy offensive. Such assessments may be made by soldiers at a relatively junior level. For it is a feature of modern war that responsibility is increasingly being devolved to lower levels. Decisions at the tactical level can also, in modern conflicts, conducted under the close scrutiny of the media, rapidly have repercussions at the theatre, strategic, and even political levels. It should be stressed that in undertaking the appraisal of consequences—at whatever level—the casualties that have to be taken into the reckoning are not just those of one's own forces but also those of the enemy and any non-combatant casualties.

The different levels of decision-making in war help explain the different degree of moral responsibility held by the various participants that we noted earlier. The political and military leaders who take the decision to go to war will bear the moral responsibility for this decision and be morally culpable if the war is unjust. But the ordinary service people who bear the brunt of the day-to-day conduct of the war bear no such responsibility.

Non-combatant immunity

As well as ensuring that any harmful consequences of military action do not outweigh the good to be achieved, combatants must not deliberately attack non-combatants: the principle of non-combatant immunity or discrimination. This requirement derived initially from the piecemeal immunities sought for particular classes of people, such as peasants tilling the field, but was later broadened to a more general requirement to protect the innocent from the ravages of war. As Christine de Pisan so vividly put it: 'The valiant and gentleman at arms ought to keep himself as much as they can that they destroy not the good simple folk.'[30]

But who are 'the good simple folk'? Who are the innocent to be protected and why should they be afforded special protection?

The answer implied by the title of the principle is that it is non-combatants, those not engaged in war, who should not be deliberately attacked. But any human life is a tragic loss, including that of a young conscript soldier, torn from the bosom of his family and friends, whose life and expectations are prematurely terminated. This account leaves unexplained why non-combatants should be awarded a special protection over and above that already afforded by the principle of proportion.

Within the classical tradition the main explanation proffered—and one that has attracted recent support—is that combatants deserve to be attacked because they share in the moral guilt of prosecuting an unjust attack.[31] But that response is unsatisfactory because, as we have already noted, ordinary service people cannot be held morally responsible for an unjust war. It also elides any moral distinction between combatants and non-combatants on the side of those prosecuting a just war, both combatants and non-combatants being on this theory equally undeserving of being attacked. But non-combatants are usually afforded a special protective status, while all combatants—even those prosecuting a just war—are deemed legitimate targets.

A better answer is, therefore, that combatants can be attacked because they are posing harm, which is what the Latin *nocens* means. The innocent are to be spared because they are not threatening harm. The objective of war is to stop harm being done, and so it is licit to use proportionate force against those—the combatants—who are threatening or inflicting harm. Force should not be used against those not posing harm, whether civilians or soldiers *hors de combat*, such as prisoners of war.

On this basis a robust distinction can be drawn between combatants and non-combatants. This does not correspond to the distinction between civilians and military, since some civilians may be involved in prosecuting the harm—for example, the politicians in charge of the war effort or workers in munitions factories—while some soldiers, incarcerated in prisoner-of-war camps, may have ceased so to do. There will also inevitably be grey areas. Those who make tanks can be classed as combatants, but what of those who make the steel from which the tanks are made? But the fact that there are grey areas and hence difficult choices to be made does not mean, as some have claimed, that, with the immense destructiveness of modern warfare and weaponry, the distinction between combatants and non-combatants has

broken down. On the contrary, as the US Catholic bishops rightly point out:
'Plainly . . . not even by the broadest definition can one naturally consider
combatants entire classes of human beings such as school children, hospital
patients, the elderly, the ill, the average industrial worker producing goods
not directly related to military purposes, farmers and many others.'[32]

A clear distinction can be drawn between combatants and non-combatants that justifies their different treatment in the conduct of war. What is
more difficult to assess is whether the immunity from attack accorded non-
combatants is an absolute immunity, admitting no exception, or whether it
is a more pragmatic injunction seeking to minimize the suffering of innocents, while recognizing that non-combatant casualties may be unavoidable
in modern warfare. We will answer this question in the next chapter.

Jus post bellum

The need to ensure justice after war—*jus post bellum*—is not a separate
condition within the classic just war tradition, but there are advantages in
making it explicit as a separate check point.[33]

The just war tradition always recognized that it was not enough for wars to
begin and be conducted justly but that they should end justly. Righting the
wrong that occasioned the war and so restoring peace is the objective sought
by 'right intention'. Moreover, the assessment that our leaders are obliged to
make before and during war of the overall balance of consequences arising
from war must necessarily also include the consequences after the war, if it
is to provide a full balance sheet. So, in a strict sense, there is no need for a
separate *jus post bellum* condition, since ensuring that there is a just settlement,
once victory is secured, is implicit in the other conditions. Nonetheless,
recent experiences have underlined the challenges still to be faced after the
conclusion of the conventional phase of military operations. This was illustrated in Kosovo following the 1999 NATO operations, and, still more, by
the challenges that coalition forces faced in Iraq as a result of the failure to plan
adequately for the *post bellum* phase of the 2003 Gulf War. There is, therefore,
some heuristic value in making *jus post bellum* a separate condition.

The rationale for this would be to remind political and military leaders
of the need to take the *post bellum* settlement fully into account in the overall
reckoning of the balance of consequences to be achieved by war. In doing so,
they should have, and they should keep up to date, revising as circumstances
change, a robust plan for dealing with the consequences of military action and

for ensuring the prompt restoration of peaceful conditions. Vitoria also wisely counsels the political leader always to remember: 'Once the war is fought and won, he must use his victory with moderation and Christian humility.'[34]

Justifying the just war principles

The just cause has a logical primacy over the just war conditions. A just cause does not suffice to make a war just, but a war cannot be just without one. Just cause determines the good aimed at by right intention, the good for which war is fought as a last resort and that against which the harmful consequences of war need to be measured. It has, therefore, recently been suggested that all the just war conditions could, concertina-like, be folded into one, that of just cause.[35]

This would, however, be a mistake. Just cause does not determine all other conditions—for example, the application of proportion and non-combatant immunity during conflict nor the requirement of competent authority before. Moreover, while the conditions of just cause and proportion applied before a war is undertaken are both closely interlinked, each test is of fundamental importance. Indeed, the conditions of just cause and proportion can in many ways be regarded as the key *jus ad bellum* tests, since together they set the boundaries by which the justice of a decision to go to war is measured: just cause specifying the good to be achieved and proportion assessing whether the harm caused will outweigh the good.

It is also one of the great strengths of the just war tradition that it provides a set of related but still discrete conditions, each of which has to be met. It is not enough for there to be a just cause; all the other conditions have also to be met for a war to be just. Full moral credit may only be earned if all the conditions are met. Nonetheless, some credit may still be gained if only some are met. The just war tradition wisely seeks to encourage all combatants, including those fighting an unjust war, to conduct the war justly and in accord with the requirements of proportion and non-combatant immunity. There is great merit in recognizing that the conditions, while related, are separate and so allowing for wars begun justly to be condemned, if fought unjustly, and unjust wars to secure credit for being fought justly.

The just war tradition sets out a robust set of rules to guide actions before, during, and after war. But what is the justification for these principles? The classic just war teaching offers two suggestions. The first and most widely canvassed view is that war is a form of punishment. Just as a government has a right to punish malefactors who threaten order within society, so may a government punish citizens of another state who threaten order from without, most obviously by an act of external aggression. St Augustine defined just wars as 'those which avenge injuries'.[36] Aquinas, quoting St Paul, declared that the political authorities are 'God's agents of punishment for retribution of the offender'.[37]

Vitoria explained the reasoning: 'A political leader cannot have greater authority over foreigners than he has over his own subjects: but he may not draw the sword against his own subjects unless they have done some wrong: therefore, he cannot do so against foreigners except in the same circumstances.'[38]

This view has recently attracted support from some just war commentators. David Rodin argues: 'It is possible to construct a justification for military action against aggression on the basis of a concept of law enforcement.'[39] The attraction of such an approach is that it provides a clear justification for the use of force. Force can legitimately be used against those who are guilty of aggression and who are hence liable to punishment or correction. But the punishment theory of war faces two fundamental objections.

The first difficulty, long recognized within the tradition, is that it casts states in the role of judge, jury, and executioner in their own case, a combination of functions regarded as a paradigm of injustice in civil jurisdiction. This difficulty may have appeared less compelling in the unified world of Christendom when kings were deemed to acquire their rights to rule from God and could readily be viewed as 'God's agents for punishment' on earth. Guidance could also be sought in the exercise of their functions from the Pope or Holy Roman Emperor. But, in our secular post-Westphalian world of horizontally organized states, no such theological underpinning or guidance from higher authority is available. There is an understandable reluctance to accord to modern states rights to wage war to punish the citizens of other states.

Rodin acknowledges this difficulty and argues that there is an urgent need to establish 'an impartial international body that is capable of enforcing a genuine international law'.[40] Unfortunately, no such body exists, nor does the United Nations yet fill the bill, for the reasons we have already examined. It may be a long time, if ever, before such an impartial international body comes into being. This leaves an acute problem over how states are to act pending its establishment. It would be unfortunate if all wars in the meantime, including the Second World War, which many regard as the paradigm of a just war, were to be judged unjust.

The second objection is that, if we assume the offence deserving punishment is the unjust resort to war, those guilty of this will be the political leaders, with their military and civilian advisers, who are not usually targeted in war. Those who are targeted—the ordinary service people prosecuting the war—cannot be reasonably regarded as guilty of this offence, since they are unlikely to have had any responsibility for or influence over the decision to go to war. This is so, even if they are volunteers, still more so if they are the possibly reluctant conscripts of some modern armies. Rodin seeks to evade this difficulty by arguing that, even if not guilty of the decision to go to war, ordinary soldiers are still guilty of its continued prosecution because they could refuse to fight. They may not be able to prevent the initial decision to resort to unjust war, 'but what they are able to prevent is their participation in the proscribed activity'.[41]

Quite how conscripts are supposed to exercise this ability is not clear, given the coercive organs of the state that may be arrayed against them. More importantly, although, as we shall explore in Chapter 12, we may reasonably require soldiers to refuse to fight in exceptional circumstances—for example, if their orders are manifestly illegal—military disobedience of the civil authorities is not our normal expectation. That is for very good reason. Civil control of the military is fundamental to securing our political liberties. Its loss would impel us on the path to military tyranny. We rightly expect, as a general norm, that the military should display loyalty and obedience to the civil authorities. The application of the concept of guilt to ordinary members of the armed forces for not refusing to fight seems, therefore, very strained. Ordinary members of the armed forces are as unlikely to have influence over, or responsibility for, the decisions to continue the war as they are over its inception. For this reason, the Nuremberg tribunal rejected the argument that all military actions undertaken by the German armed forces were war crimes because they were carried out in pursuit of an aggressive war.[42]

If war is punishment, it is not just a very rough form of punishment but rather an unjust punishment. For the guilty get off and the innocent are punished. There are sound reasons for rejecting the theory of war as punishment.

The second justification for the just war principles offered within the tradition is based on the self-defence analogy. This justification arose later in the tradition than the theory of punishment, since the earliest authorities, such as St Augustine, did not consider private individuals had a right to use force in self-defence.[43] The seventeenth-century writer Grotius explains the analogy as follows: 'What has been said by us up to this point, concerning the right to defend oneself and one's possessions ... may be made applicable also to public war, if the differences in condition are taken into account.'[44]

This is a more promising approach, for our right to defend ourselves from attack does not depend upon the guilt of the attacker. That right remains, even if the attacker is himself innocent—for example, a person induced to make an attack under the influence of drugs injected in him against his will by a third party. It depends rather on the fact that the attacker is posing harm. Force is legitimized to stop the harm occurring.

We are, as Aquinas notes, quoting Aristotle, political animals who live in communities and only through such communal life can flourish as human beings. We have a right to protect our communities from external aggression so that within them we can pursue our vision of the good life. Indeed, our rulers have a duty to protect the lives and political autonomy of the communities with whose care they are entrusted: 'It is the king's task to furnish the community subject to him with protection against enemies.'[45]

War in self-defence can thus be justified. But, as we will explore in Chapter 11, not all just wars are defensive wars and may include humanitarian interventions. Any concept of self-defence on which the just war doctrine is founded will need to be an extended concept, embracing not just defence of oneself but also of one's neighbour. Moreover, the person whom a neighbour may be called upon to help may, as in the Gospel story of the Good Samaritan, be defined, not by physical proximity, but by the urgency of his need.

Such an extended concept of the right of self-defence helps to explicate just war thinking, in particular, on what constitutes just cause. But that concept on its own is not sufficient to ground the just war principles. For not all the just war principles are reducible to that of just cause. Moreover, the right of self-defence itself, like any other right, still needs justifying. At a more fundamental level, the basis for the just war principles, and the rights and duties they enshrine, needs to be sought—as with other moral principles— from the contribution that they make to human welfare and the prevention of suffering. The just war tradition recognizes that war may, on occasion, be necessary to protect human welfare but is acutely conscious of the suffering that may be caused. Based on centuries of experience and practical wisdom, the tradition has carefully fashioned a set of rules to limit the suffering that war brings by constraining both the occasions and the conduct of war. The overriding aim is to ensure that war takes place only when more good than harm will result.

The just war tradition offers invaluable guidance for the political and military leaders who take the momentous decisions to go to war and direct its conduct. Its principles also offer crucial guidance to the ordinary service people who conduct the war and who themselves may be faced in war with decisions of far greater moment than they would ever encounter in civilian life.

Compliance with all the just war principles, at all these varying levels, is necessary for a war to be just. But how are we to ensure that everyone involved in war will comply—before, during, and after war? Indeed, can we reasonably expect that the rules will be followed, if a rule book is all the guidance we have to offer? The conclusions of our previous chapter suggest that more is needed. To account satisfactorily for the full complexity and difficulty of our moral lives requires according proper weight to all aspects of our moral lives, not just rules but also intentions, consequences, and virtues. The just war tradition, as so far enunciated, has much to offer by way of rules and calculation of consequences, the latter furnishing both justification for the rules and a key component of them. But nothing has so far been said about the role of virtues.

The virtues have been largely absent from the recent revival of the just war tradition. They were lost from sight from the sixteenth century, when lawyers and juridically minded theologians took over development of the tradition and, not surprisingly given their background, concentrated on rules and principles. But, further back in the tradition, Aquinas, drawing strength as ever from Aristotle, deemed the virtues a key element of just war teaching. There was good reason to do so. For, if a sound training and education in the virtues are essential for right conduct in other areas of conduct, how much more would this seem necessary in war, given the immense challenge of the decisions taken before, during, and after war and the many temptations to err.

We shall examine the role of virtues in just war in Chapter 6. But we need first to resolve the difficult issue of the status of the principle of non-combatant immunity.

FIVE

Is Non-Combatant Immunity Absolute?

The principle of non-combatant immunity forbids deliberate attacks on civilians. Yet civilians are frequently killed and injured in war. This is not, as is sometimes suggested, a peculiarly modern aberration. This book began with the massacre in the fifth century BC during the Peloponnesian War of the male adult population of Melos and the enslavement of all the women and children of that unhappy isle. Siege-craft was widely practised and constantly refined from ancient times through the Middle Ages and into the modern era. It culminated in the protracted siege of Leningrad in 1941–3, where a million civilians died from bombing, starvation, and disease. Killing civilians in war is not a new phenomenon. But what the combination of new technology and strategic bombing introduced in the twentieth century was an ability to kill very large numbers of civilians in a very short space of time.[1] Moreover, with the ending of the Cold War, there has been an increase in intra-state conflict, 'war amongst the people', that presents its own particular threat to civilians.[2] The civilian casualty rate in war grew exponentially in the twentieth century. So, if civilians are inevitably killed in wars, does that mean that war is morally forbidden?

Just war commentators have resisted drawing this conclusion. This would, as Vitoria notes, mean that it would 'be impossible to wage war against the guilty, thereby preventing the just side from fighting'. Hitler and the Third Reich would remain unchallenged. The solution Vitoria suggests is that, while it is absolutely forbidden intentionally to kill innocent persons, 'it is occasionally lawful to kill the innocent not by mistake but with full knowledge of what one is doing, if this is an accidental effect: for example, during the justified storming of a fortress or city'.[3] The principle of non-combatant immunity is held absolute, but its effects are mitigated by distinguishing between the 'double effects' of an action: those that are intended and those that are merely foreseen. This is the doctrine of double effect first introduced in the thirteenth century by St Thomas Aquinas.[4]

The principle of double effect

Double effect is held to be important, not only because it marks out a distinction that is held to be significant in its own right but also because it helps underpin our ability to hold some moral rules to be true without exception. Professor Anscombe explains: 'The distinction between the intended and the merely foreseen effects of a voluntary action is indeed absolutely crucial to Christian ethics. For Christianity forbids a number of things as bad in themselves but if I am answerable for the foreseen consequences of an action or refusal, as much as for the action itself, then the prohibition breaks down.'[5]

The doctrine of double effect states that it is permissible to carry out acts with foreseeable bad consequences provided:

- the act (which must itself be morally neutral) is undertaken for the sake of good effects;
- the bad consequences are merely foreseen and not intended—they are wanted neither as the means to the result aimed at nor as the end itself;
- the bad consequences are not disproportionate to the good aimed at.

According to double effect, the primary determinant of the moral quality of an act is the intention. An act that has bad effects may still be permissible provided those effects are not intended. This is qualified, however, where the effects are so bad as to be disproportionate to the good aimed at, so rendering the act bad, despite the purity of the intention.

The distinction between the consequences of our actions that are intended and those that are merely foreseen is important to our moral evaluations. Intentions usually commit us to action, and so to bring about consequences in the world, in a way that mere foresight does not. What we intend to do may also disclose more about our character, of the sort of people we are. We accordingly care about the intentions others have towards us, as they do about our intentions. There is an important moral distinction between intention and foresight.

This is illustrated by Nicholas Monserrat's account in *The Cruel Sea* of the moral dilemma facing a British corvette commander during the Second World War.[6] His task was to protect a convoy of civilian cargo ships that were being attacked by a German U-boat. A number of cargo ships had already been sunk, and survivors from their crews were swimming about in the sea. The only way to protect the remaining cargo ships was for the commander of the corvette to sink a depth charge to destroy the U-boat. The depth charge would be directed at the U-boat, but the violent commotion of the sea caused by the explosion would be very likely to drown some of the people swimming about in the sea. What should he do?

According to the doctrine of double effect, it would be permissible for the commander to sink the U-boat with the depth charge. For the act would be undertaken for the sake of good effects—saving the rest of the convoy and thousands of lives. The deaths of the convoy survivors swimming in the sea would not be directly part of the act of sinking the U-boat but rather its indirect effects. The deaths would be merely foreseen but not intended—wanted neither as a means nor as an end to the result aimed at. If a large wave had suddenly appeared and swept them to safety rather than drowning them, the commander would have been only too happy. Finally, the bad consequences—the death of a few innocents—would not be disproportionate to the good aimed at—saving thousands of lives in the rest of the convoy.

This case is different from that of the British strategic bomber in the Second World War attacking the populous city centre of Hamburg in August 1943 as part of the allied strategy of area bombing. This strategy was aimed at undermining the morale of the German population to induce them to bring pressure to bear on the German government to cease its aggression. The act of the RAF pilot, like that of the naval commander, is undertaken for the sake of good effects. But in this case the civilian deaths are not merely foreseen but intended. They are wanted as a means to the result aimed at. If the bombs had missed the civilian targets, the pilot might have felt obliged to circle round again and repeat the attack.

There is an important distinction between the effects we foresee and those we intend. But, if double effect is to be able to support a moral absolutist stance, it needs to mark out a dividing line that is not just important but that always constitutes a decisive moral boundary. That is more difficult to establish.

Consider, for example, the following cases of abortion much discussed in the philosophical literature.[7] In the first case, a hysterectomy is performed to remove a cancerous womb. The mother's life is saved, but the foetus dies. In the second case the head of a foetus becomes stuck during labour and cannot be dislodged or removed by Caesarean section. The mother's life can be saved only if the surgeon performs a craniotomy, crushing the baby's skull. In the third example, the mother's life can be saved only by altering the chemical composition of the amniotic fluid by injecting a saline solution, again with fatal results for the foetus. Let us suppose that, in all three cases, if the operation is performed, the mother will be saved but the foetus will die; if the operation is not performed, both mother and baby will die.

The consequences of the operation are identical in all three cases. But, according to the absolutist, applying the double-effect principle, only in the first case—the hysterectomy—is the death of the foetus an unintended side effect of the operation. In the other cases the death of the foetus is so intimately connected with the operation that it is deemed to be an intended consequence, wanted as a means to the end aimed at. On that basis Catholic theologians rule that abortion is permitted only in the first case. In the other cases the surgeon should allow the mother and baby to die rather than intentionally to kill the foetus.

This analysis prompts two questions: first, is the distinction in these cases between intention and foresight as clear-cut as is suggested; and, second, is the distinction as morally significant as the advocates of double effect claim?

Nigel Biggar argues that a clear distinction can be drawn in such cases based on the distinction between the effects we want and those we merely accept: 'An intended effect is one that is wanted. An accepted effect is not wanted, but is instead tolerated with an appropriate degree of manifest reluctance.'[8] He illustrates this with the example of a mother who interposes herself between her child and an attacking animal. The mother may, reluctantly, accept her mauling if that is what it takes to protect her child, but that is not what she wants and she may hope against hope that it will not happen. So she does not intend but merely foresees the mauling.[9] Her lack of any prior history of suicidal tendencies may furnish supporting evidence that she does not intend her death but only the protection of the child.[10]

If the mother's death is not certain but only a high risk, a clear distinction can be readily drawn. The mother wants to protect her child and accepts the risk to her own life in interposing herself between the animal and child. But suppose the animal is so fierce and vicious that she sees her death as the certain consequence of her action. In that case, it may seem equally plausible to claim that she does choose to die. She does not choose death as an end, as her lack of prior suicidal tendencies would attest. But she does choose death, however reluctantly, as the means to save the life of her child. Indeed, it is only if we concede this that we can appreciate the full extent of her heroic sacrifice: she lays down her life for the life of the child. So perhaps she does intend her death?

T. A. Cavanaugh, in discussing the abortion examples, offers a slightly different way of making the distinction between intention and foresight. He proposes three tests: 'Intentions characteristically: (1) cause deliberation; (2) issue in further intentions through deliberation; (3) (as further intentions) solve deliberation's problem.'[11] In the craniotomy case he argues that the surgeon deliberates how to save the mother's life (1); chooses to crush the baby's skull to preserve the mother's life (2); and crushing the skull solves deliberation's problem (3).[12] He accordingly can be said to intend the baby's death. 'In contrast, in the hysterectomy case the physician chooses to remove the cancerous, gravid uterus in order to preserve the mother's life, foreseeing that the non-viable baby will thereby die with causal necessity.'[13]

That sounds plausible. But, again, as we reflect further, it seems we could equally argue that in this case too the conditions for intentionality are met. Cavanaugh concedes: 'It is no more possible for a non-viable foetus to live when the uterus has been surgically removed from the mother than it is for a foetus to live when its head has been crushed.'[14] Given that is so, we could surely equally maintain that, in the hysterectomy case too, the surgeon deliberates how to save the mother's life (1); he chooses the baby's death as the means to save the mother's life (2); and the death solves his deliberative problem (3). He would, of course, be delighted if, following the hysterectomy, the baby did not die. But so would the surgeon in the craniotomy case. The unfortunate fact is that in neither case is that possible. In both cases death is the inevitable result of the surgeon's action.

The distinction between intention and foresight in these cases is thus not as clear-cut as it first seemed. Moreover, even if we accept that a distinction can be made, the moral weight that the absolutist places on it appears open to question. It is argued that only in the craniotomy case is the operation permitted; in the other two cases the mother and baby should be allowed to die. That conclusion appears perverse. For in all three cases the balance of good over ill is the same: without an operation, mother and foetus will die; with one, the mother can be saved.

Moreover, while in only the first case is the death of the foetus unintended, in all three cases the death is within the control of the surgeon, foreseen by him and consented to by him: even though he foresees the death as inevitable, he is still willing that it should come about as a result of his action. In all three cases the extent of the surgeon's control over and consent to the death of the foetus appears the same, while the consequences are morally identical. The similarities between the cases appear greater than the differences. The mere presence or absence of intention appears too slender a distinction to bear the moral weight that the absolutist places on it. There would, therefore, appear a strong argument for concluding that in all three cases the operation should be performed if this is the only way to save the life of the mother.

This conclusion might still be resisted by arguing that there is an important difference between the surgeon's act of killing the foetus and his failure to save the lives of the mother and foetus: the difference between an act and an omission. There are important differences between acts and omissions. But the difference on its own is not enough to sustain the different moral evaluations sought. For a hospital ward orderly, hoping to inherit from an ageing patient, seems equally culpable if he fails to switch the life-support machine on (an omission) as if he deliberately turns it off (an act). Our conclusion is that where, as in the abortion cases, the balance of good over ill is so clear-cut, it is permissible to carry out the operation even in the case where the death of the foetus is intended.

Conversely, in other cases the balance of ill over good may be so strong that, even though the bad consequences are unintended, the action is still condemned. This is illustrated by the case of *Regina v. Desmond, Barrett and others*. In 1868 the accused attempted to rescue two Fenians by blowing up the wall of Clerkenwell prison and, in consequence, killed some people living nearby. They foresaw the deaths as a probable consequence of their actions but did not intend them as a means or end of their action. If the deaths had not occurred, their escape plan could still have succeeded. Nonetheless, Lord Coleridge concluded that it is murder, 'if a man did an act not with the purpose of taking life but with knowledge or belief that life was likely to be taken'.[15]

It would be possible to concur with Lord Coleridge's judgment, while still maintaining the principle of double effect, by arguing that the action of the Fenians fails the test of proportionality: the deaths of the people living near the prison wall were disproportionate to the Fenians' end of helping their comrades escape from prison. That is so, and the end sought—escaping from prison—is hardly a morally laudable objective. We condemn the action because of its disproportionate consequences. But we also condemn the Fenians' action because, even if they did not intend the deaths, they had, in Lord Coleridge's words, 'knowledge or belief that life was likely to be taken'. They foresaw the deaths and still went ahead with the plan. They were willing that the deaths should occur. They consented to the deaths. That recognition is also part of our grounds for condemning the action.

The beliefs and feelings we attribute to others are an important part of how we view and react to them as human beings and how morally we evaluate their actions. That is why, as double effect rightly insists, there is an important difference between intended and unintended actions. But that is not the only difference that matters. There are gradations of the agent's mental state to be considered.

This can be illustrated by looking again at the hand-crushing example we considered in Chapter 3. It will be recalled that Strawson judiciously observed that:

> If someone treads on my hand accidentally, while trying to help me, the pain may be no less acute than if he treads on it in contemptuous disregard of my existence or with a malevolent wish to injure me. But I shall generally feel in the second case a kind and degree of resentment that I should not feel in the first.[16]

Let us fill out the example further. Suppose that there is a fire in a flat in an apartment block. My own flat is unaffected but, while doing some decorating, I have fallen and am trapped by a bookcase, with my arm extended into the corridor. Someone treads on my hand, causing me considerable pain. Now let us consider the following variations:

- In the first case, a neighbour, taking advantage of the confusion caused by the fire, seizes the opportunity to settle an old grievance and deliberately crushes my hand in order to hurt me.

- In the second variant, a fireman steps on my hand, while rushing along the corridor in order to rescue a neighbour from the fire. He foresees the hand-crushing and consents to it but does not intend it. It is neither a means nor an end of his action. He would be only too pleased if I had managed to withdraw my hand.

- Third, a neighbour (unaware of the fire in one of the flats) steps on my hand, while rushing along the corridor in haste to get to the pub before last orders. He foresees the hand-crushing and consents to it but does not intend it, as either a means or an end of his action.
- Finally, a neighbour steps on my hand while trying to rescue me, losing his balance as he is pushed by a crowd jostling along the corridor. The crushing is accidental: neither intended nor consented to.

In all four cases the pain felt is the same, but how the action of hand-crushing is assessed is very different. There is, as double effect notes, an important difference between the first case where the hand-crushing is intended and the other variations. But there is also an important difference between the first three examples where the crushing is within the agent's control and consented to and the fourth example where it is neither. There is also a crucial difference between the second and third cases, even though in both cases the crushing is within the agent's control and consented to by him. For in the second case the pain from the hand-crushing could be deemed to be outweighed by the benefits to the rescued neighbour, whereas in the third case there are no such good consequences to offset against the pain. Getting to the pub on time is hardly an ethically compelling objective. In this case I would justifiably feel resentment that my neighbour had, nonetheless, been willing to cause me pain and shown a callous indifference to my suffering. The hand-crushing would thus be condemned in the first and third cases but excused in the second and fourth.

What these considerations underline is that in evaluating actions we need to take into account both the mental states of the agent and the consequences of his agency. But they also suggest that, in doing so, there is not a single cut-off point between intended and unintended consequences but rather more of a graduating scale. It matters if the consequences are intended. But, even if unintended, it is still important if they are deemed to be within the agent's control and consented to by him, how important depending on the extent of the agent's control and consent. For there are degrees of control and consent, as illustrated by the many links and potential breaks in the causal chain between my sending money to Oxfam to save a child's life and its arrival in Africa to help a starving child. The agent's consent to harmful consequences, even if unintended, may still occasion resentment in the victim. Where, however, the consequences of an action are neither intended nor consented to, no blame is attributable to the agent.

These distinctions in mental state need, moreover, to be considered and weighed up together with the overall balance of good over ill consequences. This is illustrated by our condemnation of the unintended deaths in the Fenian escape plot. Conversely, where great harm could be avoided—for example, the saving of a mother's life, as in the abortion cases—we may excuse an act even where harmful consequences are intended.

This more nuanced analysis seems to reflect more accurately the complex nature of our moral reasoning where we may need to attend not just, as double effect insists, to the presence or absence of intentions, but to a variety of gradations of mental state. The analysis also offers guidance in a wider range of situations than double effect. Double effect was introduced into the just war tradition to resolve the particular problem of the unwanted bad consequences of an action undertaken with good intention, such as killing civilians during siege operations. It was not, however, designed to provide guidance for other equally difficult challenges, such as the bad consequences of our inactions. The analysis of moral reasoning that we have suggested would help provide guidance in both types of situation. For, in assessing both actions and inactions, we may need to weigh up the balance of good over ill to be achieved with gradations of the agent's mental state. We may condemn a failure to act where the consequences of inaction are of sufficient gravity, even though the consequences are not intended, provided they are foreseen, within the agent's control, and consented to. On such grounds we may condemn a negligent passer-by who, rushing to keep a business appointment, leaves a dying baby abandoned by the wayside or, even more, the failure of the international community to stop the genocide in Rwanda, as we shall examine in Chapter 11.

The doctrine of double effect was introduced not only because the distinction between intended and foreseen consequences was considered important in its own right but also because the distinction was deemed crucial to moral absolutism. Our conclusion so far is that the distinction between intended and unintended effects is important but does not always mark off a single decisive moral boundary. We need now to consider how this more nuanced approach would affect the case for moral absolutism.

Moral absolutism

The moral absolutist holds that that there are some moral rules that should
be obeyed in all circumstances without exception. These rules constitute
what Anscombe calls the 'bedrock' of morality.[17] Geach explains: 'And
legalism will further hold that if in working out the description of an action
we reach certain descriptions, e.g. that it is an act of blasphemy, or killing
the innocent, or perversion of just judgment, or perjury, or adultery; then
we need consider no further: this is already the cut-off point and the act is
ruled out.'[18]

Such a cut-off procedure may, Geach suggests, be partly justified by
prudential reasons because we doubt our ability to determine properly
when an exception may be permitted because of 'our ignorance of present
circumstances and future contingencies, and our propensity to load the scale
of judgment in favour of ourselves and those we care about'.[19] The rules are
to be held fast to without exception, since permitting exceptions to the rules
would be risky. But what if sticking to the rules is even riskier, leading to
disastrous consequences? Geach at this point falls back on theology. The
rules of morality are God's Law and so to be obeyed at all times. We must
trust in God's Providence and 'need not worry that by keeping God's Law
we could by misadventure get the world into a mess'.[20]

Some of the theological underpinning of Geach's position may seem
excessive to a natural-law approach. But the moral clarity offered by
absolutism has considerable attractions. The problem is that absolutism
can yield results that seem counter-intuitive.

In the three cases of abortion just considered, the absolutist would permit
abortion only in the case of hysterectomy, where the death of the foetus can
be considered an unintended side effect. In the other cases—craniotomy
and injection of a saline solution into the amniotic fluid—the death of the
foetus is deemed to be intended. Abortion is prohibited, since it would
breach the rule forbidding the intentional killing of the innocent, even
though in all three cases abortion is the only way to save the life of the
mother and without an operation the foetus would die anyway. These
conclusions seem at odds with our ordinary moral intuitions that such
life-saving operations should be permitted.

The absolutist would also never permit voluntary euthanasia or assisted suicide for a dying patient where the ailment is incurable and certain to lead to death, however excruciating and unendurable may be her suffering. Nor would it help that the most stringent and careful safeguards are in place to ensure that: only a medical practitioner can carry out euthanasia or assist a suicide and only after a second opinion is sought from another independent doctor; euthanasia or assisted suicide represents the explicit wish of the patient; the illness is terminal and there is no other way to relieve the patient's intolerable suffering.[21] For the absolutist, since euthanasia or suicide involves intentional killing of the innocent, it is forbidden in all circumstances, whatever the consequences in terms of prolonging the agonizing pain of a dying patient. This appears an unduly harsh conclusion. Some may dissent from this judgement, perhaps fearful of the wider consequences of sanctioning a practice that might be open to abuse—for example, by grasping relatives. Such concerns are legitimate, although they could be met by appropriately stringent safeguards of the kind just suggested. But even to enter into debate over such concerns is ruled out by the absolutist, for whom the act is to be condemned, regardless of its consequences. It is this refusal even to allow consideration of the consequences for the patient that seems to mark a defect in the absolutist's construal of the nature of moral reasoning.

The absolutist would also never countenance killing one innocent in order to save many lives. Bernard Williams introduced into the debate the much discussed example of Jim and the Indians:

> Jim finds himself in the central square of a small South American town. Tied up against the wall are a row of twenty Indians, most terrified, a few defiant, in front of them several men in uniform. A heavy man in a sweat-stained shirt turns out to be the captain in charge and, after a good deal of questioning of Jim, which establishes he got there by accident while on a botanical expedition, explains that the Indians are a random group of inhabitants who, after recent acts of protest against the government, are just about to be killed to remind other protestors of the advantages of not protesting. However, since Jim is an honoured visitor from another land, the captain is happy to offer him a guest's privilege of killing one of the Indians himself. If Jim accepts, then as a special mark of the occasion, the other Indians will be let off. Of course, if Jim refuses, then there is no special occasion and Pedro here will do what he was about to do when Jim arrived, and kill them all . . . The men against the wall, and the other villagers, understand the situation, and are obviously begging him to accept. What should he do?[22]

For the absolutist, the prohibition on killing the innocent means that Jim should decline Pedro's offer, despite the earnest pleas of the villagers that he should accept. But for other commentators such a conclusion is far from clear. Indeed, if faced with such an agonizing dilemma, it would seem wrong for Jim to put his own moral purity above the needs of others. So, provided he has good reason to believe Pedro will keep his promise, it may be permissible for him to shoot one of the Indians in order to save the lives of nineteen. The killing of one innocent is a moral harm, for which he should feel remorse and moral regret. But, if there is really no other way to save the lives of nineteen innocents, such action, however regrettable, may still be permissible, as the lesser of two evils.

Absolutists may seek to resist this conclusion by arguing that such philosophical examples are both improbable and fanciful and that it is misguided to allow such examples to distort our moral reasoning. With sufficiently weird and wonderful examples, philosophers, it is claimed, can end up justifying anything.

Philosophers are sometimes guilty of the fanciful manufacture of improbable examples. But, unfortunately, the dilemma posed for Jim is only too real. Post-11 September 2001, we no longer need to manufacture examples. We have all agonized whether it would have been right to shoot down a hijacked plane with thirty innocent hostages on board if it were about to hit the Twin Towers in New York killing many thousands. Few in America or elsewhere dispute that it would have been right so to act on 11 September, had the opportunity arisen. US Air Force pilots are now under orders to shoot down hijacked planes posing similar threats, and this publicized order has occasioned little controversy. This suggests that our ordinary moral beliefs permit taking innocent life where this is the only way to prevent very much greater harm to innocents.

An absolutist may seek to avoid this conclusion by arguing that the USAF pilot does not intend to kill the passengers but only to shoot down the plane in which they are travelling to prevent its collision with the Twin Towers. The deaths are only unintended side effects. If they could have been avoided, that would have been cause for rejoicing. The latter may be so, and the deaths were certainly not wanted as an end of the action. But the escape of the passengers was unfortunately not an available option. There was no way to avoid the civilian deaths if the plane was blown up by a missile: for to shoot down the plane would be to kill the passengers. The deaths of the passengers were as intimately connected with the blowing-up of the plane, as is the killing of the foetus with the crushing of its skull in the abortion example considered earlier. In both cases the deaths could be regarded as the means chosen, however reluctantly, to achieve the end of saving innocent lives. If the craniotomy operation constitutes intentional killing, so would the killing of the passengers on the plane. To maintain otherwise would be to miss a key element of the agonizing dilemma with which the USAF pilot, and those who authorized his action, are presented: that, in shooting down the plane, the pilot would be killing innocent passengers.

The claim that in such a case the deaths are unintended obscures key moral features of the pilot's predicament. The possibility of adducing arguments either way also underlines that the distinction between intention and foresight is not as clear-cut and decisive as the absolutist needs it to be. Moreover, with the dilemma faced by Jim and the Indians, such verbal manœuvres are not available. For killing one Indian is indisputably the chosen means to save the others, and so there can be no suggestion that the death is not intended.

Another possible response for the absolutist is to argue that, since the passengers were doomed to die anyway, the USAF pilot's decision would not determine that they should die but only how they should die. Their impending death is relevant to assessing the balance of consequences, just as is the unavoidable death of the foetus in the craniotomy case. But it is not clear that the fact the passengers would die anyway can thus be used to exculpate the agent. For that would provide too ready an escape route from moral censure. We could, for example, argue that it was permissible to rape someone who was about to be raped by others, or to sell arms to a villainous tyrant because, if we did not, others would.[23]

A variation on the Twin Towers example can quickly show that this manœuvre does not work. For suppose the deaths of the passengers were not inevitable. The al-Qaeda operatives were not suicide bombers but bombers who had hijacked the plane to drop powerful bombs on the Twin Towers, after which they planned to fly to a prearranged airfield, where an escape car was awaiting them and the passengers would be released. Even in this amended example, it would still seem permissible for the USAF pilot to shoot down the plane in order to prevent the thousands of deaths that would otherwise occur.

So, there are cases—real-life cases that are not at all fanciful or improbable—where holding fast to the prohibition on killing the innocent may lead to morally unwelcome conclusions.

It could be argued that such cases are exceptional and it would be better to accept such anomalies rather than lose the moral clarity gained by holding fast to the rules. If one breach in the rules is permitted, however individually justifiable it may seem, we would be opening the way for unscrupulous politicians and others to twist the rules to their own purpose, a risk particularly present under the heavy pressures of war.

This is a powerful argument, but one that is not in the end sustainable. Without Geach's assumption of a benevolent Providence, there is no assurance that sticking to the rules, whatever the consequences, may not lead to disastrous results. Moreover, the cases we have been considering are not so exceptional that we may reasonably hope never to encounter them. They are very real moral dilemmas we can face in our ordinary lives where sticking to the rules, regardless of consequences, may lead to the suffering and death of those we love and those to whom we have duties as our neighbours. Faced with such a proliferation of recalcitrant facts, the absolutist might still seek to adjust his theory to accommodate these facts. But the expedients to which he would need to resort would be likely to become increasingly desperate. His convolutions might come to resemble those of the Ptolemaic astronomer adding ever increasing numbers of cycles and epicycles in a vain attempt to sustain his geocentric world view in the face of the accumulating evidence that we inhabit a heliocentric planetary system.

Moreover, to pretend that a rule that we acknowledge admits of exceptions does not do so appears a morally unattractive response. Such pretence smacks of the two-tier 'Government House' morality for which utilitarians have been rightly criticized: the idea that there could be a nuanced morality for the privileged few, while they impose an immutable code on the natives outside the Government House perimeter.[24] Such manipulative duplicity seems not just impractical but alien to the nature of morality.

Absolutism fails in the end because it oversimplifies and misdescribes the nature of our moral reasoning. Moral rules could be held absolute only if there were a guarantee that they never would conflict. In the imperfect post-lapsarian world we inhabit no such guarantee is available. It is a regrettable fact but a fact nonetheless that moral rules can and do conflict. We may thus be faced with the kind of agonizing dilemmas we have been considering. Like Agamemnon at Aulis, torn between his duties as king and his duties as a father, we can be presented with situations where there 'are no ways that do not lead to ill'.[25] In such circumstances the right thing to do, however morally regrettable, may be to choose the lesser of two ills. Absolutism pretends that such dilemmas never happen. But they do. Hence, as Aeschylus recognized, derive the springs of moral tragedy.

The failure of absolutism can also be traced at a deeper level to its defective view of the nature of moral reasoning. For absolutism equips us with too few conceptual tools with which to undertake the task of moral reasoning.

The principle of double effect underlines the important distinction between the intended and unintended consequences of our actions. But there are other gradations of mental state that can also be relevant to the attribution of moral responsibility. An agent may be held responsible for the consequences of her action that, while unintended, are still within her control and consented to by her. There may, moreover, be degrees of control and consent to be attended to. Finally, at the other end of the scale, an agent who has no control over or consent to what happened is excused liability.

Absolutism also oversimplifies our moral reasoning by debarring any consideration of consequences where an act falls under one of the rules that the absolutist deems without exception. Indeed, at this level morality becomes an irrational activity, for which no reasons can be sought or given. The rules must just be obeyed and, in Geach's telling phrase, 'we need consider no further'. The combination of this prohibition on considering consequences with the priority accorded to intentions by double effect makes the agent's intention to follow or breach a moral rule the only further morally relevant feature of such acts that needs to be attended to. This has two further unfortunate consequences. First, it appears to make the mere lack of intention too readily available as an excuse for actions with very harmful, albeit unintended, consequences. Second, it accords to the agent's intention a disproportionate importance in the moral reckoning. We are debarred from taking consequences into account, however disastrous they may be. The heavens may fall, provided only our hands are clean, our intentions pure: *fiat iustitia, ruat caelum*. This exaltation of personal integrity above all else appears both morally unattractive but also dangerous, particularly in a world where nuclear technology has made the all too literal collapse of the heavens a very real possibility.

In place of the oversimplified view of moral reasoning proffered by the absolutist, moral reasoning is better construed as operating with a graduating scale on which we assess degrees of mental responsibility, judged by the extent to which the consequences are within the agent's control and consented to by him, and weigh these up together with the assessed balance of good and ill to be achieved. Where great harm may result, mere lack of intention would not excuse an act, or failure to act, whose consequences we foresaw, had control over, and consented to. Where great harm could be avoided, an act with intended harmful consequences may still be permissible.

Moral reasoning thus turns out to be more complex and difficult than the absolutist supposes. But that accurately reflects the challenges we face in our moral life. The absolutist makes an error parallel with that made by the consequentialist. It is the mistake of consequentialism to look only at consequences. The error of absolutism is to focus on intentions. A balanced assessment—as virtuous consequentialism requires—needs to consider both the interior quality of the action, as well as the external effects of agency.

Principle of non-combatant immunity reconsidered

So, where does our discussion leave the principle of non-combatant immunity? The principle forbids deliberate attacks on non-combatants, whether our own or those of the enemy. It is derived from the broader prohibition on the intentional killing of innocents, applied to the particular and difficult circumstances of war. Given the need to restrict the suffering caused by war, the prohibition of deliberate attacks on non-combatants is of fundamental importance. Any death is a moral tragedy to be avoided. The ban on killing is lifted for combatants only because they are the ones who are threatening harm. There is no licence to kill non-combatants who pose no such threat.

In what circumstances then are civilian casualties permissible? Civilian casualties may, as the principle of double effect accepts, be licit where they are the unintended side effects of legitimate military action and the harm thereby produced is not disproportionate to the good achieved. But, even where the deaths are unintended, to the extent that they are foreseen, within our control, and consented to, we bear responsibility for them.

Moreover, the harm caused is certain, while any good achieved is likely to be more speculative. Every effort should, therefore, be made to minimize civilian casualties, whether intended or foreseen. Mere lack of intention should not be available as too ready an excuse to pile up civilian deaths.

Moral principles may conflict. The prohibition on intentionally killing the innocent cannot, therefore, be held absolute, admitting no exception. But, if we are to minimize the suffering caused by war, there are very strong reasons for holding fast to non-combatant immunity as near absolute a principle as we can. For, amid the pressures and strains of war, it may otherwise be too tempting for political and military leaders to argue for exceptions in the interests of military necessity. The ban on killing non-combatants is designed to provide a powerful further constraint over and above that provided by the principle of proportion, to afford additional protection to the innocent. Any breach of the principle would, therefore, be permitted exceptionally only if this were the only way to prevent very much greater harm to innocents. On that basis, we have suggested that it would be permissible for the USAF pilot to kill the innocent passengers on board the plane about to crash into the Twin Towers, if this were the only way to save the lives of the many thousands of innocents who would otherwise be killed. But the moral presumption is always that the prohibition should be followed. No licence to kill civilians is granted for the sake of military convenience or necessity.

Civilian lives are not to be traded off in marginal calculations of proportional advantage. At all times action should be taken to minimize civilian casualties, whether intended or merely foreseen. As the seventeenth-century Puritan divine William Ames insisted: 'Charity and Aequity doth require that Warre be so managed as the innocent may bee as little damnified as possible.'[26]

Minimizing civilian casualties is a requirement of ethics. It can also be sound military strategy. The key to the success of a counter-insurgency operation is the support of the civilian population. Civilian deaths cannot, therefore, be discounted as collateral damage, the mere unintended side effects of military operations. For civilian deaths, whether intended or unintended, can alienate the support of the population and so prejudice the success of the military mission. These lessons in counter-insurgency doctrine have had to be painfully relearnt in recent years by US and UK forces operating in Iraq and Afghanistan, as we shall explore further in Chapter 8.[27]

To illustrate the application of the principle of non-combatant immunity, it may be helpful to consider two recent military operations: the Gaza conflict in 2008–9 and the NATO air campaign in Kosovo in 1999.

Conflict in Gaza

The Israeli Defence forces conducted a military campaign in Gaza, code-named Operation 'Cast Lead', against the Islamist militant group Hamas, from 27 December 2008 to 18 January 2009. The aim of the campaign was to reduce Hamas's military capability, in general, and, in particular, to stop Hamas rocket attacks on Israel's southern communities.[28] At the end of the campaign Palestinian estimates converged around 1,400 Palestinian dead, including 940 civilians. Israeli military sources estimated just under 1,200 Palestinian deaths, including 300 confirmed civilian deaths.[29] The main reason for the discrepancy was the difference in the estimates of how many of the dead were Hamas fighters and how many civilians. The Israeli government said more than 700 dead were militants. The Palestinian estimate for militant deaths was much lower. In conflict, casualty estimates can become caught up in the propaganda battle each side wages against the other. There was, however, less dispute over Israeli casualties: thirteen Israelis were killed during the conflict, including three civilians and one soldier killed by Hamas rocket attacks.

Hamas rocket attacks during the conflict hit a synagogue, schools, including a kindergarten, and apartment blocks. They were intended to kill civilians and did so. Although only 3 were killed, 918 were injured. The attacks were in clear breach of the principle of non-combatant immunity.

By contrast, the Israeli government claimed that its forces attacked only military targets. Substantial efforts were made to minimize civilian casualties, despite the difficulties involved when their enemy deliberately chose to fight from civilian centres. This included issuing warnings, by leaflets, text messages, and phone calls, to the civilian population to evacuate areas where military operations were to take place and cancellation of military attacks where the risk of civilian casualties was too high.

Nonetheless, there were substantial Palestinian civilian deaths, probably somewhere between the 300 Israeli figure and the 940 estimated by the Palestinians. These included the deaths of women and children, whose fate made particularly harrowing viewing on the worldwide, twenty-four-hour,

TV news broadcasts, which are a significant accompaniment of modern warfare.

The Israelis claimed that they did not intentionally kill the civilians. The deaths were the unintended side effects of attacks on military targets, wanted neither as a means nor as an end of the action. But the question still arises whether the Israeli Defence Forces took sufficient precautions to minimize civilian casualties. Some casualties were unavoidable, particularly since Hamas deliberately operated from civilian centres. But the military operations were prosecuted with considerable ferocity and intensity in a geographically confined area of high population density: a population of nearly one and a half million in an area of only 139 square miles. The operations also included employment of weapons, such as white phosphorus shells, whose use is deemed disproportionate in areas of civilian population.[30] Even when the populace received warnings to evacuate, there were not necessarily safe areas to which they could move. A UN Fact-Finding Mission—the Goldstone Report—subsequently concluded that the Israeli forces had 'failed to take all feasible precautions in the choice of means and method of attack with a view to avoiding and in any event minimizing incidental loss of civilian life, injury to civilians and damage to civilian objects'.[31]

While the Israelis may not have intended the civilian casualties, they could in many cases foresee that they would occur, and, by persisting in conducting the operation in the way they did, the deaths were within their control and consented to by them. Nor was it clear that there was some overriding good to be achieved by prosecuting attacks in this way that might counterbalance the manifest harm caused. The Israelis argued that they were seeking to protect the lives of innocents from Hamas rocket attacks. This was a legitimate goal, although the stated aim of stopping the attacks altogether may have been over-ambitious, given the ease with which rocket launchers could be repositioned. But it is not clear that achievement of the goal required the attacks on Hamas military infrastructure to be prosecuted with quite the intensity and ferocity employed. It is arguable that, if they had taken greater care to protect civilians, including cancelling more attacks where civilian lives were evidently at risk, they could still have achieved their military goal of degrading the military capability of Hamas.

A more careful campaign might have sacrificed some military efficiency and taken longer. But there would have been political gains. As US counter-insurgency doctrine now teaches: 'An operation that kills five insurgents is counter-productive if it leads to the recruitment of fifty men.'[32] A more carefully conducted campaign might also have enabled the Israeli goal to be achieved in a way that avoided the widespread international condemnation that the manifest suffering caused to civilians attracted. By failing to do enough to minimize civilian casualties, the Israeli Defence Forces lost political support for their operation.

The Israeli operations could thus be held to have breached the principle of non-combatant immunity.

Kosovo air campaign

Further dilemmas in applying the principle of non-combatant immunity can be illustrated by the difficult decisions that we faced during the NATO Kosovo air campaign—Operation 'Allied Force'—when I was working in the UK Cabinet Office as a defence adviser to the Prime Minister Tony Blair, a leading proponent of the allied military action.[33]

Throughout 1998 and into 1999, Milosevic's campaign of repression and violent ethnic cleansing against the Albanian population of Kosovo had intensified. By the autumn of 1998 an estimated 250,000 Kosovo Albanians had been driven from their homes. In January 1999 evidence emerged that Serbian security forces had massacred forty Albanians, including fleeing women and children, outside the village of Racak.[34] Attempts to find a political settlement at Rambouillet failed, when the Serbian delegation rejected the terms of the accord that the other parties had accepted. NATO leaders regretfully concluded that military action was the only way to bring to an end the ethnic cleansing of the Albanian Kosovars on which Milosevic's forces and supporters were engaged. NATO accordingly commenced military operations on 24 March 1999. The mission of the air campaign was, in the words of the NATO military commander, General Wesley Clark, 'to halt or disrupt a systematic campaign of ethnic cleansing'.[35] This was to be achieved by coercing Milosevic to withdraw his forces from the province of Kosovo so that NATO forces could occupy the province and it could then be administered under the auspices of the UN.

Initially, the attacks were concentrated on military targets, such as air defence facilities and tanks and artillery pieces. The targeting policy had to be approved by all nineteen NATO members, and there was considerable reluctance to sanction non-military targets. Despite the scale of the offensive, with up to a thousand allied aircraft at times engaged, these attacks were largely ineffective. Serbian tanks were easily hidden away or replaced by decoys made of old tyres, plastic sheeting and military logos. Operations against relatively small military targets were hampered by bad weather and made more challenging by NATO's reluctance to fly at low levels to minimize allied casualties. Moreover, even where the targets were hit, their strategic value to Milosevic was low. The pilots began to run out of new military targets to attack. A campaign that some had expected to be over in days began to drag on over weeks and into a second month. The campaign critically began to lose momentum.

Militarily, it was essential to be able to escalate the campaign to inflict or threaten to inflict sufficient damage on assets that Milosevic valued so that he would accede to the terms of the Rambouillet accord. But how was this to be achieved? One option would have been to supplement the air campaign with the use or, at least, threatened use of ground forces. A ground campaign could, however, have increased casualties, including among the civilian population. President Clinton had, in any case, publicly ruled this out, and only at a very late stage conceded to the forceful advocacy of Prime Minister Blair that this could be an option.[36] In theory, another option would have been an area bombing campaign hitting the cities where Milosevic supporters lived. Such a flagrant breach of the principle of non–combatant immunity would, however, have been at odds with the humanitarian objectives of the military operations and was not considered.

Instead, under pressure from the USA and UK, the other NATO Allies were persuaded to agree to a limited broadening of the target set to include military-industrial infrastructure and related strategic targets, a shift in policy that was agreed at the NATO Washington Summit on 23 April. During the later phases of the campaign, civilian infrastructure targets became increasingly the focus of attacks. These included: bridges across the Danube, factories, power stations, telecommunications facilities (including the attack on the headquarters of Serbian State TV that killed fourteen civilians), and even the headquarters of the political party run by Milosevic's wife.

These attacks brought the war home to the civilian supporters of Milosevic. Milosevic, however dictatorial his behaviour and however imperfect the post-communist Yugoslav democratic institutions, was an elected leader. As the damage to the civilian infrastructure mounted, the war became increasingly unpopular among his Serbian supporters, and Milosevic became fearful that he would lose his power base. On 12 June he accordingly accepted the terms offered by the joint Russian–Finnish mediation team and agreed to allow NATO forces to enter Kosovo.

Were these attacks wrong, since they conflicted with the principle of non-combatant immunity?

In defence, it was argued that the attacks were against dual-use targets, with both military and civilian usage. In part this claim was justified. For example, the Serbian State TV was used as a propaganda organ for Milo-sevic, while some of the factories attacked were dual use. The Sloboda vacuum-cleaner factory at Cacak housed a tank-repair facility. But that claim is only part of the picture. For in some cases the strategic value in attacking the targets was not primarily military but rather designed to cause harm to the civilian population—for example, through power blackouts and economic disruption, so that the war would become unpopular and Milosevic's supporters would bring pressure on him to desist. The damage to civilian infrastructure was not a side effect of attacks on military targets but rather one of the objectives of the attacks. The attacks were intended to inconvenience the civilian population and so make them realize the costs of their continued support for the war. But they were not intended to cause civilian deaths. Every effort was made to minimize civilian casualties and deaths. Factories were, for example, attacked at night rather than in the daytime, when they would have been full of workers. Some civilian deaths were, however, recognized as inevitable. Human Rights Watch estimated at the end of hostilities that, as a result of the military operation as a whole, between 489 and 528 civilians had been killed,[37] and NATO accepted the figure could have been higher.[38]

The attacks did not breach the prohibition on intentional killing of the innocent, but they did cause civilian suffering. The Geneva Conventions forbid not just direct attacks on civilians but also attacks on 'civilian objects' that do not 'make an effective contribution to military action'.[39] On a strict interpretation of the principle of non-combatant immunity, the attacks could be held to be unjustified. Yet they made a decisive contribution to ending the war and so ending the suffering of the Albanian people. If the campaign had remained restricted to purely military targets, the war would have dragged on or even failed in its objective, so prolonging and increasing the suffering of the Albanian people in Kosovo. Their suffering was, more-over, real enough. For example, the UN reported that by April 850,000 people, mostly Albanians, had fled their homes. A report to the International Criminal Tribunal for Former Yugoslavia estimated that during March–June

1999 alone over 10,000 civilians had been killed as a result of ethnic cleansing, the grisly evidence for which was attested by the mass graves uncovered following the end of hostilities.[40]

The limited suffering of innocents caused by the NATO military action would thus seem justified by the massive suffering of innocents averted. This conclusion would accord with the principle of non-combatant immunity, as we have suggested it should be interpreted. There is a strong moral prohibition against any direct attack on civilians but this can—exceptionally—be breached if this is the only way to avert very much greater harm to innocents. Moreover, at all times, every effort should be made to minimize non-combatant deaths, whether direct or indirect. On that basis, a bombing campaign attacking centres of population aimed at causing civilian casualties as a way of bringing pressure to bear on Milosevic would not have been permissible. But the more discriminate approach adopted by the NATO Kosovo air campaign, which, while seeking to cause inconvenience to civilians, did not deliberately target civilian deaths and made every effort to minimize civilian casualties, would appear justified, as the only way to end Milosevic's brutal ethnic-cleansing campaign.

This completes our survey of the just war principles. These principles are designed to furnish guidance to all those—including politicians, civil servants, and military personnel—who are involved in the momentous decisions whether or not to go to war and how war should be conducted. For a war to be just, all the principles have to be met. But, as we have suggested, if all the just war tradition has to offer is a book of rules, it may be open to question whether this guidance, however important, is enough to ensure, in practice, that the right decisions will be taken before, during, and after war, particularly given the many contrary pressures on decision-makers. We need, therefore, to consider next what role the virtues may play in helping to reinforce and supplement the just war principles.

SIX

Virtues

PROSPERO: Yet with my nobler reason 'gainst my fury
Do I take part: the rarer action is
In virtue than in vengeance.

The Tempest, Act V, sc. i

T here has been a recent revival of interest among philosophers in the virtues. But in ordinary discourse and practice the virtues have largely fallen out of fashion. From ancient to medieval times and beyond, the virtues were key features of our moral lives. But from the Reformation the pre-eminence of the virtues (and their corresponding vices) declined. By Victorian times the terms had begun to acquire a narrowly sexual connotation. This decline in meaning was noted by Alasdair MacIntyre: '"immoral" and "vice" become associated in the nineteenth century with whatever threatens the sanctity of Victorian marriage—that last refuge of those who, outside the domestic sphere, were quite prepared to be scoundrels.'[1]

This usage has persisted into the modern era, as illustrated by the way the London Metropolitan Police Vice Squad is hardly noted for its efforts to discourage cowardice or root out injustice.

There has been a general decline in the popularity of the virtues. But one notable exception is the military profession. This point was observed by the British General, Sir John Hackett:

Thus, while you may hope to meet these virtues in every walk of life . . . in the profession of arms they are functionally indispensable. The training, the group organisations, the whole pattern of life of the professional man at arms is designed in a deliberate effort to foster them, not just because they are morally desirable in themselves, but because they contribute to military efficiency. A digest of Cicero's *De Officiis* might well figure as a military training manual.[2]

Soldiers need virtues to make them effective soldiers. Hackett suggested that, given equally advanced military techniques, a force in which virtues, such as courage, fortitude, and loyalty, were more highly developed will usually defeat a stronger force in which they are less so. Hackett's encomium of the virtues was recorded in a lecture in 1962, but the importance of the virtues would be endorsed by the British Army today.

Before we examine the role of the virtues in military life, we need first to explore what virtue is.

What is virtue?

According to Aristotle: *'Virtue is a character trait that manifests itself in choice, lying in a mean that is relative to us, this being determined by a rational principle by which the man of practical wisdom would determine it.'*[3] To the modern ear these words may seem strange and difficult to understand. Let us consider each part of the definition in turn.

Virtue is a 'character trait' or 'state of character'. For Aristotle, character is not a mysterious concept. A person's character is straightforwardly the sort of person he is. If called upon to describe a man's character—for example, for a testimonial—we would typically list not only his abilities but also his character traits, including his virtues: Jones is industrious, considerate, and generous. Our capacities—for example, a good memory—are inherited, but crucially for Aristotle our character is acquired. Character is not inherited and immutable in the way that some philosophers, such as Schopenhauer, have supposed. Nature may contribute to our character formation. We may have natural skills and abilities. We may even have 'natural virtues'—for example, a natural fondness for giving presents. But without the appropriate exercise of choice we would not yet have the virtue of generosity.

Our choices are the primary determinant of our characters. A person's character is the sort of person she is; and the sort of person she is, is the person she has become through her past choices and actions. As states of character, the virtues are acquired; and acquired through dint of long training and practice—the exercise of past choices. Just as the virtues are acquired, so too—and rather more readily—are the vices. As William James gloomily observed:

Could the young but realise how soon they will become mere walking bundles of habits, they would give more heed to their conduct while in the plastic state. We are spinning our own fates, good and evil, never to be undone. Every smallest stroke of virtue or vice leaves its never so little scar. The drunken Rip Van Winkle, in Jefferson's play, excuses himself for every fresh dereliction by saying, 'I won't count this time.' Well! He may not count it, and a kind Heaven may not count it; but it is being counted nonetheless . . . As we become permanent drunkards by so many separate drinks, so we become saints in the moral, and authorities and experts in the practical and scientific spheres, by so many acts and hours of work.[4]

'With mere good intentions', as James reminds us, 'hell is proverbially paved'.[5] To be confident of our own or others' right conduct, that conduct needs to have become to us second nature. Virtues are like habits in that we acquire them by constant practice and habituation. But they are unlike habits in that they are not the result of unreflective habitual action. The exercise of virtue always requires careful thought, attention, and, above all, the exercise of choice. The habits that the person of virtue needs to acquire are 'reflective habits'.

Virtues are often described as dispositions. There are important analogies between virtues and dispositions. To say that a glass is brittle is to say that it would break if it were hit by a hard object, such as a brick. The inner dispositional quality of brittleness is manifested by external occurrences, such as the breaking of the glass. But the external manifestations do not exhaust the concept. For to say that glass is brittle is not merely to say how it would behave under certain circumstances but also implies that it does so because of its nature—in this case its molecular structure. It is this assumption about its underlying nature that supports the counterfactual claim about how it would behave if it were hit by a brick. As Ross explains: 'There is no such thing as a potentiality that is not rooted in actuality.'[6]

Just so, to say that a man is courageous is not merely to say that he is the sort of person who, when faced with danger, would act courageously but implies that he does so because of the sort of person he is and has—through his previous choices—become. It is to say something about his underlying character. The virtues are the inner states of a man's being that incline him towards virtuous conduct

Like dispositional properties, these inner states are manifested in external behaviour. But, unlike other dispositional qualities, the inner states are not definable in terms of the external behaviour but rather the reverse.

A disposition to catch colds is defined in terms of the readily identifiable act of 'catching a cold'. To say that an act is courageous may tell us something of its external features. A Greek soldier knew that breaking the line in battle would not be a courageous act. But the description does not necessarily tell us much about the external qualities of the act and may tell us nothing at all. For a courageous act is not defined in terms of a particular externally recognizable activity or act. Courage does not name a specific activity, in the way that angling is the characteristic activity of the angler. There is no activity of 'courageing'. Nor is there a class of externally recognizable acts of courage.[7] Indeed, there may be no externally discernible common quality to various acts of courage. Chasing a handbag-snatcher in the street or jumping into a cold river to save a drowning child may both be acts of courage. The same is true with other virtues. Giving money or withholding it (to avoid placing someone under an obligation she cannot fulfil) may both be acts of generosity. There is no externally recognizable category of acts or activities that corresponds to each virtue.

Unlike other dispositional qualities, the virtues are not identified by reference to the actions in which they issue. Rather, the actions are identified by reference to the virtues from which they spring. This is illustrated by the following example.[8] A woman, laden with shopping and a crying child, gets on to a crowded bus. Smith offers her a seat out of concern for her and the child's welfare. Jones also offers her a seat without feeling such concern but because he wants to do his duty. Fraser offers her a seat but in his case simply because of concern that others will criticize him. Each of the agents performs an externally similar act—giving up his seat to the mother and child. But, depending on the reasons from which each acts, what he does may be the performance either of a different virtue (in Smith's case kindness; in Jones's case conscientiousness) or of none at all (Fraser's behaviour).

Acts of virtue are identified according to the reasons—the desires and beliefs of the agent—for which they are undertaken. The names of the virtues classify actions according to the reasons for which they are undertaken: a classificatory role that they share with other motive terms. The names of the virtues are, however, more than simply terms for classifying actions. They also name the inner states of character from which such actions issue.

These observations are not an exercise in conceptual analysis for its own sake. For what the analysis illuminates is the key role played by choice in the exercise of the virtues. '*Virtue is a character trait that manifests itself in choice.*'

We can now see from the difference between the virtues and other dispositional qualities why choice is so important. It is because there is no externally recognizable category of acts or activities corresponding to each virtue that choice becomes crucial. We cannot discern in advance what an act of courage would look like. It all depends on the circumstances and, crucially, the beliefs and desires of the agent. As von Wright notes: 'The path of virtue is never laid out in advance. It is for the man of virtue to determine where it goes in a particular case.'[9]

Virtue manifests itself in choice. But not all situations in which a choice needs to be made call for the exercise of a virtue. The virtues are intimately connected with the promotion or protection of human welfare. The situations that require the exercise of virtues are those where the good or welfare of an agent is at stake: whether that of the agent herself, requiring the exercise of a self-regarding virtue; or those of another agent, requiring the exercise of an other-regarding virtue. So, for example, choosing a dish at a dinner party may not normally call upon the exercise of a virtue. But it may do so if the good of some person is at stake. The guest who calls for a second helping of Peking duck may need to exercise forbearance if the additional helping would put her digestive processes at risk. For the sake of her own health, she would need to practise temperance. Alternatively, if by demanding a second helping she would deprive others of a first helping, consideration for others might enjoin her abstinence.

Choice is crucial to the exercise of virtue, but what is it that the person of virtue chooses to do? Aristotle thought that he had the answer with his doctrine of the mean: *'Virtue is a character trait that manifest itself in choice, lying in a mean that is relative to us.'* The virtuous person chooses what is intermediate between opposing extremes. For example, in situations of great danger, the man of courage does not choose to ignore danger and act in a foolhardy way but nor does he allow himself to be paralysed by fear and act in a cowardly way. In avoiding either extreme and choosing the middle path, he chooses the courageous thing to do. Similarly, the person of temperance avoids the extremes of both excessive abstinence and of gluttony—the vice from which our dinner-party guest was just rescued in the last example.

With some of the virtues, Aristotle's doctrine of the mean offers helpful illumination. But with other virtues—such as justice and practical wisdom—it is less easy to discern what are the twin vices to which each virtue corresponds. Moreover, in all cases the advice 'to follow the mean' may offer less than pellucid practical guidance on what one is supposed to do. This is a difficulty Aristotle himself recognized. For, at times, he comes close to defining 'following the mean' as 'doing the right thing': 'To feel at the right time, about the right objects, towards the right people, with the right intention and in the right way, is what is both intermediate and best. This—which applies similarly to actions—is characteristic of virtue.'[10]

This definition helpfully reminds us of the complexity of moral decision-making and the number of features of the situation that need to be attended to. But to be told that the mean thing to feel and to do is the right thing to feel and to do is not as helpful advice as we may have hoped for, when it is the doctrine of the mean that is supposed to explain what is the right thing to do!

The doctrine of the mean turns out to be either inapplicable to all virtues or, if so emaciated as to apply to all, it becomes empty of content. It does not offer the help that Aristotle thought it would. We need, therefore, to abandon the doctrine and answer the question that we posed earlier by saying that what the man of virtue chooses to do is the right thing. But without guidance from the doctrine of the mean how does he decide what is the right thing to do?

As well as the doctrine of the mean, Aristotle offers another, more helpful, account of how we determine what is the right thing to do. The man of practical wisdom, we are told, is the man who is good at deliberating about 'what conduces to the good life as a whole'[11] and who 'takes his aim at what is best for man'.[12] Any theory of the virtues needs to be reinforced with a theory of the good. To determine what is the right thing to do we need to consider which of the available actions would better promote human welfare (whether of the agent or of others whose interests are affected) or prevent harm. In some cases this doctrine and that of the mean may neatly coincide. The person of self-control chooses a moderate diet, avoiding the excesses of gluttony and abstinence, and thereby promotes her own health and welfare. The doctrines do not, however, always coincide. Where they do not, deliberation about what conduces to human welfare provides more illuminating guidance on how to act than does the doctrine of the mean. But how does the person of virtue determine what will promote welfare or prevent harm?

First, and most importantly, she can seek guidance from the moral principles, in which she will have been soundly educated. It is a mistake to concentrate exclusively on the virtues and to ignore other features of our moral lives. Virtuous consequentialism insists rather that to address satisfactorily the challenge of our moral lives requires attending to all the relevant features, including the moral rules that encapsulate the wisdom of our forebears on how human welfare is best promoted. These rules provide the signposts for the person of virtue to follow in determining what is the right thing to do.

This is important. But the rules may conflict, may not apply clearly to a particular situation, or may not apply at all. The rules are also inevitably of a degree of generality. They provide signposts that indicate the direction but do not necessarily specify the precise path to be followed in each case. The challenge then becomes how to determine whether and, if so, how the principles apply in particular cases; and, where they do not, how, nonetheless, we should act best to promote human welfare.

To determine this, the man of virtue will need to assess the consequences of his agency. But such appraisal too is easier said than done. If he is to choose the right thing to do, he will, crucially, need practical wisdom, the wisdom that enables him to deliberate well about what conduces to human welfare. The right thing to do—reverting once again to Aristotle's definition of virtue is '*determined by a rational principle by which the man of practical wisdom would determine it*'. The concluding words of Aristotle's definition provide the crucial missing link disclosing how the man of virtue has learnt to choose rightly.

According to the modern myth, our right choices spring fully formed from empty heads like the fully girt Athena from the head of Zeus. In contrast to this, Aristotle perceived, with rather more plausibility, that to choose to act rightly we need to have cultivated both the appropriate desires and feelings—so that we want to promote the welfare of others, as of ourselves—and also to have developed practical insight into what, in the varying circumstances of life, constitutes human good and how it is best achieved. We need, in other words, to have cultivated the virtues. But the path of virtue is never precisely laid out in advance. The man of practical wisdom is the man who can discern amid all the varied circumstances of life what are the likely consequences of his acts (or omissions), whose interests are affected and hence which results of his agency would be beneficial (whether to himself or others) and which harmful.

Practical wisdom is applied at different levels. The moral principles are themselves the product of practical wisdom. But practical wisdom is also needed to guide individual actions. Practical wisdom may be required to determine how the rule should be applied in the particular case. Where no rules offer guidance or rules conflict, a more fundamental calculation of what will promote welfare or prevent harm will be needed. Even if clear guidance from moral principles is lacking, the person of practical wisdom is not left to choose the right action in a vacuum. For, as well as the moral rules, the virtues too help guide our choices. Past practice in the virtues guides the choice of future virtuous action. The person of practical wisdom will have built up practical knowledge relevant to the varying challenges she may face. She will have learnt what moral rules are appropriate to the area of conduct under consideration. She will also have learnt how to apply them in practical situations. Drawing from both her own previous experience and the examples of others, she will have learnt the kind of choices and behaviour that each of the virtues requires and how the virtuous person acts and reacts in a variety of situations. Such practical knowledge will help guide her choice in addressing the particular challenge with which she is faced. Nor will she hesitate to consult the wisdom of others where her own practical knowledge may be lacking.

The person of virtue may have developed specialist knowledge and skills to help in making right choices. For example, the courageous soldier seeking to save the lives of his comrades will have acquired particular military knowledge and skills that he can bring to bear to assist him. The temperate person will know what is beneficial for health and how this is to be achieved. She will know not just that she should eat healthy foods and want to do so, but will have learnt which foods are healthy. She will know, in Aristotle's example, that light foods are good for her, that chicken is a light food, and so chicken is good for her.[13] She will also know in what quantities food or drink should be consumed. The virtuous person will have acquired stores of practical knowledge from which to draw and to apply to particular situations; stores that will vary, depending which virtue is appropriate. The practical knowledge of the person of courage will vary from that of the temperate person.

Practical wisdom is not acquired easily. It requires sound education and training; attending to the teachings of the wise and, what is even more difficult, following their advice; learning from examples, including a readiness to learn from the mistakes both of others and of ourselves; and, finally and crucially, constant practice. Only thus will the man of practical wisdom learn to develop, in Geach's phrase, 'a habit of sound judgment about practical situations'[14] and a habit that is attuned to the relevant features of different situations, applying to each the appropriate practical knowledge. Such sound reasoning is crucial to the moral life. For Aristotle, it is the key to all virtuous conduct: for 'it is not possible to be good without practical wisdom'.[15] Practical wisdom is mutually intertwined with the other virtues. We need practical wisdom to exercise the virtues and, through practice in the virtues, we develop further our practical wisdom.

Practical wisdom has to be exercised, despite the conflicting desires and emotions that may be present. An important role of the virtues—as von Wright stressed—is to counteract the obscuring effect that such counter-vailing passions may have upon the agent's practical judgement of what is harmful or beneficial.[16] The man of virtue has learnt how to make a dispassionate assessment of the benefits and disbenefits of his agency. This does not mean that he ceases to have such passions but that he has learnt how to control them.

This can again be illustrated by considering the dilemma faced by a soldier who has just learnt that enemy forces are about to capture the position occupied by his comrades. If their lives are to be saved, a message must be sent to them to withdraw. As a man of courage, he will want to save the lives of his comrades, but he will also have learnt how to control the fear he may feel so that it does not impede his judgement of what to do. He will neither ignore the danger, for example, by shouting out to his comrades in a way that would expose their position to enemy fire; but nor will he succumb to his fear and turn and flee in panic. The man of courage has not learnt to avoid all feeling of fear. If he felt no fear, he could not be said to act courageously. Rather, what he has learnt is not to allow his feeling of fear to obscure his judgement of what it is necessary to do in situations of great danger to prevent harm befalling himself and his comrades. This ability is acquired only by careful training and practice.

In the light of this discussion we can offer a revised definition of virtue, based on that of Aristotle, but without the doctrine of the mean: '*Virtue is a character trait that manifests itself in choosing the right action—the action that will better promote the welfare of those affected or prevent harm than available alternatives—determined by a rational principle that the person of practical wisdom would apply.*'

The virtuous person is someone whose character inclines her towards right conduct and who chooses what is the right thing to do in the particular circumstances through the judicious exercise of practical wisdom.

So, having defined virtue, let us consider next the role of the virtues in military life.

Military virtues

The just war tradition sets out the principles that need to be followed if war is to be just. But in war, as elsewhere in our moral decision-making, applying general principles to particular situations and then abiding by them can present a considerable challenge. That challenge is particularly daunting where the decisions need to be made, often quickly, amid all the passions, fog, and fury generated by war; and where the stakes—and costs in human suffering of wrong decisions—may be much higher than elsewhere. It is not surprising that the virtues are regarded as especially critical in the military sphere. The virtues are crucial if we are to have any hope of ensuring that all those involved with war will act justly. So what virtues do the military need?

Virtues are character traits needed for our welfare as human beings. As circumstances change, there may be shifts of emphasis on the qualities required for our welfare. The importance of chastity as a virtue has declined as the ready availability of contraception has furnished other ways of avoiding the suffering caused by unwanted pregnancies. But, while there may be changes at the margins, the importance of the core virtues to our welfare has remained constant. Chief among such virtues are the four virtues traditionally regarded as fundamental to our moral life: the cardinal virtues of justice, practical wisdom, courage, and self-control. These are the virtues that are essential for our ability to live well together. They are, according to Geach, 'needed for any large-scale worthy enterprise, just as health and sanity are'.[17] Let us begin our examination of the virtues needed by the military with the cardinal virtues.

Justice

Justice would appear a prime candidate for ensuring the just conduct of war. But justice has always been a difficult virtue to pin down. Aristotle had problems fitting it into his conceptual scheme. He also noted that we use the term in three different senses. We use the word 'just' as a general ethical concept rather like the term 'moral' or 'morally good', covering a wide range of behaviour based on showing respect for others and concern to promote their welfare. Such justice is the virtue that governs our relations with others. It is, Aristotle notes in uncharacteristically poetic mode, 're-garded as the sovran virtue, "more wonderful than the evening or morning star," and we have a proverb: "All virtue is summed up in dealing justly."'[18] It is in this broad sense that moral sceptics from Thrasymachus onward have demanded to know, 'Why should I be just?' It is this broad sense that the Prophet Micah used when he summarized the ethical code:

> God has told you what is good:
> And what is it that the Lord asks of you?
> Only to act justly, to love loyalty,
> To walk wisely before your God.[19]

There are also two specialized senses of 'just'. The first is justice as fairness: the virtue we look to when goods or resources are distributed to ensure the distribution is fair. The second is the justice of the law courts, often called 'corrective' or 'retributive' justice. It is the virtue we require of judges when they mete out punishments to those who have broken the law.

For the medieval just war theorists who viewed war as a form of extra-territorial punishment it was this retributive sense of justice that they had primarily in mind. But, as argued in Chapter 4, it is difficult to sustain a theory of war as punishment when, in modern conflicts, the innocent are more likely to be punished, while the guilty are let free. Individual crimes committed before and during war may, nonetheless, be subject to punish-ment, as with the crimes against humanity and other charges with which Milosevic was charged by the International Criminal Tribunal for the Former Yugoslavia. Retributive justice may need to be exercised during, and especially after, war, to ensure just judgements are reached in such cases. But we can no longer regard retributive justice as the primary virtue of the just warrior.

Nor is justice as fairness. There will be distributions of goods in war that will require this virtue to be exercised. Achilles was angered that Agamem-non had failed to exercise this virtue in stealing from him the beautiful captured handmaiden, Briseis. This led to Achilles' withdrawal from the Greek ranks besieging Troy, with the disastrous consequences that furnish the central plot of the Iliad. Justice as fairness is important in war, as elsewhere. But it is not the primary virtue required in war.

We are left with the more general sense of justice, as morally good, respecting others and promoting their welfare. It is this more general sense that would now seem most appropriate in just war theory. The just war principles are designed to mitigate the suffering caused by war and to ensure that war is undertaken only if it contributes to human welfare. The principles set out the criteria to be met if war is to be morally permissible in its inception, conduct, and end. To enable us to meet this challenging demand requires that we learn and practise the virtue of justice, respecting and promoting the welfare of others. We also need the other cardinal virtues.

Practical wisdom

First and foremost we need practical wisdom. The just war principles themselves embody practical wisdom built up over the centuries. But they are inevitably of a general nature. Practical wisdom is required to ensure the correct application of the principles. The challenge is to relate the general to the particular: to recognize which principle applies to which particular situation, to discern how it applies and what action it requires.

Aquinas notes three kinds of practical wisdom, or prudence, required in political and military affairs. First is the practical wisdom of the ruler, called statesmanship.[20] This is the virtue that the ruler needs if he is to serve the common good, whether by enacting wise laws or protecting the state from external aggression. This is the highest or architectonic form of practical wisdom. Second is the political practical wisdom that the subjects in a state need to exercise if they are to play their, albeit lesser, part in promoting the common good.[21] The third variant of practical wisdom is called military. It is the virtue needed to ensure that 'war is managed by due ordering': 'Actual fighting calls for courage, but its direction calls for prudence, especially that of the good generalship of the officer commanding.'[22]

Aquinas rightly notes that practical wisdom needs to be exercised at different levels in the hierarchy of responsibility. It needs to be exercised, above all, by the political leaders, together with their military and civilian advisers, who take the fateful decision whether or not to go to war. It is they, after all, who decide whether there is a just cause for war. It is they who must calculate the consequences of their action and determine whether more good than ill will prevail, taking into account the prospects of success. These are daunting tasks, with many temptations to stray, particularly amid all the passions and fury generated by conflict. The cool exercise of practical wisdom by our leaders is critical.

Practical wisdom also needs to be exercised by the ruled. The political duties of subjects in the princely kingdoms that Aquinas takes as the norm were limited but important. How much more important is the practical wisdom required of citizens in a democracy who can choose their leaders and the policies they support, as well as those in the media, academe, or non-governmental organizations who may have influence on the formation of opinions. We should choose leaders with a proven track record of practical wisdom, 'a habit of sound judgment about practical situations'. Discerning such leaders will require us to exercise practical wisdom, as will the fulfilment of our other political responsibilities as citizens. We cannot shift all the blame or responsibility onto the rulers. For in democracy, we get, to an extent, the rulers we deserve.

Aquinas attributes military practical wisdom chiefly to the general commanding the army. Generals directing warfare at the strategic and theatre levels of command need, by careful training and experience, to have acquired and exercise practical wisdom. They will need this to enable them to assess correctly whether the course of military action proposed will achieve its objectives and whether it will bring about more good than harm.

But it is a feature of modern warfare that responsibility is devolved to ever lower levels. Practical wisdom needs also to be exercised at the tactical level, often by service people of junior rank. The 'strategic corporal' is responsible for taking life and death decisions. It is he who may have to decide whether the woman with a bulging robe in the crowded Afghan marketplace is a suicide bomber or an innocent to be protected by the principle of non-combatant immunity. The modern battlefield demands of all its participants an increasing range of skills, with activities capable of shifting within the space of three city blocks from war-fighting through peace support operations to humanitarian relief—the so-called Three Block War. Practical wisdom needs to include an ability to adapt rapidly to changing situations and to respond with resourceful innovativeness. Since the decisions may be required in split seconds, the exercise of practical wisdom needs to have become, through long training and practice, second nature, an ingrained habit of sound reasoning.

Practical wisdom is thus exercised at a variety of levels, ranging from that of the statesman who seeks to promote the common good to that of the humble soldier who seeks to avert the suffering of his comrades. The translation of the just war principles into practice requires, above all, the virtue of practical wisdom. But the just conduct of war also requires the other cardinal virtues of courage and temperance.

Courage

We have examined courage already. It is the virtue we need to enable us to persevere in the face of difficulty and danger, not allowing fear to obscure our judgement of what needs to be done. Courage is the virtue of the warrior on the battlefield, but it is also a virtue required in peacetime. It is a virtue for which we should look in our politicians. The courageous political decision may be not to go to war, despite the popular clamour or pressure from allies to do so. Courage is also a virtue that may be required of us all in the humblest situations. The enduring necessity of courage is well summarized by Geach: 'Courage is the virtue of the end: what makes a man endure to the end and in the extremity of evil. Courage is what we all need in the end; we all have to die and for none of us can the possibility be excluded of dying nastily: in great pain or after a long disabling illness.'[23]

Self-control

As well as courage, soldiers need the cardinal virtue of temperance or self-control. In order to achieve and maintain the physical fitness required to undertake their duties, soldiers need to exercise self-control, eating enough to build up their physical strength but avoiding over-indulging their bodily appetites. But self-control is, like practical wisdom, a virtue that is needed in support of the exercise of other virtues. It is the character trait that helps a man never lose his head, whether through anger or fear or lust for pleasure and so always to exercise a dispassionate judgement of what is the right thing to do. Self-control is a key virtue on the battlefield. The US Marines in Haditha who went on a rampage of revenge, enraged by the death of their comrade, displayed, among other failings, a lack of self-control. Self-control is an important military virtue. It is also a virtue that those outside the military profession require. This includes our political leaders and their advisers, who need to take decisions on war and peace without allowing anger, greed, or other passions to obscure their judgement.

Other military virtues

What other virtues do soldiers need? Lists of military virtues may, like lists of virtues more generally, vary at the margins. Different emphases may be accorded different qualities at different times. During the Cold-War era of mutual nuclear deterrence, courage was of less importance to the captain of a Trident submarine than obedience; while, conversely, the practical wisdom of the political leaders whose orders the serviceman obeyed was at the highest premium. There have been shifts of emphasis, but what is more striking is the extent of agreement on a common set of core values required for military life. This is well illustrated by the British Army's statement of its Core Values. These are: selfless commitment, courage, discipline, integrity, loyalty, and respect for others.[24] Few would dispute the importance of these virtues for military life.

Courage we have already considered, as we have respect for others, which is a key feature of the virtue of justice. Selfless commitment is the requirement for the individual to place the interests of the group within which he operates above his own interests. Discipline is necessary to ensure the prompt execution of orders on which the lives of others may depend in the heat of battle. Obedience, which presupposes the practical wisdom of those issuing orders, needs to be reflective and cannot be invoked for orders that are manifestly illegal or immoral. Integrity is about honesty and truthfulness, which can be crucial to the saving of lives where inaccurate information can put those lives at risk. It is also about, and best summarized as, consistency between principle and practice: meaning what one says, saying what one means, and doing what one says. Integrity is the virtue that a leader needs if he is to earn the trust of those he commands. Finally, loyalty to one's comrades and to the military unit in which one serves is a virtue much needed on the battlefield. It is the virtue that impels the soldier to go back and rescue a comrade, even though this may endanger his own life. The British Army's Core Values well summarize most of the qualities needed by the military. But we need to add to them the cardinal virtues of self-control and practical wisdom, which are as crucial to military, as to non-military, life.

The virtues have to be learned and practised. Their importance can too easily be forgotten in the heat of battle. They can also be abused, if used to serve wrong ends.

Uses and abuses of the virtues

Actions are virtuous only if undertaken for the sake of a good end. As Aristotle observes, the brave man endures danger for the sake of what is good[25] and chooses so to act because it is good.[26] The soldier on the battlefield will, Aquinas adds, have a good end in view 'in so far as one defends the common good by just warfare'.[27] A soldier acting justly in a war undertaken for a just cause behaves virtuously.

But what if the soldier is on the side that is pursuing an unjust end? Can courage then never be exercised? That would be too stern a judgement. We admire the bravery of Rommel and other members of the Afrika Corps in how they conducted their campaign in northern Africa, recognizing that their immediate objectives—for example, saving comrades from death—may have been good, even though the campaign was ultimately in support of an evil end. But we show no such admiration for the soldiers in the special SS units—the SD-Einsatzkommando and Sonderkommando—who were tasked in 1941 with executing Jews and Communist party officials in the wake of the victorious advance of the German Sixth Army across Russia.[28] For both their immediate and their ultimate objectives were evil. They may have persevered in the grim task in the face of great dangers and difficulties. But whatever character trait they exhibited it was not the virtue of courage.

A moving account of military virtue in action is provided by John Baynes in his history of the exploits of the battalion of the Second Scottish Rifles in the Battle of Neuve Chapelle in March 1915. Of the 700 men of the battalion who went over the top on 10 March, 469 were killed, wounded, or missing in action, including all but one of the officers. Most of the casualties were suffered in the first hour of action. Despite the high casualties and loss of its officers, the battalion stood its ground until withdrawn from action six days later when the overall British offensive was called off. Baynes attributes the heroic action of the soldiers to their high morale: 'a quality of mind and spirit which combines courage, self-discipline and endurance.'[29] The main ingredients of high morale are: loyalty to the regiment, mutual trust between the men and their officers, strong discipline, a sense of duty in all ranks developed by their training, and the sound administration of the battalion, ensuring the soldiers were well fed and armoured. 'Here was the essence of the battalion's morale. Thus equipped, the Second Scottish Rifles marched up the line through the darkness to the Battle of Neuve Chapelle.'[30]

The ability of the battalion to retain its military effectiveness despite the high casualties sustained in a short space of time is proof of both the virtuous conduct of the soldiers and the importance of the virtues to their conduct. But the Battle of Neuve Chapelle was a strategic failure. It was called off after six days amid steeply mounting British casualties—583 officers and 12,309 other ranks killed, wounded, and missing. It failed to achieve its aim of a strategic breakout towards Lille. The brave men of the Scottish Rifles lost their lives with little, if anything, to show for it. They had displayed supreme virtue but to what end? The First World War was fought for a just cause—the defence of Belgium and France against German aggression. The soldiers had a good ultimate end. What is less clear is whether those fighting at Neuve Chapelle had a reasonable prospect of achieving their proximate objectives without disproportionate casualties. In view of the high attrition suffered without strategic gain, we may wonder whether the soldiers' virtues were employed to best effect in the battle of Neuve Chapelle.

Even if the virtues of the Scottish soldiers were not employed to best effect, they remained, nonetheless, men of virtue. If there was a failure of virtue, it was not on the part of the members of the Second Scottish Rifles battalion but rather among the higher command, the generals whose poor strategic decisions displayed their lack of the military variant of practical wisdom extolled by Aquinas.

Ordinary virtues can be misused but still remain virtues. But, at the extreme, abuse of the virtues may not only turn the habits of character usually associated with the virtues into vices, but those character traits may themselves contribute to the vicious activity. This is illustrated by the wartime activities of the German Reserve Police Battalion 101, whose exploits have been examined by Christopher Browning.[31] These reserve policemen were not trained mass murderers like the special SS units in Russia. They were respectable middle-aged citizens of Hamburg who had become reserve policemen to avoid more arduous military duties.

On 13 July 1942 the battalion received an order to round up all the Jews in the Polish village of Jozefow and kill all those not of working age: 1,500 Jews, mainly the elderly, women, and children, were shot in the forest outside the village. Individual policemen were not compelled to undertake the task. No punishment was meted out to those who refused. But 85 per cent of the 500 strong battalion acquiesced without undue complaint. The battalion assisted on a number of subsequent occasions in the deportation and execution of Jews. After some initial squeamishness, recounts Browning, they 'became increasingly efficient and calloused executioners'.[32] What motivated them was not Nazi fervour and anti-Semitism but a natural propensity for obedience to authority and the influence of peer pressure and comradeship, including not wanting to let down their comrades by refusing their share of an unpleasant task. Character traits that, if properly directed, would conduce to virtuous activity were thus misdirected and subverted into the service of vice.

These examples underline that the virtues, while necessary for morality, are not, on their own, sufficient. Virtuous actions are virtuous only if undertaken for the sake of a good end. We need a clear understanding of the good to be achieved by our actions, of how our actions will promote human welfare or prevent suffering. Such understanding is furnished in the first instance by the moral principles whose guidance we should seek and follow. But, where rules conflict or offer unclear or no guidance, deeper deliberation may be needed, requiring the exercise of the virtue of practical wisdom.

Our next example of the use and abuse of virtue is from more recent history.

What went wrong in Basra in 2003–4

In the autumn of 2003 and early 2004 there were a number of cases of abuse by British soldiers of Iraqis who had been detained during the looting and breakdown of order that took place following the invasion in March 2003 and subsequent overthrow of Saddam's regime. Compared with the number of troops deployed, the cases were few, but they were of considerable concern, not least since such abuse was at variance with the avowed objective of helping the Iraqi people. One of the most notorious of these cases was the death in custody of Baha Mousa and the ill-treatment of eight other Iraqis that took place in September 2003.

Baha Mousa was working as a hotel receptionist in Basra when on 14 September British troops raided the hotel, acting on a tip-off that there were arms on the premises. The troops arrested Baha Mousa and eight other Iraqis. They were taken to a nearby military base for interrogation. In the course of their interrogation they were deprived of sleep, hooded, and beaten. The beating of Baha Mousa was so severe that two days later he died. Seven members of the Queen's Lancashire Regiment were charged with offences arising from the incident. But, apart from a corporal who admitted inhumane treatment and was sentenced to a year's imprisonment and dismissed from the service, the rest had the charges against them dropped because of lack of evidence.

This case is now the subject of a public enquiry. But the internal British Army report into what went wrong with these cases—the Aitken Report—noted many failings that had contributed to these events.[33] These included the lack of training for soldiers in handling civilian detainees, a task that elsewhere would have been undertaken by civilian police. There were gaps in the instructions given to the troops on what interrogation techniques were or were not permissible. In 1972 the British government had prohibited the five 'deep-interrogation' techniques whose employment in Northern Ireland had provoked moral outrage. These were: wall-standing, hooding, subjection to noise, sleep deprivation, and deprivation of food and drink. That prohibition remained in force, but no explicit instruction reminding troops of this had been reissued in 2003. The report notes that 'exactly how and when specific direction in 1972 came to be lost in 2003 would have to be a matter for a separate investigation'.[34]

What is of most interest to our enquiry is the way the report frankly admits the moral failings that led to these abuses, a failing that it attributes to both a lack of virtues and an abuse of virtues. It is worth quoting the report's conclusions on this in full:

> The Army's Core Values—Selfless Commitment, Courage, Discipline, Integrity, Loyalty and Respect for Others—articulate the code of conduct within which the Army conducts its business. They reflect the moral virtues and ethical principles which underpin any decent society, but which are particularly important for members of an institution with the responsibility of conducting military operations—including the use of lethal force—on behalf of the Nation. The Army requires that all its people understand these Values and live up to their associated Standards. It does this in part by mandating annual training for all ranks, but also by requiring its leaders to set a personal example to their subordinates.
>
> The evidence from the cases of deliberate abuse with which this report is concerned suggests that there was a failure to live up to those Values and Standards by some of those involved—not just the accused but the other individuals involved on the periphery of the investigations; and not just the

soldiers but the commanders as well. A particular example of this failing was the lack of cooperation experienced by the Service police in conducting the investigations, and what the judge in the Baha Musa case referred to as the 'wall of silence' from some of those who gave evidence. This is not a form of behaviour limited only to the Army; but it is perhaps exacerbated in an organisation that trains people in the virtues of loyalty, and which stresses the importance of cohesion. The challenge is to educate our people to understand that lying to the Service Police, or having 'selective memory loss' in court, in order to protect other members of their unit, are not forms of loyalty, but rather a lack of integrity. Respect for others means respecting all others—and that includes people who may be your enemies. Courage includes having the moral courage to challenge unacceptable behaviour whenever it is encountered.[35]

This exemplary self-criticism by the Army of the Army provides an illuminating insight into the uses and abuses of the virtues and why the virtues are important to the military. Hackett, whom we quoted earlier, emphasized that soldiers need the virtues to be effective soldiers. That is true. But society wants its soldiers to be not only effective soldiers but also good people. We entrust them, as Brigadier Aitken notes, with the conduct of military operations on behalf of the nation, including, crucially, the use of lethal force. If the force is used justly and in support of a just aim, good can be achieved and human welfare promoted. But if the military are bad people and abuse that trust by using force for bad ends, harmful consequences ensue.

The soldiers in Basra who ill-treated the detainees displayed a lack of virtue, including that of self-control and the respect for others required by justice. Their lack of virtue led to the death of an innocent man and the ill-treatment of eight others. Further harm was caused by their comrades through their lack of courage in challenging such unacceptable behaviour and their abuse of the virtue of loyalty. The misplaced loyalty of their colleagues who protected them from punishment by their collective amnesia was misplaced because it was focused too narrowly. The colleagues were concerned only with the interests of their immediate comrades. They ignored the wider interests of the regiment and Army in which they served, whose reputation they besmirched by their mendacity, and of the society in whose service they were employed. Lying to the investigators may have shown loyalty to some but it displayed disloyalty to many more. The failings displayed at the tactical level both by those who committed the crimes and those who covered them up had profoundly adverse consequences at the strategic level by undermining the wider humanitarian objectives of the mission.

The virtues are needed in military life, as elsewhere, because of the contribution they can make to human flourishing; and because their absence or abuse can lead to suffering and death. The difference is that, in war, the stakes, and hence the costs, if things go wrong, may be higher than elsewhere. So, society rightly places a high premium on military virtues.

But there is also a further reason why the military need virtues. We ask the military to perform tasks that in civilian life they would be forbidden to undertake: in particular, the killing of other human beings. It is crucial for both the internal self-respect of the military and our external pride as a nation in their achievements that they are able to distinguish themselves from assassins or murderers. As a Colonel in the US Special Forces remarked: 'Our guys have got to be confident in their ability to use lethal force. But they've got to be principled enough to know when not to use it. We're not training pirates.'[36] The soldiers will return at some stage, possibly after only a few years, into civilian life, where they will need to be able to look back on what they did in military service with pride rather than the horror and shame that unlicensed killing would provoke. The military need a code of conduct that enables them to distinguish themselves from pirates, and see themselves rather as warriors in a noble tradition of service on behalf of the state. The military virtues constitute a core element of such a code. The code needs to be internalized so that the virtues become deeply engrained habits of conduct, to which we can appeal to ensure just conduct, even in the split-second decisions of the battlefield.

This is well illustrated by the story of a young enlisted Marine in the Vietnam War who was enraged by the death of his comrades. An officer found the youth 'with his rifle at the head of a Vietnamese woman' about to kill a non-combatant in cold blood.[37] The officer had only seconds to defuse the situation. He could have lectured the Marine on the principles of the just war and, in particular, its prohibition of the killing of non-combatants. That might have worked. But in the heat and fury of battle it probably would not have done. Instead, the officer tried a different tack. He simply said in a calm voice, 'Marines don't do that.' As Shannon French notes: 'Jarred out of his berserk state and recalled to his place in a long-standing warrior tradition, the Marine stepped back and lowered his weapon.'[38] Where an appeal to the just war principles would have failed, an appeal to the military virtues embodied in the Marine's own code of honour worked. Marines do not kill innocent women. Marines are not murderers but just warriors. The woman's life was saved.

The virtues are needed in military life to ensure that soldiers are effective soldiers. But they are also needed to ensure that our service people are good people who deploy the lethal force with which society entrusts them only for the sake of a good end and in ways of which they and the society whom they serve can be justifiably proud; and that they are able to act thus even amid all the pressures and passions of war.

Teaching justice

In his introduction to the Aitken Report, the then Head of the British Army, General Sir Richard Dannatt, notes that 'we need to find better ways to inculcate our core values'.[39] At the start of this millennium, I was Director of the Defence Training Review, a major strategic review of training and education for the British Armed Forces and civilians working in defence. The Defence Training Review was designed to ensure that the military and defence civilians were equipped with the skills needed to meet the challenges of the twenty-first century. For the military, training is intensely important. The armed forces spend most of their professional lives training. They do so because the success of a military mission and their lives may depend on the training they have received. As a young corporal serving in Sierra Leone in September 2000 told the review team: 'This is the only firefight I've ever been in. This company is a very young company and none of us had ever experienced it before. But when the battle started the training just took over.'[40]

The Defence Training Review ranged widely, looking at the training required by our forces: for peace support and humanitarian operations; for joint operations with other services and with other nations in multinational formations; and for the whole range of skills needed to cope with the changing nature of war in the twenty-first century and the challenges of an increasingly digitised battle space. But what the Review did not do was to consider what training was needed by our servicemen and women in moral skills. This was the missing chapter of the Defence Training Review. As the British Army's experiences in Iraq have subsequently underlined, further reform is needed to ensure that our forces are provided with the necessary moral education and training.

Since the events in Basra, improvements in ethical training have been made.[41] All ranks are now required to undertake training in the Laws of Armed Conflict, once annually and during pre-deployment training. This training includes the main features of the laws of war based on the Hague and Geneva Conventions, including detailed guidance on the treatment of prisoners of war and—since the Basra incidents—the handling of civilian detainees. Such training also covers the Army's Values and Standards, together with its policies on bullying and harassment.

These developments are important. But the failures in Basra, as the then Head of the British Army underlined, point to the need for a radical overhaul of the way values and standards are taught within the military. Morality needs to be afforded high priority and salience within the military curriculum. Ethical teaching should include not just the laws of war, such as the Geneva conventions, of which our soldiers seemed so sadly unaware. It should also embrace the wider body of just war teaching, whose practical wisdom and insights should be expounded not just to officers but to all ranks. For it is, as we have noted, a feature of the way conventional wars are fought today that responsibility is devolved to ever lower levels. Just war principles need to become staple fare in the classrooms of both officers and other ranks.

But morality cannot be taught just in the classroom. Morality needs to be expounded not as an abstract set of principles but as a practical guide to daily living, taught by precept, personal example, and practice. The example set by the military leader is crucial. Examples of virtuous behaviour need to be studied from both living and historical exemplars. It is also important to recall that morality is taught not just by what we say and do but what we fail to say and do. It was striking how Lynndie England, one of the participants in the Abu Ghraib abuses, claimed in her defence that she had assumed the abusive practices were acceptable because no one had told her otherwise: 'When we first got there, we were like, what's going on? Then you see staff sergeants walking around not saying anything (about the abuses). You think, OK, obviously it's normal.'[42]

The just war principles need not just to be expounded in our classrooms but embedded in the daily practice and experience of the barracks and battlefield. Moral training needs to become an integral part of the very fabric of service life. For it is not enough that our service people have a theoretical understanding of the conduct of just war. What matters is that they behave morally. Learning the rules and codes of war is necessary for the ethical behaviour of those involved with war. But rules alone are not sufficient to ensure that the right decisions are taken before, during, and after war. Just as an artillery officer needs both an understanding of the science of gunnery and to be drilled in the daily tasks of artillery warfare, so too our service people need to be equipped with both the theory and the practice of morality. Our service people need moral *education* so that they know and understand the principles of morality in general and those relating to the conduct of war in particular. But they also need to be *trained* so that they have the appropriate traits of character and skills to apply the principles in practice to the diverse challenges and tasks with which they may be faced, even when under pressure and with time running out. It is important too that they are able rapidly to adapt their behaviour to the shifting battlefield, as tasks change from those of conflict to those of peaceful reconstruction, a shift in behaviour that the soldiers whose exploits in Basra we examined failed to achieve.

All those involved in decisions about peace and war, from the highest level down to the ordinary service person, need to have been educated and trained to confront the moral challenges with the appropriate beliefs, desires, and feelings and to have acquired the necessary skills and practical wisdom to enable them to behave morally. Our service people need, in other words, to have been schooled and practised in the virtues, so that ethical conduct becomes for them second nature, as deeply engrained as habits of thought and action as may be the drills with which the soldiers wield their weapons. Like the corporal in Sierra Leone, we need the training just to 'take over'. Only thus will there be any prospect that the right decisions will be taken in the split seconds in which life or death decisions may have to be taken, amid the heat and passion of war.

This presents a considerable challenge for military education and training. It is, moreover, a challenge that cannot be met by reforms within the military establishment alone. For the challenge facing the military is made more difficult by the lack of moral education and training that our servicemen are likely to have received within the civilian community prior to recruitment. This reflects and is a consequence of the widespread moral scepticism in society, which we traced in Chapter 2. This presents an added challenge for the military, as was underlined by General Sir Richard Dannatt: 'In past generations it was assumed that young men and women coming into the armed forces would have absorbed an understanding of the values and standards required by the military from their family or from within the wider community. Such a presumption cannot be made today.'[43]

Nor is this lack of moral awareness a challenge just for the British Army. A survey by the US Army Surgeon General of soldiers and Marines serving in Iraq in 2006 found that 'less than half of the soldiers and Marines believed that non-combatants should be treated with dignity and respect'.[44]

The challenge of moral reform will be met only if it is supported and reinforced by society as a whole. This will be achieved only if society recovers its confidence in the rationality and teachability of morality. Such recovery of our moral self-confidence is essential for the wider reasons noted in Chapter 2. But there are two particular reasons why it is needed if we are to ensure the just conduct of war. First, it is impractical for the military to operate as a moral community within a society that is itself morally sceptical or indifferent. Without a consensus on morality within society, it would be difficult to establish what the military should be taught. Military leaders are required to set a personal example to their subordinates. But they will not be effective in inculcating values in which they themselves have received insufficient grounding. An ethical military needs the support and guidance of the wider community from whom they are drawn and whose interests they are called upon to serve. Second, a society that attaches insufficient importance to the moral education and training of its citizens will not be able to produce and nurture the practically wise and virtuous politicians and other leaders whom we need if just decisions are to be taken on the crucial choices between peace and war.

'Marines don't do that' is an appeal that successfully recalled a soldier from immoral action. But if we were to make such an appeal to the politician's code of honour—'Politicians do not do that'—our appeal would provoke contemptuous mirth, so devalued has become the politician's craft. Yet we need our politicians and their advisers to be as schooled in virtue as we need our military to be. Indeed, our political leaders need to be schooled in the very highest form of practical wisdom, given the scale and weight of their responsibilities. Is this a forlorn hope? Not quite.

For there is one appeal in the political field that still has resonance: 'Statesmen do not do that.' Statesmanship, as Aquinas reminds us, is the highest form of practical wisdom. Like other virtues, it is acquired through education, training, and experience. It requires attending to the counsels of the wise. The statesman will have built up his own practical store of knowledge in statecraft from which to draw. But a statesman will also choose, consult, and act upon the advice of wise advisers. The statesman is not driven by considerations of party interest or personal profit but desires to serve only the common good. He has learnt through teaching and experience what constitutes the common good and how it is best promoted. He exercises his judgement on how best to achieve the common good dispassionately, with his judgement not obscured by passion or emotion. We have thus not entirely lost our ideal of how politicians should behave and how they need to behave if they are to be entrusted with making just decisions on our behalf on matters as momentous as those of peace and war.

Just war teaching needs, therefore, to become not just the staple fare of our military academies. Just war counsels should also ring out in the Cabinet war rooms of our political leaders. Just war doctrine should become a key ingredient of public debate on war and the crucial yardstick against which the actions of both politicians and the military are measured before, during, and after war.

Conclusion

The virtues play a key role in both military and political life, as they do in our wider moral lives. The just war tradition furnishes the principles to guide our choices on how to begin, conduct, and end wars justly. But the successful application of the principles to concrete practical situations requires the exercise of the virtues, including, above all, that of practical wisdom. All those involved in decisions about peace and war—from the politicians, generals, and civil servants at the highest levels down to the ordinary service people facing the challenges of combat on the ground—need to be schooled in the virtues, so that virtuous conduct becomes for them second nature. For only thus will there be any prospect that the right decisions are taken in the heat and passion of war.

SEVEN

Virtuous Consequentialism

For much of the twentieth century, Anglo-Saxon philosophy was dominated by schools of ethical thought that held morality to be a fundamentally irrational activity, unconstrained by facts; at best, a matter of personal preferences or choices, at worst, the mere expression of feelings or emotions. In the preceding chapters I have sought to show that this view is mistaken and that morality is a rational activity. Man is not the solipsistic egoist that the moral sceptics presupposed but is, as Aristotle insists, a political animal: a being that lives and thrives in communities and for whom the good of others furnishes a reason for action just as does his own. Concern for others, on which morality is based, is thus not irrational. Morality is necessary for our flourishing as humans, not because it is a disguised form of egoism, but because to flourish as humans is to live well together in communities.

It is, moreover, a key feature of morality that it extends its claims progressively further out through ever-widening concentric circles of the communities to which we belong, starting from the family and extending outwards even towards the international community. Indeed, it was a key contribution of the sixteenth-century theologian, Vitoria, to the development of just war thinking to recognize that the constraints on warfare, embodied in the just war tradition, were not just private rules applying only between Christian princes in Europe but applied everywhere, including to the Indians in the New World.

Morality is thus neither mysterious nor irrational but furnishes the necessary guidelines for how we can flourish as humans: how we can promote human welfare and prevent suffering. Moral scepticism, in seeking to deny such a rational basis to morality, has had a deeply pernicious influence on our society. For, if there is no rational basis for morality, it becomes difficult to resist a slide towards a universal relativism in which any moral view goes and which ends up unable to distinguish the wisdom of Socrates from the wickedness of a Hitler or Stalin. This has, in turn, undermined our confidence in our own moral values. We no longer believe in moral wisdom nor do we feel able to teach morality. This has had harmful results throughout society, including on the moral behaviour of those of our citizens who serve in the armed forces. We expect our servicemen to behave morally. Yet new recruits to the services can no longer be presumed to have any prior grounding in moral values or an ethical code.

We need, therefore, a different approach to moral thinking. We should reject moral scepticism. But the options on offer from those philosophers who are prepared to accord a serious role to moral reasoning are, as we explored in the previous chapters, still riven by deep divides and disagreements. On the one hand are the deontologists and virtue ethicists, who agree among themselves that what matters are the interior qualities of our moral actions but disagree whether the key moral features are the rules under which the actions fall or the virtues displayed in the actions. Against both of these are the consequentialists, who hold that it is mistaken so to extol the personal integrity of the agent and that all that matters—or all that really matters—are the consequences of actions. We are faced with a bewildering choice. So how are we to decide?

Virtuous consequentialism is based on the simple insight that each of these theories is partly right but each is profoundly wrong. Adherents of the theories are right in respectively perceiving that intentions, rules, consequences, or virtues are important to our moral lives. But they are wrong in failing to recognize that all these features are important and instead supposing that their own preferred ethical feature is all that matters, or at least what matters most, in our moral decisions. Such accounts fail to do justice to both the complexity and the difficulty of our ethical decision-making. Virtuous consequentialism insists rather that, if we are to account for the complexity and richness of our moral lives, each of these features—intentions, rules, consequences, and virtues—needs to be given appropriate weight. We need also to draw on all these resources if we are to have any prospect of taking the right decision amid all the countervailing temptations and pressures. Virtuous consequentialism provides a basis both for appraising the ethical behaviour of others, as well as for guiding our own ethical conduct.

The obvious rejoinder to such an approach is that, by mixing up all these different features from different ethical traditions, we will simply end up with an indigestible farrago, an incoherent ragbag of ethical insights that will not offer clear or consistent guidance to our moral behaviour.

A rich farrago of concepts may, however, be what we need to describe our ethical life. For there is no reason why ethics should be simple. Indeed, as Bernard Williams once observed, 'Perhaps we need as many concepts to describe it as we find we need and no fewer.'[1] It is also important to recognize the different roles played by each of the features, which come into play at different points and levels in the reasoning process: the rules guide our actions, training in the virtues enables us to become adept in practical reasoning and to enact the rules in our daily lives, while both consequences and mental states need to be attended to in determining the moral quality of our actions. More fundamentally, since the aim of morality is to enable us to live well together in communities, it is this that furnishes the overall unifying principle that guides our ethical deliberations. The crucial test that has to be applied is whether an action will or will not contribute to the flourishing of those affected by our decisions. How many are so affected depends on the level and nature of the decision. The decisions of statesmen typically affect more than those of private individuals but not always and, as we have seen, the decisions of junior soldiers can critically affect the welfare of many others.

The variety of factors—both the internal states of the agent and the external consequences of his agency—that need to be taken into account in determining the moral quality of an action reflects the complexity and richness of our moral lives. For, as was underlined in Chapter 3, to live well is to live well together in a community, not as passive recipients of pleasure but as active contributors to the common welfare, where our flourishing depends not just on what happens to us but on what we do and how we view and are viewed by others. There is no inconsistency between the different factors, since they all contribute in their different ways to our flourishing as humans.

Far from collapsing into incoherence, virtuous consequentialism, as I hope the previous chapters have shown, offers a powerful tool not only for explicating how we ordinarily think about morality but also for guiding our ethical thought towards sound conclusions, avoiding paradoxical conclusions to which other theories may be drawn. Moreover, it offers such practical guidance, as we shall explore further in the next part of the book, even in the very difficult area of war. The importance of this area for ethical thought was rightly underlined by Michael Walzer: 'For war is the hardest place: if comprehensive and consistent moral judgments are possible there, they are possible everywhere.'[2]

A key weakness of both consequentialism, on the one hand, and deontology and virtue ethics, on the other, is that these theories oversimplify the complexity of moral reasoning. They bring too few conceptual tools to equip us for the task of ethical thought. Consequences are crucial to our ethical assessment of actions but they are not all that matter. If my hand is crushed, the pain caused is an important feature of my moral assessment. But I will view the action very differently depending upon whether the pain was produced intentionally; or, if unintentionally, whether it was foreseen but within the agent's control and consented to; or was the result of an accident—the agent tripped and fell.

So the intentions of the agent are important, but they are not all that matter. For, as this example also illustrates, it may matter that the agent, even if he did not intend the result, was still willing that it should happen, still consented to its occurrence. This feature may, moreover, be particularly important where the consequences are very harmful, as with the case that we examined in Chapter 5 of the Fenian bombers, who, to effect their comrades' escape from Clerkenwell prison in 1868, blew up a prison wall, even though there was a house nearby. They did not intend the deaths of its inhabitants, but they foresaw them and were still willing that they should happen. Part of the reason for condemning their action is that the consequences—the deaths of the nearby inhabitants—are judged disproportionate to the objective sought—escaping from the prison. But the mental state of the Fenian bombers is also relevant to our assessment: we condemn them for their indifference to the fate of the inhabitants. This is an important part of our reason for condemning their action. Intentions are not the only mental state that may be relevant to our ethical assessment. There may be gradations of mental state to consider.

Mental states are thus important. Deontologists go, however, too far in arguing that, if an act falls under a particular absolute moral rule, such as the prohibition on killing the innocent, we should consider only the agent's intentions and ignore the consequences. This too is to oversimplify our moral reasoning in which both mental states but also consequences play an important role. If we are debarred from taking consequences into account, we risk once again rendering morality an irrational activity, for whose rules and virtuous practices we can afford no reasons, and which furnishes no basis for decisions when—as may happen—the rules conflict or offer unclear or no guidance.

Such an absolutist approach can lead to conclusions that may seem paradoxical and harsh in cases where there is a conflict between principles, such as the prohibition on taking life and the injunction to save life or prevent undue suffering. The absolutist would, for example, forbid an abortion even where, as with the craniotomy case explored in Chapter 5, this is the only way to save the mother's life and without the operation both mother and baby will die. That conclusion appears perverse. Absolutism would also never permit assisted suicide or voluntary euthanasia for a dying patient where the ailment is incurable and certain to lead to death, however stringent the safeguards and however excruciating and unendurable may be her suffering. Indeed, even to consider such consequences is ruled out. Absolutism commits us to sticking to rules, regardless of the consequences—however disastrous they may be—and regardless of the pain and suffering thereby caused. This seems at odds with our ordinary moral consciousness. For there may be occasions when the moral rules are in conflict and where, exceptionally, it may be permissible to breach a moral rule if this is the only way to prevent very much greater harm.

Virtuous consequentialism suggests rather that moral reasoning is better construed as a matter of balancing both mental states and consequences in determining whether or not an action will contribute to the welfare of those it may affect. This is done not by applying some simple, black or white, cut-off procedure, determined solely by the presence or absence of intentions. We need rather to apply a graduating scale in which we assess degrees of mental responsibility, ranging from intention through consent to lack of consent; and weigh these up together with the assessed balance of good and ill to be achieved, taking into account both the nature of the consequences and the probability of their occurrence. Where great harm may result, as in the case of the Fenian bombers, mere lack of intention would not excuse an act whose consequences we foresaw and consented to. Where great harm could be avoided, as with the abortion case, an act with intended harmful consequences may still be permissible. Conversely, the internal quality of an act may be so bad as to be precluded even where beneficial consequences would thereby be achieved, as we shall explore further in considering torture in Chapter 9. For consequentialists, consequences may always override intentions; and for the absolutist, intentions override consequences. Virtuous consequentialism insists on the importance of both mental states and consequences.

Such an approach may add to the difficulty and complexity of moral reasoning but seems more accurately to describe its nature. It avoids the unwelcome conclusions to which, as we have just seen, the absolutist can be drawn. It also avoids paradoxes to which consequentialism can give rise.

For consequentialism can extend our moral responsibility in ways that are at odds with our ordinary moral judgements and may seem to impose impossibly excessive demands. This can be illustrated by the following examples:

- A Chinese father kills a new born infant. The child is a girl and, within the prescribed limit of only one child per family set by the Chinese government, he wants a boy. It is estimated that there are forty-four million fewer women in China than we should expect, with infanticide a major contributory factor to such discrepancy.[3]

- A desperate mother, with no money to look after her infant herself, abandons her child in an alleyway. A stranger passes by and notices the package with a baby but is in a hurry for a late appointment. He does nothing, hoping that someone else will deal with it. No one does, and the baby dies.

- On our TV screen we see the image of a starving child in Africa. We are invited by Oxfam to donate £50 to save the child's life. We do nothing, and the child dies.

On a consequentialist view, all these cases may seem morally indistinguishable. There are some differences. The death in the first case results from an act and in the others from omissions. But the distinction between an act and an omission does not of itself necessarily furnish grounds for a major moral distinction. Consequentialism lacks, however, other conceptual resources to mark the moral difference. For in each case the consequence is the same: a baby dies. In each case the agent is causally responsible for the death. If he had behaved differently, the baby would not have died. An act and a deliberate omission with identical consequences are for the consequentialist deemed to be morally equivalent.[4] If all that matters are consequences, the agent is as responsible for the death of the child in Africa, as for the child left in the alleyway, as for the death of the infant girl in China.

This view elides moral distinctions to which common sense attaches importance. For there is a world of difference between a child murderer, an uncaring passer-by, and a negligent aid-giver.

An ethic in which a failure to save the life of a starving infant in Africa is equated with murder may appear laudable. But its demands can also appear excessive. For, if our own good is to be traded off on equal terms against each of the potentially hundreds of thousands of the world's starving infants who could be helped by our action, it may be difficult to establish a robust cut-off point beyond which we are entitled to desist from offering help. But, without a robust cut-off point, we risk becoming gradually enveloped in an impractical feeling of universal guilt, like the guilt-ridden younger brother of Father Zossima in *The Brothers Karamazov*, for whom 'everyone of us is responsible for everyone else, and I most of all'.[5]

We want to avoid an impractical universal responsibility. But equally we want our ethics to be demanding. If intentions are what matter most, it may seem that only where the death is intended is the agent morally responsible. Where, as with the starving child in Africa, the death is unintended, we bear no responsibility. So we need feel no guilt for the starving child in Africa. But such an ethic would seem insufficiently challenging. Mere lack of intention should not be allowed to furnish too easy an excuse for our failure to help the plight of the children suffering in Africa.

Virtuous consequentialism seeks to reflect more accurately the nuances of our moral reasoning. For it discerns variations in moral culpability reflecting both the gradations of mental state and the assessed balance of good and ill that may result. These range from intention in the first case of female infanticide, where the baby's death is fully within the agent's control and consented to by him and the evil is outweighed by any good achieved. In the case of the passer-by, the extent of his control over and consent to the death of the infant in the alleyway may be less—the death was not certain and he hoped others would attend to the baby. But his behaviour is still deemed culpable, since he had some control and consented to what happened. The ill effects of his haste are disproportionate to any good achieved, such as reaching an important appointment on time. Towards the other end of the graduating scale is the aid-giver, where the considerably more attenuated control and consent reflect the many links and potential breaks in the causal chain between her sending money to Oxfam and its arrival in Africa to help a starving child.

Virtuous consequentialism would suggest that, where we have no knowledge of or control over a child's death in Africa, we have no moral blame.
But, conversely, someone who intentionally kills a child rightly bears all the
moral opprobrium of a child murderer. In between these extremes there
will be variations in moral responsibility, depending on the degree of
consent and control, with responsibility reducing as the causal chain lengthens and becomes gappier so that our control and consent diminish. We do
not escape responsibility for the death of the African child on our TV screen
about which we knew and could have done something. But our behaviour
is not equated with murder.

Any balanced ethical assessment needs to attend to both the internal and
the external aspects of agency, to the mental states of the agent and the
consequences of his actions. But that is still not enough. For the next
important insight, on which virtuous consequentialism is based, is that our
moral life is not only more complex than other theories suggest but is also
more difficult. It is very hard to be good. We need, therefore, all the help
we can get.

Help is provided first by the moral rules or principles that embody the
practical wisdom of our forebears on the conduct required to promote
human welfare or prevent human suffering. One of the mistakes of consequentialism is to belittle the value provided by such rules, so leaving us
bereft of guidance amid the many complexities and challenges of our moral
life other than that furnished by our own calculation of consequences.
Where the rules conflict or provide unclear or no guidance, we may be
obliged to undertake such calculation in order to assess which of the
available actions would better promote human welfare or avoid suffering.
Philosophers rightly attend to the resolution of such difficult cases. But in
doing so they can give a misleading impression of our moral lives. For most
of the time the rules do provide clear and consistent guidance. And where
they do, the strong moral presumption is that they should be followed.

In the case of the fateful decisions on war and peace, the rules are
furnished by the just war tradition. These rules have evolved over time
and reflect the practical wisdom and hard-won experience of our forebears,
in response to the diverse and difficult challenges set by war. A politician or
soldier who ignores these rules, or who thinks that in the midst of conflict
he could fashion better ones, would be either wicked or foolish. History
has, however, as we explored in Chapter 1, regretfully furnished only too
many examples of individuals who supposed they could do so.

The just war tradition also itself exemplifies the complex interplay between the various features of moral reasoning: rules, consequences, intentions, and virtues. The just war rules are justified by their beneficial consequences in promoting human welfare and preventing human suffering. The principle of proportion applied before and during war requires us to assess the consequences of our actions to ensure that more good than harm will arise. The principle of right intention insists that it is not enough for there to be a just cause but that the war must be undertaken for the sake of that just cause and so undertaken with a rightful intention.

But even the guidance of these principles is not enough. For, unless we have developed a sound habit of both reasoning and practice, the chances of our making the right decision amid all the many contrary pressures will be very remote. Such pressures may, moreover, be particularly intense in the heat and fog that precede and attend war. Hence derives the importance of the virtues not just in our ordinary lives but, in particular, for military life. The virtues—lost to sight in recent just war thinking—need to be rediscovered and to reinforce the just war principles, just as they did in the teachings of Aquinas in the thirteenth century.

If we are to choose and then follow the right course of action in the many difficult practical situations with which we may be faced and amid the many varying temptations to stray, we need to be well practised in the virtues, so that we confront the practical challenges of our moral life with the appropriate beliefs, desires, and feelings and have acquired a habit of sound reasoning in practical matters, not deflected from our purposes by passion. Indeed, if we are to have any prospect of reaching even the starting line for sound ethical decisions—let alone of completing the course—we need to have been educated in the importance and role of the virtues and trained in their daily practice. The virtues are crucial to our moral lives.

But even the virtues are not sufficient. Virtuous actions are virtuous only if undertaken for the sake of a good end. We need, therefore, a clear understanding and vision of the good to be achieved by our actions, of how our actions will promote human welfare or prevent suffering. To assist in determining this we need the guidance of the moral principles. But we also need to exercise our own practical wisdom to enable us to apply those general principles to concrete practical situations and to help guide our actions when the principles conflict or offer unclear or no guidance. Only thus, when faced with such difficult decisions, will we have the appropriate mental state and be able to assess correctly the relevant consequences of our agency and judge how best to act to promote welfare or prevent suffering.

Virtuous consequentialism accordingly insists that the complexity and challenge of our moral lives can be properly addressed only if we give appropriate weight to all facets of moral agency: to both the internal qualities and the external consequences of our actions, as well as to the principles that guide those actions and the virtues needed to enact the principles in our daily lives.

Virtuous consequentialism can thus satisfactorily explain how moral judgements are made. It can also do so in a way that maintains the essential moral unity between the private and public realms.

Public and private morality

From G. E. Moore onwards, the focus of moral philosophy for much of the twentieth century was primarily on our private lives. Moral philosophers had little to say about public affairs. Indeed, it is striking how silent were moral philosophers during the two global wars of the twentieth century, as they were even during the holocaust. Bertrand Russell was an egregious exception, but he was primarily a logician rather than a moral philosopher, and his opposition to war derived from his pacifist beliefs. Poets, not moral philosophers, led the criticism of the carnage of the trenches in the First World War. Bishops, not philosophers, criticized area bombing in the Second World War. Apart from Father John Ford's article on 'The Morality of Obliteration Bombing' in 1944, there was little interest in the just war tradition until its revival many years after the war, primarily in the context of the debate over nuclear deterrence that raged from the 1960s.[6]

Moreover, when in the latter half of the century moral philosophers began to discuss public affairs, their approach was initially hesitant and uncertain. This was perceptively noted by Bernard Williams in a collection of essays on *Public and Private Morality* published in 1978. He observed that the whole subject of public morality notoriously elicited 'an uncertain tone from academics, who tend to be either over-embarrassed or under-embarrassed by moralizing in the face of power'.[7]

What was perhaps most surprising was the way philosophers appeared only too ready to concede to politicians the right to behave in ways that would not be permitted in private morality. Stuart Hampshire, the editor and main contributor to the collection of essays in which Williams's article had appeared, argued that love and friendship and appeals to intuitions of right and wrong had a natural place in private morality.[8] But public morality was different. It was necessarily consequentialist, with the gravity of the consequences justifying a degree of licence over the means chosen: 'A degree of fastidiousness about the means employed, appropriate in personal relations, is a moral dereliction in a politician.'[9]

In another essay in the same volume, revealingly entitled 'Ruthlessness in Public Life', Thomas Nagel argued in a similar vein that, 'within appropriate limits, public decisions will be justifiably more consequentialist than private ones'.[10] In public life 'officials can do what would be unsuitable in private life'.[11] In private life, more weight is accorded to the internal qualities of the action. In public life, 'action-centred constraints will not be absent: there will still be restrictions on means. But those restrictions may be weaker in relation to the results than they are for individuals.'[12] Politicians may, accordingly, behave with greater ruthlessness than private individuals: 'public actors may have to get their hands dirty.'[13] This was 'the problem of dirty hands' to which Michael Walzer had already alluded in his seminal article of that name in 1973.[14]

These views have persisted. Most recently, Philip Bobbitt has argued the need for a divorce between public and private morality in his book *Terror and Consent* published in 2008. Bobbitt claims that, whatever may be an official's private moral beliefs: 'the moral rules that govern the official of a state of consent impose a "duty of consequentialism"—that is any contemplated course of action must be measured in terms of the foreseeable costs and benefits that are its result and not any absolute or categorical rule, including those regarding intentions.'[15] In private, we may be absolutists; in private, we may afford importance to intentions. But in public, our reasoning should be consequentialist.

The readiness of philosophers to accept that both the standards and the nature of moral reasoning are different in public and private life is surprising in a number of ways. This was the doctrine that Machiavelli counselled princes to adopt, urging that, 'if a prince wants to maintain his rule he must be prepared not to be virtuous'.[16] Some political leaders have been only too ready to follow Machiavelli's counsel. But this is not—despite the apparent academic presumption to the contrary—a view widely held in public life, at least not on the basis of my experience of a career in public service in the UK. Nor is it self-evidently in the interests of the citizens in a democracy that they should encourage such unscrupulousness on the part of their political leaders and public servants. Machiavelli may have admired the murderous exploits of Cesare Borgia, but few share his predilections. 'Machiavellian' is usually regarded as an epithet of condemnation rather than praise. There is good reason for this, since the concession to public officials of a right to behave in ways not licensed to individuals is a dangerous move. For there is always the risk that politicians will exploit such licence to a degree and in ways other than we, as citizens, would wish. This is no idle concern but a real fear. For the major criminals of the twentieth century, responsible for the deaths of many millions of innocents, have been just such political leaders who believed that ordinary moral constraints did not apply to them: leaders such as Stalin, Hitler, and Pol Pot—to name but three from a dismally lengthy list.

The dangers in conceding that different standards might apply in public and private life are only too evident. So the arguments for divorcing the two moral realms would need to be very strong to justify such a move. Let us consider each of the grounds suggested for making such a distinction.

There are differences between the public and private realms. In public life, the consequences tend to be larger and affect many more people than our private decisions. Public officials have particular duties and responsibilities that go with the office they hold. For example, particular requirements are placed on a judge to uphold the impartial administration of the law. Related to the different roles they perform, different virtues may come to the fore in the different realms. Hampshire suggests that the seriousness of politics 'requires priority for duties of careful and responsible calculation, for the virtues of prudence and "cleverness"'.[17] For the military, obedience has an importance that it lacks elsewhere. It has been claimed that 'the rule of obedience is simply the expression of that one among the military virtues upon which all others depend'.[18] Few would accord such a pre-eminent role to obedience in civilian life.

There are differences in the subject matter between the public and private realms. This is most apparent in the area of war. We cede to the governments of states, and to the military and police who act on their behalf, a monopoly in the use of organized force. Only states, not individuals, can go to war. Soldiers are permitted to use violence on a scale and in circumstances that are not permitted to individuals. The rules of war govern the behaviour of public officials, not of private individuals.

These differences are important. But do they oblige us to conclude that public and private morality are so different that different principles of morality apply and that the very nature of moral reasoning diverges between the two spheres?

The consequences of public decisions tend to be on a larger scale affecting many more lives. Morality extends its claims progressively further out through ever-widening concentric circles of the communities to which we belong. The communities for which as individuals we may bear responsibilities may be smaller than those for which public officials have responsibility. But this broadening of perspective can be viewed as a difference of degree rather than of principle.

Decisions taken in public life may, because of their scale, have a greater import than some private decisions. But it does not follow that the nature of moral reasoning is different between the two realms. What does follow is that it is crucial that our political leaders take ethically correct decisions. Consequences are important in politics. But consequences are also important and may be equally momentous in private life. As we noted in Chapter 5, following the terrorist attacks on 11 September 2001, the US President authorized United States Air Force pilots to shoot down any hijacked airliner posing a similar threat to that which had crashed into the Twin Towers. This was a momentous decision, with the lives of many thousands potentially affected. But on 11 September the brave individuals on board the hijacked airliner, United Airlines Flight 93, agonizing whether to try to seize control of the plane from the terrorists, faced an equally challenging and momentous decision, with the lives of many, including—tragically—their own, at stake.

Public officials have particular duties deriving from their roles. But so too do individuals. A mother has duties towards her own children. But we do not suppose that the basic rules of morality apply differently within and outside a family. Nor should we assume that they apply differently within and outside the public sphere because of the particular duties that may attach to public life. According to the differing roles we assume, the relative importance of virtues may shift. Obedience has an especial importance for military life. Practical wisdom is crucial for the statesman. But, while there may be shifts of emphasis, all the virtues still have relevance in both realms, and the four cardinal virtues, in particular, are as crucial in private, as in public, life. In our ordinary everyday affairs we still need to acquire and exercise practical wisdom, as we do justice, courage, and self-control.

The difference in subject matter between the public and private realms is important, most evidently in the area of war. Soldiers defending their countries from attack are licensed to use violence on a scale and in circumstances where individuals, acting in self-defence, are not. But, as we argued in Chapter 4, this difference in treatment reflects the different nature of the threat posed in domestic and international violence, rather than a disparity in the ethical basis. For the domestic threat is typically from an isolated single act of violence, whereas in war the threat extends over time and space and involves a number of people. We are permitted to attack a withdrawing or sleeping soldier because, when he returns or awakes, he may resume his attack on us. Consistent with the right of self-defence, more force may accordingly be licensed in war than in the domestic situation.

The differences between public and private morality can be viewed as differences of degree, perspective and subject matter, without needing to suppose that the nature of moral reasoning and the basic precepts of ethics differ between the two realms. So why have some philosophers, nonetheless, perceived a need to divorce the realms?

Part of the answer stems from the wider view they have taken of the nature of moral reasoning. If morality is primarily focused on our private lives and deemed to be a matter of absolute moral rules, admitting no exception, such a view may, indeed, be challenged when presented with the complexity and difficulties of public life. For in public life principles may only too often conflict. So, too, if morality is regarded as primarily a matter of personal feelings and the internal qualities of acts, this may furnish too impoverished a conceptual framework in which satisfactorily to explain the decisions of the public official who necessarily has to address consequences. It may then seem necessary to suppose that the nature of moral reasoning changes between the private and the public realms. But that conclusion would be mistaken. We should rather conclude that there is a weakness in the underlying ethical theories. For principles can conflict in private, as in public, life. A theory is deficient that highlights only some but not all of the conceptual features to which we need to attend in reaching moral decisions. Such a divergence between the public and private realms can be avoided if we recognize that consequences are important in both our private and public decisions.

But we need also to recognize that consequences are not all that matter in the public, any more than in the private, realms. Institutions and states are not individuals, but they are made up of individuals. The character of the agents and the internal quality of their actions are also important to the ethical assessment. This is recognized in the just war tradition by the importance accorded to right intention. We shall also examine in Chapter 9 how difficult it is to explain the moral repugnance we have for torture if we attend only to the consequences of the action and do not give appropriate regard to the mental states and moral character of the agent.

If we are to address the complexity and difficulty of our moral choices in the public, as in the private, realms, we need, therefore, to deploy the full range of resources identified by virtuous consequentialism. Drawing on such resources, virtuous consequentialism is able adequately to account for our moral reasoning in both the private and the public realms. It thus avoids the need for any schism between the two worlds. Morality extends rather as a seamless web between the private and the public spheres. We can, accordingly, hold our politicians and public officials to account against the same basic moral principles and deploying the same moral reasoning as we do in our private lives. There is no licence for the unscrupulous politician; no need to concede to public officials a right to display a ruthlessness that elsewhere we would disdain.

In no area is there a more pressing need to hold politicians and officials morally to account than in the area of war. The just war tradition provides the principles against which their conduct can be judged. In understanding, applying, and implementing the principles, we also need to draw guidance from the broader ethical framework that underpins our ordinary moral reasoning—the framework of virtuous consequentialism. I shall consider in Part Two how just war thinking, as so developed and reinforced, can help guide both policy-makers and ordinary service people in meeting the difficult security challenges of the twenty-first century. I shall begin by examining the changing nature of war.

PART TWO

War

EIGHT

The Protean Nature of War

An era of strategic stability

For forty years—from 1949, when Russia acquired its own nuclear weapons, to 1989, when the Berlin Wall fell—strategic stability prevailed. This was the period of the Cold War, when the Eastern and Western blocs confronted each other with a massive array of armaments but did nothing. Each was mutually deterred from attacking the other because of the risk of escalation to the nuclear level. The advent of nuclear weapons in 1945 had transformed the nature of war, inflating its cost to such unimaginable levels that force, even at the lowest conventional level, seemed barely usable because of the risk of nuclear escalation. Writing in 1945 shortly after the atomic detonations at Hiroshima and Nagasaki, Bernard Brodie, the strategic prophet of the nuclear age, declared: 'Thus far the chief purpose of our military establishments has been to win wars. From now its chief purpose must be to avert them.'[1]

Military forces continued to train for large-scale, conventional wars of the kind fought already twice on a global scale in the twentieth century. The aim was, however, no longer that the forces should be used but that an adversary should believe they might be used. For not just nuclear but conventional forces too had a primary deterrent role within NATO's overall strategy of flexible response. Within the European theatre of operations—the prime focus for East–West rivalry—force was no longer deemed to be usable by Western governments, except at the margin—for example, operations in support of the civil power in Northern Ireland. So, when the Soviet Union invaded Hungary in 1956 or Czechoslovakia in 1968, the West declined to intervene, preferring that those countries should remain 'red' rather than risk our becoming 'dead'. There were interventions elsewhere, most notably that by the USA in Vietnam from 1964 to 1973. But the failure of that intervention left the USA with a distaste for foreign military adventure. The West accordingly failed to intervene to prevent the genocide of 1.7 million Cambodians by the Khmer Rouge during their brutal reign of 1975–9.

The fall of the Berlin Wall in November 1989 put a dramatic and unexpected end to this period of strategic stability. Some of my continental, particularly German, colleagues in NATO, where I was representing the UK at the time as Defence Counsellor, thought that the end of the Cold War would presage a new era of peace, with the obsolete NATO alliance disbanded and its swords turned into ploughshares. Alas that was not to be. Indeed, as the salience of nuclear deterrence declined, with the easing of East–West tensions, so the utility of conventional force was rediscovered. During the heyday of nuclear deterrence we had hoped that war might for ever become unwageable. But now, as the risk of nuclear escalation receded, so war became once more a thinkable option.

The first sign of the renewed utility of conventional force came when Saddam Hussein invaded Kuwait on 2 August 1990. Saddam had not expected any military response from the international community, any more than there had been when he had invaded Iran in 1980. This was not an unreasonable expectation given the general US reluctance to intervene since the failed intervention in Vietnam. But what Saddam had omitted to notice was the shift in the strategic tectonic plates that had occurred when the Berlin Wall fell. Far from acquiescing in this breach of international law, the USA rapidly assembled a broad coalition of nations that from 16 January to 28 February 1991 successfully expelled the Iraqi forces from Kuwait.

This return to conventional conflict seemed to some to be merely a last hurrah of the old regime before the 'new world order'—proclaimed by President Bush (senior) in his January 1991 State of the Union Speech— would prevail: 'What is at stake is more than one small country: it is a big idea: a new world order—where diverse nations are drawn together in common cause, to achieve the universal aspirations of mankind: peace and security, freedom and the rule of law.'[2] But the new world order was of very short duration. In late 1991 and early 1992 unrest broke out in the Balkans, erupting into open conflict when a Serbian sniper fired into a crowd of demonstrators in Sarajevo on 5 April 1992. This signalled another change brought about by the ending of the Cold War. As the permafrost that had gripped Europe in frozen immobility thawed and political bonds loosened, so ancient ethnic rivalries resurfaced in the very centre of Europe. Croats, Serbs, and Bosnian Muslims began to fight each other for control over the former territory of Yugoslavia, once rigidly unified by President Tito. The immediate target was control of the disputed territory of the newly independent Bosnia-Herzegovina.

New wars

These events took Western governments by surprise. They did not know how to react. Civilians were being slaughtered in the very heart of Europe. So the cry went up that 'Something must be done!' But what? No one was sure. The mood of perplexity was well captured in a cartoon in the British *Guardian* newspaper entitled 'The Bosnian Drill'. This showed a squad of soldiers being drilled by a sergeant who is bellowing out the command: 'On the order "Something", Do Something!'

During the long years of the Cold War, Western governments had become accustomed to the notion that the only use of military forces was in defence of their own territory and, even then, the aim was to ensure—through the threat of use—that the non-use of force was maintained. Such was the essence of deterrence. There was deep reluctance to become involved in a conflict in which the direct defence of home territory was not involved. Bismarck had remarked that the Balkans were not worth the life of one Pomeranian Grenadier. So in the UK there were dark mutterings that the life of a single British Grenadier was not worth risking for the sake of 'a quarrel in a far-away country between people of whom we know nothing'.[3] In the Cold-War period there had been a degree of moral clarity, as the Western democracies sought to defend their way of life from the aggressive ambitions of a Marxist, totalitarian dictator. But now moral confusion and even panic reigned, as there was no longer a clearly charted path forward.

There was also conceptual confusion over the kind of war being fought in the Balkans. It was initially viewed as an inter-state war but fought on a mini-scale, with the Serbs perceived as conventional aggressors. Only slowly was it appreciated that the states involved were failed states and that many of the primary actors were non-state players, including the marauding bands of thugs such as Arkan's Tigers. Similarly, it took time for it to be realized that the attacks on civilians perpetrated by such bands

and the military forces with whom they collaborated were not the unfortunate side effects of conventional military actions but were rather the primary
objective of the military activity. A new term—ethnic cleansing—was
coined to describe such activity. It is symptomatic of the prevalent confusion that even this term was apparently introduced as a result of a journalist's
mistranslation of the words used by a Serbian commander that, in fact,
described his 'mopping-up' operations.[4] Rather than seizing territory by
military force, the new tactic of ethnic cleansing was designed to gain
control of territory by changing the ethnic mix of the population, displacing
populations so that the ethnic mix eventually matched that of the displacer.

Thrown into confusion by the advent of this new kind of warfare,
Western governments reacted uncertainly. The US government chose to
sit on the sidelines, issuing edicts, while the European governments chose to
intervene at the lowest possible end of the spectrum, as peacekeepers. The
United Nations Protection Force (UNPROFOR) was deployed to Croatia
in February 1992 and to Bosnia-Herzegovina in June 1992 'to support
efforts by the United Nations High Commissioner for Refugees
(UNHCR) to deliver humanitarian relief, and, in particular, to provide
protection, at UNHCR's request, where and when UNHCR considered
such protection necessary'.[5] Western governments thought they had clev-
erly limited the scope and scale of their involvement.

In fact, they had chosen to intervene in a way that was both ineffective at
preventing the civilian atrocities that were taking place but also dangerous
both for the troops deployed and for those whom they were sent to protect.
For the peacekeepers, plunged into the midst of a complex and bitter three-
way civil strife between Serbs, Croats, and Bosnian Muslims, rapidly ceased
to be shields offering protection to the civilian population. Instead, they
themselves became hostages, vulnerable to the threats of the rival military
factions, particularly the Serbs, but unable to take effective military action
against them. The lowest point of this policy came in July 1995 when Dutch
peacekeepers stood idly by while Serbian forces seized Srebrenica. In the
next few days Serbian forces massacred 8,000 Bosnian men and teenage boys
and buried them in mass graves around the city.[6] The West was finally
galvanized into action by this atrocity. Following the shelling of Sarajevo
market by Serbian forces on 28 August, the UN commander, General
Rupert Smith, ordered into action an Anglo-French Rapid Reaction
Force that had been deployed to Mount Igman overlooking the city.
Their skilful artillery bombardment of Serb positions, carefully coordinated

with NATO air-force operations, finally induced the Serbs in September to desist from their attacks and accept a ceasefire. The terms for the ceasefire were negotiated by the US diplomat Richard Holbrooke, the USA having belatedly realized that this was a conflict from which they could not stand aside.[7]

The 1992–5 Balkans conflict was an excruciatingly difficult learning experience for Western leaders, as they too slowly came to grips with the new kind of warfare being fought and how best to respond to it. The conceptual confusion was illustrated by the confusion of military language, with no one quite sure even what to call the new kind of military operations, so settling for the cumbersome and un-descriptive 'Operations Other than War'. So impressed have been some commentators and participants with the need to develop a new approach to deal with Balkan-type conflicts that they have spoken of the Balkans conflict as marking the end of the era of 'old wars'—industrial inter-state wars—inaugurated by Napoleon's introduction of the *levée en masse* in 1793 and culminating in the two world wars of the twentieth century. Instead, the Balkans conflict would provide the model for all future 'new wars'. Such was the thesis of Mary Kaldor's book *New and Old Wars*.[8] Meanwhile, General Rupert Smith, himself a protagonist in the Balkan conflict, prophetically declaimed: 'For it must never be forgotten: war no longer exists . . . We now are engaged, constantly and in many permutations, in war amongst the people.'[9]

Key features of the new form of warfare are that it is fought among the people, with civilians often the direct object of attack, and the primary participants are non-state actors. These may be, on the one side, the remnants of a failed state and, on the other, the international coalition of forces arrayed against them. War is no longer between states. It is also a feature of the new conflicts that the use of military force is no longer designed on its own to produce a strategic outcome, as was achieved, for example, by the physical destruction of Hitler's forces in 1945. Wars are now fought not to achieve a strategic outcome but to create conditions in which that outcome can be achieved by other means. Military force is but one of a number of tools to be employed alongside others, such as diplomacy, economic reconstruction, improved political governance, and aid programmes. Equipped with such a variety of tools, a political leader can take an appropriately 'comprehensive approach', as it is now termed, to conflict resolution.

These are all important features of the way wars, or at least some wars, are currently fought. Whether, however, the Balkans conflict really provides an exclusive and enduring paradigm for the new face of war seems unlikely. For not all new wars are like the Balkans conflict. The First Gulf War, for example, was more like a classic inter-state war, fought in self-defence. Moreover, even some of the Balkan-style 'new wars' bear striking similarities to some old wars. Thucydides would have recognized many of the features of Balkan ethnic cleansing from his experience of the civil strife in Corcyra in 427 BC:

> The Corcyraeans continued to massacre those of their own citizens whom they considered to be their enemies. Their victims were accused of conspiring to overthrow the democracy, but in fact were often killed on grounds of personal hatred or else because of the money they owed. There was death in every shape and form. And, as usually happens in such situations, people went to every extreme and beyond it. There were fathers who killed their own sons; men were dragged from the temples or butchered on the very altars; some were actually walled up in the temple of Dionysius and died there.[10]

The protean nature of war

Rather than supposing that, through the Balkans conflict, we have finally uncovered the true and permanent new face of war, war is better regarded, as John Keegan judiciously observed, as 'a protean activity'. Like the Greek sea monster Proteus, 'it changes form, often unpredictably . . . Like disease, it exhibits the capacity to mutate, and mutates faster in the face of efforts to control or eliminate it.'[11] It may be as mistaken to suppose that the latest mutation of war is the form war will henceforward take for ever, as it was mistaken for the traditionalists to suppose that the paradigm of industrial war, for which they had been trained, would itself dominate for ever.

Moreover, war has continued to mutate since the Balkans conflict, with a striking feature being how one and the same conflict may exhibit several modes of war. So the conventional campaigns fought against the Taliban in Afghanistan in October–December 2001 and against Saddam's forces in Iraq in March–April 2003 have both mutated into counter-insurgency campaigns of a kind recognizable from that fought by the British in Malaya in 1948–58. Such campaigns also illustrate the variety of military operations

For the USA, the 9/11 attack, as it became christened, was the first significant direct attack upon the US homeland since the Japanese attack on Pearl Harbor in 1941. One of the apparent lessons of the Balkans conflict—that the new wars would be fought at a distance from home, with relatively low risk to one's own forces, and in support of broader national interests than self-defence—had been quickly falsified. For the terrorists now appeared to be directly threatening civilian lives on the US mainland. The coalition military operations that swiftly followed in October 2001 against the Taliban and al-Qaeda in Afghanistan, albeit fought at a distance, were conducted under the self-defence provisions of Article 51 of the UN Charter. The direct threat to American lives presented by al-Qaeda terrorists also ended the previous US reluctance, as evidenced in the Kosovo campaign, to engage with ground troops, as the ensuing operations in both Afghanistan and Iraq have demonstrated. In combating terrorist-inspired insurgency operations, US troops have had to learn to accept more risk to their own forces and that force protection is no longer an absolute.[17]

The 9/11 attack had other novel features. It exploited the terrorists' suicidal propensities to spectacular effect by turning a civilian airliner into a weapon of mass destruction. The attack underlined the terrorists' readiness to inflict large-scale civilian casualties, undeterred by fear of alienating the public or their supporters or by considerations of personal survival. But it was still a conventional attack. Concern, nonetheless, grew that, in the strategic confusion of the post-Cold-War world, including the ineffective controls initially exercised over the armouries of the former Soviet Union, terrorists might be able to acquire, indeed, might have already acquired, chemical, biological, or even crude nuclear devices with which very much greater damage could be caused. This is far from an imaginary fear, as the sarin gas attack by terrorists in the Tokyo subway on 20 March 1995 had illustrated. Osama bin Laden had, moreover, openly proclaimed in 1998, when asked about acquiring chemical or nuclear weapons, that 'acquiring such weapons for the defence of Muslims is a religious duty'.[18]

Concern over nuclear proliferation had further increased with the uncovering by the British Secret Intelligence Service, working in conjunction with the CIA, of the worldwide network run by A. Q. Khan, the father of the Pakistani nuclear bomb, illegally to export nuclear technology for profit.[19] Khan had himself stolen nuclear technology from the European company URENCO, for which he had worked, to assist in the development of Pakistan's bomb. He had been involved in illegally exporting nuclear technology from 1976, with customers including North Korea, Iran, South Africa, and Libya. There had been contacts in 2001 between rogue Pakistani nuclear scientists, associated with Khan's programme, and al-Qaeda.[20] Khan's activities finally came to an end on 4 October 2003 when agents boarded the *BBC China*, a ship flying a German flag, in the Italian port of Taranto and seized thousands of centrifuge components. Illicit nuclear proliferation was no longer a fearful possibility but a reality.

A further disturbing feature, illustrated by the 9/11 and subsequent attacks, is the effectiveness of al-Qaeda's global network. Al-Qaeda is not a super- or supra-national state. But it does have global reach. It achieves this through outsourcing its terrorist operations to local groups for whom al-Qaeda provides training and financial, logistic, and planning support, as well as the al-Qaeda brand. It is adept at exploiting modern communications technology, including the Internet, not just for recruiting and training but also for publicizing its atrocities worldwide. These characteristics mark, as Philip Bobbitt has argued, a worrying shift from the nation-state terrorists, with whom we have grown familiar, to globally active 'market state terrorists'.[21]

The final and, in many ways, most concerning feature of the new terrorism is the huge breadth and ideological ambition of the terrorists' objectives. In the various *fatwas* and declarations that Osama bin Laden has issued, he has proclaimed that 'to kill the Americans and their allies— civilians and military—is an individual duty for every Muslim who can do it in any country in which it is possible'.[22] The justifications offered for such indiscriminate slaughter are, however, multifarious. Some of the objectives sought by al-Qaeda are achievable, such as the removal of US forces and bases from Saudi Arabia. But others, such as the conversion of the American people to Islam, an end to democracy, and the establishment of a universal caliphate and sharia law, hanker for a return to a pre-Enlightenment past that, even if desirable, would appear beyond the realms of practical possibility.[23] So long as their objectives remain so diffuse, the scope for a negotiated settlement—which is how terrorist campaigns have often been concluded—appears limited.

In the face of such an extreme terrorist threat, it has been argued, not least by the previous US Administration of George Bush (junior), that the West is justified in taking extreme measures to defend itself and its civilians from such attacks. The US government proclaimed a new strategic doctrine of pre-emption—attacking the terrorist enemy before he attacks us, in order to

prevent harm to our country and people.[24] Other measures include operations to capture and detain terrorists and to secure information from them
by coercive interrogation. We shall consider in the next chapter whether
such measures can be justified against the just war criteria.

The two decades since the fall of the Berlin Wall have not heralded the
era of peace that had been hoped for. Over this period British forces, like
those of the USA and, to a lesser extent, those of other allies, have been
more actively engaged in military operations worldwide than at any time
since the Second World War. This was illustrated by the award in 2008 to
British servicemen and women of twenty-eight Military Crosses for service
in the preceding year, the highest number awarded in any year since the end
of the Second World War.[25]

Let us consider some of the morally relevant features of the way war has
changed its nature over this period.

Moral features of the new wars

It is often claimed that wars now fought are wars of choice, rather than of
necessity. This is an oversimplification. Governments may consider they
have little choice but to defend their people from the direct attacks of
terrorists, such as the threats posed by al-Qaeda. Conversely, all wars are a
matter of choice, even wars in self-defence. It is, in principle, open to
governments to decline to participate even in wars of self-defence, although
this may, in practice, be difficult, particularly if their own territory is under
attack. So, for example, in 1982 the Argentine government expected the
UK to choose not to defend the Falkland Isles. This proved to be a strategic
miscalculation, but it was not an unreasonable expectation, given the
apparent signals the British government had given in the preceding months
of its declining interest in the islands. Moreover, even the decision by the
British government to continue the fight against Hitler after the fall of
France was far from a foregone conclusion, as testified by the intense
three-day debate of the War Cabinet during 25–28 May 1940.[26] So even
with wars of self-defence there are degrees of choice available. It is, nonetheless, true that, in the post-Cold-War era, Western governments have
more choice about whether, when, and how they should engage in military
operations than they did earlier in the twentieth century, when faced with

the threats to the existence of their states posed by Nazism or Soviet Communism.

This shift from wars of necessity to wars of choice has been accompanied by a move throughout Europe and elsewhere from large conscript to smaller, more flexible, professional forces, a trend initiated in earlier decades by the US and UK governments. Such forces are better configured to the new modes of warfare. But one consequence of the ending of conscription is that experience of military life, still less collective memories of war, such as those of the Second World War, are no longer shared by the wider citizen body. This relative isolation of the military from wider society can add to the challenges of morally educating our service people. It can lead within the isolated group to the development of codes of practice that are at odds with the moral norms of wider society. It can lead, for example, as we explored in Chapter 6, to loyalty that is too narrowly focused between members of a regiment and so ignores the wider interests of the society they are serving.

The agony of choosing whether or not to go to war was well illustrated by the convoluted and painful deliberations of Western governments over their involvement in the Balkans conflict in the early 1990s. Without the strategic certainties and moral clarity of the Cold-War period, there is uncertainty and confusion about when interventions should be undertaken. The changing nature of war and, in particular, the demise of the industrial inter-state model of war, have also led some to question the continued utility of just war thinking. If war no longer exists, how can just war teaching still be helpful?

Such criticism misunderstands both the nature of war and just war thinking. War has always had and will continue to have its protean qualities. The just war tradition does not presuppose a particular model of war, such as industrial inter-state war. The tradition, as we traced in Chapter 4, long pre-dates the establishment of the modern state system at the Treaty of Westphalia or the arrival of industrial war. Just war thinking provides guidance on when and how force should be used, in whatever mutation the protean monster may assume. Moreover, the very strategic confusion of the post–Cold-War era underlines the importance of having clear criteria, as furnished by the just war tradition, for deciding whether, when, and how military interventions should be undertaken. We shall assess in subsequent chapters how useful that guidance is in helping to chart a path through the bewildering security challenges of the twenty-first century.

The fact that wars may now be undertaken for reasons other than self-defence reinforces the importance of the ethical behaviour of the soldiers involved. For soldiers, despatched to undertake a humanitarian mission, will undermine the objective of that mission if they ill-treat the people they are sent to protect. Moreover, since the support of the civilian population is the key to the success of counter-insurgency operations, the protection of civilians may be not only a moral duty but a military necessity. This message is underlined by the new *US Army and Marine Corps Counterinsurgency Field Manual*: 'At its core, counterinsurgency is a struggle for the population's support. The protection, welfare and support of the people are vital to success.'[27]

Sarah Sewall argues in her introduction to the manual: 'The doctrine's most important insight is that even—perhaps especially—in counterinsurgency, America must align its ethical principles with the nation's strategic requirements.'[28] In such contexts to fight well is to fight in accordance with moral requirements. These developments emphasize the need to ensure that our soldiers are not only well versed in the principles of the just war but are also well trained in and habituated to practise the virtues. Virtuous conduct needs to become for them second nature, enabling them to respond correctly, even amidst the heat and fury of war, and with only seconds to decide matters of life or death.

The importance of ethical conduct is further underlined by the way mistakes at the tactical level can rapidly assume strategic importance as a result of the media domination of modern conflicts. Rupert Smith noted: 'Whoever coined the phrase "the theatre of operations" was very prescient. We are conducting operations now as though we were on stage, in an amphitheatre or Roman arena.'[29] The actors on stage play to the gallery and among those seated in the gallery are the world's media, conveying news around the world and around the clock, 24/7. Terrorists have become adept at playing to the global gallery. Forces seeking to counter terrorist operations need, in turn, to be ever mindful of the potential global impact of their actions. The media are now part of military operations. Information is a key tool of warfare. The reports that the media file on the conflict may critically influence the struggle for the hearts and minds of the people on which the success or failure of a counter-insurgency operation may depend. They can also have a key influence on the support for operations from the people back home. Unethical military conduct at the tactical level, such as the ill-treatment of civilians detained in Basra that we examined in Chapter 6, can undermine the strategic objectives of the campaign.

The comprehensive approach required by modern warfare, in which humanitarian, peace support, and warlike activities can take place simultaneously or in quick succession, necessitates a wide range of skills from the military and for them to work in close cooperation with the civilian agencies responsible for reconstruction. Moreover, until civilian agencies are able to take over the tasks, ground forces engaged in counter-insurgency may, according to the US *Counterinsurgency Field Manual*, even have 'to assume the roles of mayor, trash collector and public works employer'.[30] A multiplicity of skills is also required at all levels. For it is a feature of modern warfare that responsibility is devolved to ever lower levels, with the 'strategic corporal' taking decisions on a street corner or at a vehicle checkpoint that can affect the welfare of many others and have strategic impact on the campaign. Practical wisdom is no longer, as Aquinas thought, the prerequisite of generals. Moral training needs to extend from the highest general to the lowest private.

The nature of modern conflicts—war among the people—also points to the continuing threat to civilian populations. It has been estimated that at the start of the twentieth century 85–95 per cent of casualties were military. By the end of the century these proportions had been almost exactly reversed, with approximately 80 per cent of all casualties civilian.[31] Such statistics need to be treated with caution, since the protean nature of war is ever to mutate and the massacre of civilians is not just a feature of modern warfare. But war in the late twentieth and early twenty-first centuries poses its own particular deadly threat to civilians, ranging from the indiscriminate attacks of al-Qaeda suicide bombers in Western cities, through the ethnic cleansing of populations in the Balkans to the genocidal massacres in Rwanda and Darfur.[32] Civilian populations have been and are being attacked in ways that no possible interpretation of the principle of non-combatant immunity could justify. The protection of civilians from the ravages of war—a central concern of the just war tradition—remains an ever fragile but crucial norm of restraint on which the international community needs to insist. The protection of civilians may, moreover, not only be a necessary constraint on the way in which war is conducted but also furnish just cause for the inception of military operations to prevent massacres taking place. We shall examine the case for such humanitarian intervention in Chapter 11.

Conclusion

War is a protean activity, constantly changing. It is never safe to assume that we have finally discovered its true and permanent nature. The strategic stability of the Cold-War period has been replaced by a period of transience, change, and confusion, in which various kinds of wars among the people are being conducted. Amid such strategic confusion, the importance both of moral clarity on why war is being undertaken and of virtuous behaviour by all involved in its conduct has never been greater. The realists who claimed that war and morality should have nothing to do with each other were, for the reasons examined at the start of this book, always profoundly mistaken. But their views look even less plausible today when morality not only provides a necessary external constraint on war but may also furnish both the ground for undertaking military operations and a vital internal tool for their successful conduct. In such circumstances, to fight well is to fight justly, to fight in accordance with the constraints of morality.

NINE
Extreme Times, Extreme Measures

History returns

The terrorist attack on New York and Washington on 11 September 2001 created panic among decision-makers in the USA. For the attack came as a terrible and unexpected shock. With the ending of the Cold War, the USA had emerged as the sole military superpower. Americans had begun to settle down to enjoy the fruits of what one commentator dubbed the 'end of history'—a new quiet period in which the ideals of democracy and the market economy would peacefully predominate over the spent forces of totalitarianism and communism.[1] Just when all appeared safe and secure, so literally came a bolt from the blue. Out of the blue September skies terrorists crashed civilian airliners into the Twin Towers in New York and the Pentagon in Washington, killing 3,000 innocent civilians. The terrorists hailed from an extremist Islamist group—al-Qaeda—that were inspired by a hatred of America and the West and everything for which they stood—including democracy and the market economy. History had returned with a vengeance.

The attack was the first significant direct attack on the American homeland since Pearl Harbor. The attack had been designed to maximize the deaths of innocent civilians, with the terrorists spectacularly succeeding in this objective because of their readiness to act without regard to their own safety or fear of alienating the public or their own supporters. The devastation had been achieved by exploiting to deadly effect the destructive potential of a commercial airliner. But how much more devastation might have been caused should such determined terrorists acquire—as was their avowed aim—weapons of mass destruction. A new and deadly enemy had appeared; and an enemy who acted without regard to ethical or legal constraints. To counter such an extreme threat, a radical reappraisal of security policy was required. In extreme times, extreme measures had to be considered.

A new strategic doctrine: pre-emption

An early task was to revise US defence policy. In the past, massing of armies and armour had been the signs of impending attack. But terrorists could now mount devastating attacks, anywhere in the world, clandestinely, swiftly, and without visible preparations. Effective defence against the new scourge of terrorism could not be assured, as had been evidenced by the spectacular success of the 9/11 attack. But nor could deterrence be relied on to dissuade would-be terrorists from mounting attacks. The new adversary possessed no territory that could be targeted and was prepared to commit suicide in pursuit of his objectives. During the Cold War peace had been maintained through deterrence, based on a threat of massive reprisal. Pre-emptive action had been generally viewed with disfavour because it threatened the stability of deterrence. But the cool, calculating rationality, based on mutual self-interest, that had underpinned such deterrence no longer seemed to apply to the new threat posed by terrorists who might welcome self-immolating martyrdom.

So neither defence nor deterrence through threatened reprisal could be relied on to counter the new terrorist threat. Was there then no choice but to wait until after an attack had taken place and only then to take action against those who had perpetrated it? When the victims of the attack could be many thousands of innocent civilians, a policy of 'wait and see' had little appeal to a democratic government whose duty was to protect its citizens. In order to avoid this agonizing dilemma, a new doctrine of pre-emption was forged. It was not acceptable to wait until an attack had taken place. Philip Bobbitt, accordingly, advocated 'preclusive' action against threats of sufficient gravity to imperil international security, even where not imminent. For, as he explains, 'once a terrorist mass atrocity is actually executed in Manhattan, only tragedy and terror will follow'.[2] In an era 'of disguised attack using terrorist networks, the proliferation of WMD can make pre-emption an absolute necessity'.[3] 'Preclusion is the new deterrence.'[4]

The US Government's new strategic doctrine of pre-emption was trailed in President Bush's State of the Union address in January 2002 and set out in full in *The National Security Strategy of the United States of America*, published in September 2002.

The National Security Strategy explains the new doctrine of pre-emption as follows:

> For centuries, international law recognized that nations need not suffer an attack before they can lawfully take action to defend themselves against forces that present an imminent danger of attack. Legal scholars and international jurists often conditioned the legitimacy of preemption on the existence of an imminent threat—most often a visible mobilization of armies, navies, and air forces preparing to attack.
>
> We must adapt the concept of imminent threat to the capabilities and objectives of today's adversaries. Rogue states and terrorists do not seek to attack using conventional means. They know such attacks would fail. Instead, they rely on acts of terror and, potentially, the use of weapons of mass destruction—weapons that can be easily concealed, delivered covertly, and used without warning.
>
> The targets of these attacks are our military forces and our civilian population, in direct violation of one of the principal norms of the law of warfare. As was demonstrated by the losses on September 11, 2001, mass civilian casualties is the specific objective of terrorists and these losses would be exponentially more severe if terrorists acquired and used weapons of mass destruction.
>
> The United States has long maintained the option of preemptive attacks to counter a sufficient threat to our national security. The greater the threat, the greater is the risk of inaction—and the more compelling the case for taking anticipatory action to defend ourselves, even if uncertainty remains as to the time and place of the enemy's attack.
>
> To forestall or prevent such hostile acts by our adversaries, the United States will, if necessary, act preemptively.[5]

The National Security Strategy presents the doctrine of pre-emption as a development of the just war tradition. That tradition takes self-defence to be the paradigm just cause. But it also recognizes that there might be exceptional circumstances where a state need not wait to suffer an attack before it takes action. Mindful, however, how open to abuse might be the concession of a right of pre-emption, classical just war theorists sought to constrain tightly the occasions on which it might be exercised. All the conditions of the just war would need to be met, including that of proportionality, requiring that military action should be undertaken only if more good than harm is judged likely to ensue. Pre-emptive action in self-defence could, however, be permissible if the threat were immediate and certain.

The new US doctrine concedes that in the past the immediacy or imminence of the threat was an appropriate criterion. But it argues that the changed nature of the threat now posed by terrorists—who may be covertly armed with weapons of mass destruction and able to strike swiftly and decisively—requires that the criteria should be changed. The sufficiency of the threat would justify military action 'even if uncertainty remains as to the time and place of the enemy's attack'. According to Bobbitt, what justifies a shift towards preclusion is 'the potential threat to civilians... posed by arming, with whatever weapons, groups and states openly dedicated to mass killing'.[6]

The doctrine of pre-emption was formulated under the Bush Administration and drew criticism from Democrats, not least because of its unilateralist approach. But pre-emption has not been without attraction to Democrats. It was President Clinton who in December 1998 launched pre-emptive military action to impede the build-up of Saddam's WMD capability in the US–UK air operation, code-named 'Desert Fox'. President Obama's *National Security Strategy* no longer proclaims a doctrine of pre-emption but nor does it forgo the right to act pre-emptively. President Obama, while offering Iran dialogue, has not ruled out pre-emptive military action to prevent that country's acquisition of a nuclear capability.[7] Pre-emption attracts great powers. But is it justified?

The new doctrine would permit pre-emptive action in a much wider range of circumstances than international law currently licenses. The test for lawful pre-emptive action was formulated in the nineteenth century following the *Caroline* affair. In 1837 British marines boarded a private schooner, the *Caroline*, that was engaged in gun running from the USA to Canadian rebels. The marines set the ship on fire and cast it adrift. The action was justified by the British ambassador as an act of pre-emptive self-defence. In the acrimonious debate that ensued, the generally accepted test set for pre-emptive self-defence was that proposed by Daniel Webster, the US Secretary of State, in his response to the British Ambassador: 'the necessity of that self-defence is instant, overwhelming, and leaving no choice of means, and no moment for deliberation.'[8] The inconsistency of the new doctrine with international law would, however, cut no ice with advocates of pre-emption. For this would merely show that international law is out of date and needs to be reformed to reflect what Bobbitt calls 'the new changing strategic context'.[9] We need to consider whether the change, even if not currently legal, could still be morally justified according to just war thinking.

One objection that was immediately raised to the new doctrine of pre-emption is its unabashed unilateralism: 'We will not hesitate to act alone, if necessary.' 'The United States will, if necessary, act pre-emptively.' Such unilateralism would seem at odds with the just war requirement of right authority. If the USA, as a sovereign state, arrogates a right of pre-emption to itself, why should not other states do so similarly? Indeed, even North Korea could do so. With such a proliferation of pre-emptive rights, international anarchy would threaten.

It might be countered that the new terrorist threat was aimed—as al-Qaeda's leaders made clear—particularly at the USA, as the leader of the Western world whose values al-Qaeda rejected.[10] So, as the principal target for the new terrorism, it could be argued that the USA should have particular rights to take defensive action. That is perhaps so. But other states also face terrorist threats. The rights need, therefore, to be specified in terms that would be equally applicable to any other state similarly threatened with terrorist attacks. If the USA had a right to act unilaterally in such circumstances, so would any other nation similarly threatened. Our concern might then be whether other states, to whom such a right were conceded, would exercise it responsibly. This might then lead us to insist that pre-emptive action should require prior international consultation and approval in order to meet the requirement of right authority.

It is unrealistic to insist that a state should always secure the backing of the UN Security Council before any kind of pre-emptive military action is taken. The Security Council is itself made up of sovereign states who do not always act from the best of motives and are driven by their own considerations of realpolitik. Pre-emptive military action may take a variety of forms, ranging from the mere deployment (without use) of military force through a single missile attack up to a full-scale military operation. We might be prepared to concede that actions, particularly at the lower end of the scale, where there is a need to act swiftly, decisively, and on the basis of intelligence that could not be widely shared without compromising sources or losing surprise, could, exceptionally, be undertaken without such authorization. But, even if we were prepared to make such a concession, the way the new doctrine of pre-emption was formulated still seems objectionable because of its apparent presumption in favour of unilateralism. At the least, the requirement of right authority would suggest that this presumption should be reversed. So, even if, exceptionally, unilateral action is permitted, the presumption should be in favour of a multilateral approach, with any action preferably endorsed by the UN Security Council.

But should pre-emptive military action as envisaged in the *US National Security Strategy* be permitted at all? Some critics have sought to draw a distinction between pre-emption, aimed at grave threats that are imminent, and prevention, aimed at threats that, while equally grave or graver, are as yet more distant. The former, it is suggested, may be morally permitted, while the latter remains forbidden.[11] On such grounds it could be argued that the new doctrine of 'pre-emption' should be rejected. For, while it was labelled a doctrine of pre-emption (that could be justified), it was actually a doctrine of prevention aimed at countering threats that were not necessarily imminent. The label was misleading. The doctrine was accordingly unjustified.

This criticism proceeds, however, too briskly. It also relies on a distinction between 'pre-emption' and 'prevention' that is not supported by our ordinary usage of these words.[12] In ordinary parlance 'prevention' is not somehow regarded as bad, while 'pre-emption' is acceptable. Indeed, if anything the reverse is the case. So let us look more closely at just war teaching.

The clearest guidance on pre-emption is provided by Grotius:

> War in defence of life is permissible only when the danger is immediate and certain, not when it is merely assumed.[13]
>
> Fear with respect to a neighbouring power is not sufficient cause. For in order that defence may be lawful it must be necessary and it is not necessary unless we are certain not only regarding the power of our neighbour but also regarding his intent, the degree of certainty being what is accepted in moral matters.[14]

The just war tradition permits pre-emptive action where the threat is immediate and certain. On such grounds there was general sympathy for the pre-emptive air strikes launched by the Israeli Air Force on 5 June 1967. For there was compelling evidence that Egypt and Syria were not only uttering bellicose threats but also taking active military preparations to launch an imminent attack against Israel. The threat to Israel was judged to be both serious and imminent and so to constitute just cause for action.

But is the imminence or immediacy of the threat always necessary? Grotius' argument would suggest not. It is rather 'the degree of certainty being what is accepted in moral matters'. The seriousness of a threat is assessed by both the gravity of the event and the probability of its occurrence. This has to be compared with the expected damage arising from military action. Since military action is almost certain to cause substantial harm, it can be justified only to avert a harm that is greater and of high probability. Imminence or immediacy may provide a useful practical guide to what kind of threat would justify action. But the temporal imminence or immediacy of a threat is not important in itself. It is important because, if a threat is imminent, our knowledge of both its gravity and its high probability will usually be more securely founded than if the threat is still distant. With an imminent threat there is also likely to be less opportunity to counter it by other means, so enabling the condition of last resort to be met.

So, if there were a serious emerging threat, that was not immediate but of which our knowledge was securely founded, and against which no other means were available, the just war tradition would concede, in principle, that it would be permissible to counter it pre-emptively. The action would be justified not just by the gravity of the threat but by the high probability of its occurrence. The justifiable scepticism would, however, be how all these conditions could be met, in practice, if the threat were not imminent.

One possible historical example where the conditions were met was the Israeli attack on the Iraq nuclear reactor at Osirak on 7 June 1981. The Israelis had learnt that the reactor was about to go live, after which it could not be attacked without risk of radiation fall-out. They had good reason to believe that the reactor would be used to make nuclear weapons, since oil-rich Iraq had no need for nuclear power to generate its electricity or other fuel needs; and that the nuclear weapons might be targeted against what the Saddam regime proclaimed was the Zionist enemy. The day chosen for the attack was a Sunday, when the French engineers building the plant were expected to be absent. So the attack was launched. One French technician who had returned unexpectedly to the site was killed. There were no other casualties.

The attack was universally condemned at the time but, in retrospect, could be deemed a justified attack.[15] The threat was not imminent, but there were good grounds for supposing it to be serious, as judged by both the damage that could be caused and the high probability of its occurrence. The opportunity to counter it was time limited. So it could be argued that there was just cause. A just cause does not on its own justify military action, since all the other just war conditions need also to be met. But, given the intransigent nature of the Iraqi regime, the Israelis could reasonably argue that there were no other options available, while military action would be too risky once the reactor had gone live. So the condition of last resort was met. There was at the time little prospect of the United Nations, its deliberations still immobilized by Cold-War rivalries, taking any effective action. The Israelis could argue that they had competent authority. They could also argue that, with an attack on a Sunday, when nobody was expected to be present and before the reactor had gone live, casualties would be minimal, so permitting the conditions of proportion and discrimination to be met. So, overall, the attack might appear justified.

This example suggests that a sufficient threat can provide just cause, even if it is not imminent. But the rather exceptional chain of circumstances in this case also shows how difficult it may be, in practice, for such pre-emptive action to meet the just war conditions. The threat must be sufficiently serious to justify military action. The military means selected must also be appropriately fashioned so that any harm caused is not disproportionate to the harm averted. For, otherwise, we risk the action causing more harm than good. Intelligence that a one-off attack was to be mounted by terrorists to destroy a prestigious architectural monument might justify a pre-emptive raid on the house where the plotters were at work. It would not justify a military invasion of the country from which the attack was planned. Crucially, there must be reliable grounds for believing in both the gravity of the threat and the high likelihood of its occurrence. There should also be no alternative means available to counter the threat. The future is usually uncertain and hard to predict. Such grounds for confidence in the threat, as well as the lack of alternative means to counter it, are, therefore, much more likely to be justified if the threat is imminent than if it is distant. 'Fear', as Grotius stressed, 'is not enough'. What matters is 'the degree of certainty'.

It has been argued that a further objection to pre-emptive attacks is that, because they take place before war has started and before military action has commenced, they will necessarily be aimed at the innocent and so be indiscriminate. A pre-emptive attack would thus be unjust and should be ruled out. Jeff McMahan, for example, argues that the people attacked are likely to be the ordinary soldiers, not the generals and politicians plotting the harm.[16] Since the ordinary soldiers do not share moral responsibility for an unjust threat, they should not be liable to attack. But this objection is too strong. For, if such moral desert is a requirement before attacks can legit-imately be undertaken, it would be not just pre-emptive action but any military action that would be ruled out, since the ordinary soldiers engaged in non-pre-emptive military action are also unlikely to share responsibility for initiating an unjust attack and so do not deserve to be attacked. That is why in Chapter 4 we argued that the appropriate grounds for distinguishing between the combatants who can legitimately be attacked and the non-combatants who are to be spared are that the former, but not the latter, are posing a threat of harm and, in that sense, are judged to be not innocent. Nor does the just war tradition require that those attacked are, at the moment they are attacked, engaged in hostile military action. The tradition permits attacks against military forces not engaged in action in recognition that they may be so engaged at a later date and so can be deemed still to present a threat.

Nonetheless, these considerations constrain who can legitimately be attacked by pre-emptive action, since those attacked must be those who are posing a threat of harm. The threat needs to be evidenced, as Grotius insists, not merely by capability or power but also by intent. Such intent could, for example, be reasonably inferred if there were good grounds for believing that terrorists were actively planning an attack to kill innocent civilians; while the capability would be judged by evidence of the weapons at their disposal. Taken together, such evidence of intent and capability would help support belief in both the gravity of the harm threatened and the high probability of its occurrence. On such grounds, the terrorists could be deemed to be posing a threat, action to counter which in order to save innocent lives would be justified. Such action could be judged discriminate provided it were launched against those posing the threat: the terrorist plotters and those actively assisting the planned attack.

So, if there had been reliable intelligence prior to 9/11 of the planned al-Qaeda attacks on New York and Washington, this could have justified pre-emptive action against the terrorists plotting the attacks, and their supporters among the Taliban, in order to prevent the attacks and the substantial loss of civilian life. This might, for example, have justified an attack on a terrorist training camp in Afghanistan or an attack such as that launched in October 2002 in the Yemen when an armed US surveillance drone launched a missile that killed six al-Qaeda suspects travelling in an automobile. What it would not have justified would have been a bombing raid on Kabul aimed at killing innocent civilians in advance retaliation for the murder of New Yorkers.

The just war tradition recognizes that a threat may be so serious that action needs to be taken to counter it, even if it is not imminent. To counter a threat to innocent civilians by terrorists, potentially armed with weapons of mass destruction, pre-emptive action may be justified. But for such a threat to constitute a just cause we need to be very sure not only that the threat exists but that it is as serious as is claimed, as assessed not only by the gravity of what is threatened but by the high probability of its occurrence. We need, as the just war criteria insist, 'a degree of certainty' about the threat. Such certainty is less likely to be available with threats that are not imminent. Moreover, before action can legitimately be taken to counter the threat, all the other just war conditions need to be met, including the requirement of last resort. That condition too may be difficult to satisfy, if the threat is not imminent, since it is likely that other means will be available to counter it.

The doctrine of pre-emption was launched in September 2002 and first put into effect with the invasion of Iraq in March 2003. This first outing of the doctrine, as we shall explore in the next chapter, proved to be hugely controversial, with much of the concern arising because the belief that there was a serious threat posed by Saddam's possession of weapons of mass destructions proved to be ill founded.

The just war tradition acknowledges a right of pre-emption, but the conditions that need to be satisfied are strict and, in practice, particularly if the threat is not imminent, difficult to meet. We should, therefore, be wary of the claims of political leaders to see into the future with a clarity of vision that is only rarely available. Just war teaching would accordingly not licence an unqualified right of unilateral pre-emption of the kind that the US government arrogated to itself in its *National Security Strategy* in September 2002.

New interrogation techniques

As well as a new strategic doctrine, the attacks of 9/11 generated demands for a new approach to the acquisition of information. In the Cold War the USA had relied heavily on technical intelligence, including surveillance satellites, to track the weapons and military dispositions of its adversaries.

But the new adversary did not rely on massive stockpiles of armaments. The terrorist's weapons were few, well concealed, and deadly. The information needed to forestall the next 9/11 assault was not on the ground but in the terrorist's head. Extracting such information from terrorist suspects was the new top priority. The task was judged to be increasingly urgent during 2002, as the first anniversary of 9/11 approached, with the fear that this would prompt another devastating attack. Extracting information was proving a task that was increasingly difficult with the detainees in US custody, some of whom had been trained in techniques of resisting inter-rogation, such as those set out in the so-called Manchester manual, discov-ered by British police in the UK city of that name.

Lawyers and officials began in 2002 to consider how this new intelligence challenge could be addressed. They were aware that torture and 'outrages upon personal dignity, in particular, humiliating and degrading treatment' were prohibited under Common Article 3 of the 1949 Geneva Convention, a ban further reinforced by the 1987 UN Convention against Torture. But, as one of the lawyers, Alberto Gonzales, Counsel to President Bush, advised the President, the war against terrorism was 'a new kind of war': 'This new paradigm renders obsolete Geneva's strict limits on questioning of enemy prisoners and renders quaint some of its provisions.'[17]

To counter the new threat a new form of interrogation was required. A new method of interrogation was devised, called 'Counter-Resistance Techniques'. This was deemed by the lawyers consulted to be not torture, but coercive interrogation. Physical violence was not allowed. But the permitted techniques included: stress positions, such as standing for a maximum of four hours; isolation for up to thirty days; deprivation of light and auditory stimuli; hooding during transport and questioning; twen-ty-four-hour interrogations; removal of religious and other comfort items; removal of clothing; forced grooming, including removal of facial hair; use of individual phobias like dogs to induce stress; and the use of 'mild, non-injurious contact', like grabbing, poking, and light pushing. William Haynes, the General Counsel at the Defense Department, sought approval on 27 November 2002 from the Secretary for Defense, Donald Rumsfeld, for the use of these techniques against selected detainees at Guantanamo Bay. This was granted on 2 December 2002.

We remarked in Chapter 8 how the so-called new wars often resemble old wars. Just so, many of the new interrogation techniques bear striking similarities to the 'deep-interrogation' techniques—wall standing, hooding, subjection to noise, sleep deprivation, and relative deprivation of food and drink (a strict regime of bread and water)—employed by the British Army in its counter-insurgency campaign in Aden and in 1971 against the IRA in Northern Ireland. The so-called five techniques had been banned by the British government in 1972 and declared by the European Court of Human Rights in 1978 to constitute a practice of inhuman and degrading treatment, which, although not amounting to torture, was still in breach of Article 3 of the Geneva Convention.[18]

Such precedents were conveniently forgotten or, if remembered, dismissed as irrelevant to the new exigencies facing America in 2002. A suspected terrorist held at Guantanamo Bay was selected for use of the new techniques. He was known as Detainee 063, subsequently identified as Mohammed al-Qahtani. Arrested in Afghanistan in November 2001, he was transferred to Guantanamo in January 2002. He was thought to be the 'twentieth terrorist' from the 9/11 gang, potentially aware of other planned attacks against the United States. He had so far been resistant to all efforts to persuade him to talk. On 2 December 2002 a new phase of his interrogation was instituted.

In the succeeding six weeks all the new techniques were employed against him. A log was kept meticulously recording his daily treatment during the 42 days. The log was leaked to *Time* magazine and published on 3 March 2006. It is summarized by Philippe Sands:

> The pattern was always the same . . . Sleep deprivation appears as a regular and central theme, along with stress positions and constant humiliation, including sexual humiliation, These techniques were supplemented by the use of water, regular bouts of dehydration, the use of IV (intravenous) tubes, loud noise and white noise, nudity, female contact, humiliation with girly mags. An interrogator even tied a leash to him, led him around the room and forced him to perform dog tricks. He was forced to wear a woman's bra and a thong was placed on his head. And so it goes on.[19]

Doctors performed regular checks of his medical condition.

The process was halted on 15 January 2003 after doubts had been expressed over the legality of the techniques employed by other senior lawyers within the Pentagon, who had not been consulted when the practice was first authorized. It is not clear how valuable was the information obtained from the interrogation of Detainee 063. But at the end of the process an army investigator who went to see him recorded: 'He looks like hell . . . he has got black coals for eyes.'[20]

The special techniques were authorized only for use at Guantanamo Bay for forty-two days. But their practice was more widespread. The CIA programme of extraordinary rendition—flying detainees into the custody of states where torture may be practised either by the officials of that state or by the CIA itself—reflects a similar belief that extreme times call for extreme measures. In secret locations outside the USA, CIA operatives 'employed enhanced techniques to varying degrees in the interrogation of 28 . . . detainees'.[21] They drew from a repertoire of 'enhanced techniques' even more extensive than that deployed at Guantanamo. Additional refinements included 'walling' (pushing the detainee against a false wall), confinement in a cramped space, together, in one case, with an insect of which the detainee had a phobia, and water-boarding.[22] On 5 February 2008, the CIA Director, Michael Hayden, told the US Congress that the CIA had used water-boarding, a technique involving simulated drowning, on three al-Qaeda prisoners during 2002 and 2003.[23] The water-board was used on numerous occasions against two of the prisoners, allegedly yielding valuable information.[24]

It is striking how the unauthorized abuses at Abu Ghraib prison in the autumn of 2003, the photographic images of which reverberated around the world, seemed to mirror, albeit in a grotesque, exaggerated, and extreme version, some of the Guantanamo Bay techniques—for example the hooding, the use of dogs, and the sexual humiliation. Similarly, the five techniques banned by the British government in 1972 reappeared and were taken to extremes by British soldiers in the abuse of Baha Mousa and the other eight Iraqi detainees in Basra in September 2003. There is perhaps substance to the claim that torture, once regularized, becomes regular.

So, did the extreme times justify such extreme measures? Might coercive interrogation or, at the extreme, even torture be justified to help us cope with extreme emergencies?

Can torture ever be justified?

The techniques employed to assist interrogation may range from the infliction of mild discomfort through to the full panoply of the Spanish Inquisition. No one is, hopefully, arguing for a reintroduction of the medieval torture chamber. But serious voices have been raised to justify the kind of coercive interrogation techniques employed by the US Army

in Guantanamo Bay and the water-boarding and other methods used by
the CIA. So can such coercive interrogation—'torture lite' as it has been
termed—be justified?

Some philosophers and lawyers have found it surprisingly easy to imagine
circumstances in which, in order to prevent catastrophic consequences,
torture might seem justified.

Michael Walzer introduced the so-called ticking-bomb example into the
modern debate. He imagined a political leader, recently elected on a policy
of decolonization and opposed to torture, paying his first visit to the capital
of the colony to which he proposes to grant independence. The city is in the
grip of a terrorist campaign.

> The first decision the new leader faces is this: he is asked to authorize the
> torture of a captured rebel leader who knows or probably knows the location
> of a number of bombs hidden in apartment buildings around the city, set to go
> off within the next twenty-four hours. He orders the man tortured, convinced
> that he must do so for the sake of the people who might otherwise die in the
> explosions—even though he believes that torture is wrong, indeed abomina-
> ble, not just sometimes, but always.[25]

The agony can be piled up further. The terrorist might be one of the al-
Qaeda gang about to launch the attack on the Twin Towers, such as Zacarias
Moussaouri. He was briefly detained by the Immigration and Naturalization
Service several weeks before 11 September, after flight instructors reported
suspicious statements he had made while taking flying lessons for which he
had paid with large sums of cash.[26] Suppose that, instead of being released, he
had been detained and subjected to special interrogation. By his coercive
interrogation we might have been able to prevent the Twin Towers disaster.
Threats of comparable or even worse devastation can be imagined. Suppose
that we have captured a terrorist who has planted a bomb in an elementary
school that, if let off, will kill all 400 children. There are many elementary
schools in the city, and we do not know in which the bomb has been
placed.[27] Or suppose the captured terrorist knows where a 10-kiloton nuclear
device is about to be detonated in New York.[28] In each case the terrorist
knows where the attack will be or where the bomb is hidden but refuses to
speak. Time is running out. The only way to obtain the information and save
thousands of lives is to torture the terrorist. So should we torture him?

Our first reaction when faced with such examples might be to try to avoid
answering the question. We might point to the 'fancifully hypothetical'

nature of the cases and hence the improbability of all the circumstances coming together in just the way described.[29] We might demur at the stipulated certainty or near-certainty that the interrogatee has the information we require and will truthfully and quickly reveal this, if only a modicum of torture is applied. We might note how those interrogated could be tempted to invent information to satisfy their interrogators and so put an end to their ordeals. We might observe that those interrogated are terrorist suspects, not yet proven guilty. We might contrast the clarity, certainty, and swift decisiveness of the philosophers' examples with the messy uncertainties of real-life examples, such as the prolonged interrogation of Detainee 063, whose knowledge of future terrorist attacks and readiness to disclose this was far from certain at the start, and perhaps even the end, of his special interrogation.

Such doubts are real and important. But, in the aftermath of the 9/11 attacks, it is difficult to rule out altogether that we might exceptionally be faced with the kind of dilemma described in the ticking-bomb examples. So, however unlikely may be the concatenation of circumstances, what should our response be?

For an absolutist the answer is easy. Intentionally to torture another human being is wrong. Torture—even in its moderate 'torture-lite' variants—is forbidden and we should not do it, regardless of the consequences, regardless of however many lives may be saved. Such was the view of some of those who gave evidence to the inquiry set up by the British government into the deep interrogation techniques employed in 1971 in Northern Ireland. The report of the inquiry notes: 'They took the line that, even though innocent lives could be and had been saved by the use of the techniques . . . a civilised society should never use them.'[30]

The absolutist response has an attractive simplicity. But it makes the decision in the ticking-bomb examples appear easier than it is. For, as the disastrous consequences of inaction are piled up, so the absolutist's insistence on maintaining his personal integrity, keeping his own hands clean, may begin to look less attractive. With the pleas of the schoolchildren's parents in our ears, it becomes progressively more difficult to resist the conclusion that it may, exceptionally, be right to apply non-lethal torture to a terrorist suspect, if this is the only way to save the lives of many innocents, whether schoolchildren, New Yorkers, or even—if the nuclear threat is grave enough—most of the inhabitants of the world. Indeed, for a consequentialist, such a conclusion might then seem as easy to reach as it is for the absolutist to draw the opposite conclusion. Such ease should give us pause. For in reality such a decision would and should be agonizingly difficult. If difficult decisions are made to look easy, this suggests that something is wrong with the structure of the moral argument being employed.

The ticking-bomb examples look easier to decide than they are because we are usually invited to consider only selected features of the situation, whether the intention to breach a rule on which the absolutist focuses, or the consequences of our action or inaction to which the consequentialist directs our attention. We condemn torture because of its harmful consequences—the pain and suffering, both physical and mental, inflicted on the victim. But the external consequences provide only part of our reason for condemning torture. For our antipathy to torture may seem surprising, and even irrational, if we attend only to the consequences of torture.

Non-lethal torture of its nature does less harm than killing someone. We are prepared to justify killing those threatening us harm in the prosecution of a just war to defend our country from attack. So, it might appear relatively easy to concede that torture of a suspected terrorist could be justified, if this is the only way to secure information to prevent a terrorist attack killing many innocents. If consequences were all that mattered, all that we would need to do would be to weigh up the pain caused to the victim—which, as in the ticking-bomb examples, might be quite limited and far less severe than death—and compare this with the much greater pain and suffering we were preventing. Moreover, even if the wider adverse consequences of the precedent thereby set were taken into account, these might still seem to be outweighed by the catastrophic consequences we were preventing, particularly since the examples, as described, relate to an exceptional concatenation of circumstances. It might thus appear a rather obvious and easy decision that we should use torture.

But even though we might accept that torture could exceptionally be justified to prevent catastrophic consequences, we reach such a conclusion reluctantly and with great difficulty. The decision appears easier than it is only if we focus on selected features of the dilemma, whether the intentions of the agent or the consequences of his agency. To understand our moral repugnance to torture, we need rather to attend to all the relevant features of our moral agency: to both the internal qualities and external consequences of our actions, as well as to the principles that guide those actions and the virtues needed to enact the principles in our daily lives. We need, in other words, to deploy all the conceptual resources that virtuous consequentialism insists are required to explain the complexity and difficulty of our moral choices in both our private and public lives.

So why is torture wrong? There is, first and foremost, a strong moral prohibition against torture. This is not just a bedrock principle of morality but is also enshrined in international law. Common Article 3 of the Geneva Conventions (1949) prohibits cruel treatment and torture, as well as 'outrages upon personal dignity, in particular, humiliating and degrading treatment'.[31] Even if interrogation techniques do not amount to torture, they are still contrary to the Geneva Convention if they involve humiliating and degrading treatment. The Geneva Convention was further reinforced in 1987 by the UN Convention against Torture and Other Cruel, Inhuman and Degrading Acts. Article 1 defines torture as 'any act by which severe pain or suffering, whether physical or mental, is intentionally inflicted on a person for such purposes as obtaining from him or a third person information or a confession'. Article 2 makes clear that 'no exceptional circumstances whatsoever, whether a state of war or a threat of war, internal political instability or any other public emergency, may be invoked as a justification of torture'.[32] Nor is torture justified because of any guilt on the part of the person tortured.

The moral and legal prohibitions on torture and any kind of 'humiliating and degrading treatment' create an immense moral presumption against such actions. Torture is judged wrong because of its harmful consequences—the 'severe pain or suffering, whether physical or mental' that it causes. But that is only part of the explanation. We also condemn torture because of its internal qualities. Indeed, we may find torture repugnant because of its internal qualities, even where minimal or no harmful consequences ensue. One of the most chilling portraits of evil from twentieth-century fiction is C. S. Lewis's portrait of the diabolical astronaut, Weston, in his novel *Voyage to Venus*. We first discern the full depths of Weston's wickedness when he is discovered, amid the enchanting landscape of the prelapsarian world of Venus, torturing frogs. At the end of a trail of mutilated frog bodies, he is found 'tearing a frog—quietly and almost surgically inserting his forefinger, with its long sharp nail, under the skin behind the creature's head and ripping it open'.[33] The consequences of his actions—except for the frogs—were minimal, and yet the malicious spitefulness of his actions is presented as an illustration of the extremity of evil.

Our moral antipathy to torture stems, in part, from the malevolent mental states that it necessarily requires of the torturer. In state-sanctioned torture the ultimate objective of the torturer, unlike that of Weston, may be noble: extracting information to save lives. But the proximate intentions of the torturer—the means by which he achieves his ends—are not. For the torturer intends not just to inflict pain. He also intends to control, humiliate, and degrade the victim. As we noted earlier from the summary of the interrogation log of Detainee 063: 'The pattern was always the same . . . constant humiliation, including sexual humiliation.'

Torture adversely affects the character of those involved in the process: both the torturers and the tortured. We are, therefore, rightly concerned over the sort of people that the public officials, whom we appoint to conduct special interrogations on our behalf, may become through their practice of torture. Virtues are crucial to our moral lives. We want our public servants to be men or women of virtue. Yet we need our special interrogators to be—professionally—men or women of vice. If they are to excel in their profession, they will need to learn to become in the exercise of their official duties, at best, indifferent to the pain of those whom they are interrogating and, at worst, adept in the vice of cruelty.

Torture also adversely affects the character of the victim. It may inspire the victim with intense and lasting hatred of those who tortured him. It may also have more profoundly unsettling effects. Jean Amery was arrested in Brussels in 1943 for distributing tracts in German urging German soldiers of the occupation to desert. He was tortured in a Belgian jail by the SS, employing the full Nazi panoply of torture, before being shipped off to Auschwitz. In his account of his ordeal, written twenty years later, he noted that a tortured man always stays tortured: 'Someone who has been tortured is never capable of being at home with the world again.'[34] What was worse than the memory of the pain was the moral shock of seeing other human beings reducing him to a carcass of meat.

Torture is for all these reasons profoundly wrong. Our concern over the corrosive internal qualities of torture explains our reluctance to contemplate its use even when beneficial consequences might ensue. This also explains why, even when, as in the ticking-bomb examples, it is the only way to prevent catastrophic consequences, we conclude only with great reluctance that torture might then be justified and insist that those involved have, in Walzer's words, 'dirty hands'.[35] For, even if there might be such exceptional circumstances where torture was justified in order to prevent truly cata-strophic consequences, this would not mean that in those circumstances torture ceased to be wrong. Torture would remain wrong, even if it were deemed to be necessary as the lesser evil. The moral prohibition on torture would remain, but we would concede that there might be exceptional circumstances where sticking to the rule would have such disastrous consequences that it might be licit to break the rule.

Should torture be legal?

But, even if we concede that an individual act of torture might exceptionally be justified, are we then committed to legalize the practice of torture in such cases? Should torture be legal?

Alan Dershowitz has argued forcefully that it should.[36] He argues that it is hypocritical to accept that torture might in certain circumstances be justified, but not then allow for it in our legal system. To refuse to legalize torture but to tolerate its occurrence in a 'twilight zone which is outside the law',[37] 'off the books and below the radar screen',[38] is contrary to the open accountability that democracy requires of its public servants. He reminds us that 'President Nixon's creation of a group of plumbers led to Watergate'.[39] He argues that it is inconsistent to permit killing to save lives, while not sanctioning non-lethal torture for the same purpose.

We need, moreover, publicly to reach a decision on this well before any such situation arises. For it is both risky and unfair to leave a decision on whether to torture until a ticking-bomb case has occurred. It is risky because decisions of such moment are better taken openly and in advance rather than secretly and in the heat of battle. It is unfair to leave such weighty decisions to low-level officials and for the legality of their decision to be judged in the courts only after the event by a jury of peers. He, therefore, proposes that non-lethal torture, to prevent massive terrorist attacks, should be legalized but its exercise should be controlled by requiring that in each case the torture is authorized in advance by a judicial warrant. He believes that such a system of judicial warrants would reduce the incidence of torture.

In raising these issues Dershowitz incurred the ireful abuse of the liberal establishment on both sides of the Atlantic, even earning for himself the sobriquet *Torquemada* after the founder of the Spanish Inquisition.[40] But his concerns are legitimate. So let us examine each of his arguments in turn.

First, would legalization reduce the incidence of torture? That is possible. But it is more plausible to suppose that it would have the reverse effect. As

Richard Prosner pointed out: 'The practice, once it were thus regularised, would be likely to become regular.'[41] This claim would appear to be supported by the way the special interrogation procedures briefly authorized for use in Guantanamo Bay came to be practised more widely, albeit in unauthorized procedures, at Abu Ghraib and Basra.

Moreover, however carefully we seek to constrain the particular interrogation techniques we license, those involved, operating under the cloak of secrecy and under pressure to extract urgently needed information, are likely to be tempted to utilize the procedures right up to and even beyond the limits authorized. Not all slopes are slippery. But the slide from coercive interrogation to torture has proved to be particularly lubricious; and a slope on which it has proved, in practice, difficult to enforce an effective braking mechanism. This difficulty was illustrated by the way the detainees interrogated in depth in Northern Ireland in 1971 were kept hooded, standing against a wall, and subject to noise for periods far in excess of that envisaged by those who had trained the soldiers in the techniques. Commenting on this discrepancy, the report commissioned by the British government somberly observed that 'there is a risk that the techniques will be applied to a greater degree than is justified'.[42]

The widespread criticism provoked by revelation of the malpractices at Abu Ghraib and Basra also underlines how the practice of torture, whether authorized or unauthorized, can be counter-productive in other ways. For it can hand to the terrorists a potent propaganda weapon for exposing the alleged discrepancy between the values espoused by a liberal democracy and the means adopted to defend these values; between the avowed humanitarian objectives of a military mission and the anti-humanitarian means employed in its pursuit. It can promote a martyrdom culture in which terrorists welcome torture as proof of the wickedness of their inquisitors. Just so, US practices at Guantanamo Bay and its programme of extraordinary rendition—whatever tactical successes they have achieved—have proved strategic failures. For Guantanamo Bay has acted as a powerful recruiting sergeant for al-Qaeda. Torture can fuel the terrorist cause that its use is designed to counter.

It would be hypocritical to denounce torture, while turning a blind eye to its increasing use. It would also be contrary to democratic accountability to tolerate such a practice in a sub-judicial twilight zone. But there is no hypocrisy nor offence to democratic accountability in maintaining that, while in extreme, exceptional, and hence unlikely circumstances, torture might be morally licit, the practice should be and should remain illegal, with every effort made to ensure it does not happen. For hard cases, it is well known, make bad law.

Moreover, it is a crucial presupposition of Dershowitz's argument that torture, even if unauthorized, is bound to take place and, in these dangerous times, is likely to take place only too frequently. So, since we cannot prevent it, we should do what we can to control it and reduce its incidence. But the choice he presents of either judicially controlling torture or turning a blind eye to its increasing use is a false one. For torture is not inevitable. Torture can be stopped. Democracies can survive without its practice. It is noteworthy that during the long and difficult years of the Second World War when the survival of democracy was at stake, the British government did not find it necessary to employ torture. The deep interrogation techniques that the British Army employed were developed only subsequently for use against far less grave threats posed by insurgents in colonial struggles. The public outcry that attended the revelation of their use within the British Isles quickly prompted the British government to ban the techniques in 1972. That ban remains in force and has been successfully enforced and complied with by the British Armed Forces worldwide, at least until the unauthorized lapse in the autumn of 2003 in Basra. That lapse underlines the need for regular reminders to soldiers of the laws of war, including the illegality of torture, and for an anti-torture culture to be deeply embedded in the soldiers' training. But it does not show that bans are unenforceable.

Dershowitz argues that it is too late to wait and only decide what to do after a ticking-bomb case has arisen. We can agree that the principles and issues involved need to be openly and publicly debated in advance. But from that it hardly follows that the practice of torture should be legally authorized in advance. Dershowitz argues that decisions of such moment should be taken by 'the highest ranking public official' and that it is not right to 'leave each individual member of the security services in the position of having to guess how a court would ultimately resolve his case. That is unfair to such investigators.'[43] He criticizes the Israeli Supreme Court for banning torture but allowing that a plea of necessity might be used by an official found guilty of torture, not to justify, but in mitigation of his offence.[44]

Decisions of such import should, indeed, not be left to junior officials but taken, if at all, by the highest-ranking public official. It is in the nature of the ticking-bomb examples that the decision is hypothesized to be of such world-saving moment that it would need to be taken by the highest-ranking public official. Were a ticking-bomb example ever to occur in real life, it would place an enormous burden on the high-ranking official to have to decide whether, in such exceptional circumstances, a breach of the law could be justified and to face the moral and legal consequences of such a decision. This may place an unfair burden on political leaders. But it is preferable to accept a remote risk of such unfairness than all the many and certain adverse consequences of officially sanctioning a practice of torture. Taking difficult decisions is, after all, part of a politician's job. As Walzer observed: 'No one succeeds in politics without getting his hands dirty.'[45]

Finally, is it inconsistent to sanction justified killing in war but not non-lethal torture? We argued in Chapter 5 that, in order to prevent a Twin Towers attack, it would be permissible for a USAF pilot to shoot down a hijacked plane, killing both the terrorists and passengers, if this were the only way to save the lives of many more innocents. Since non-lethal torture causes less harm to its victims than killing, it might seem uncontentious that we should be prepared to license torture of a terrorist suspect to save the lives of many innocents. Should the exceptional circumstances postulated in the ticking—bomb examples ever occur, then it might, indeed, be appropriate to conclude that in order to save many thousands of innocents it might exceptionally be licit to breach a moral rule by an individual act of coercive interrogation. But the policy conclusions to be drawn from the USAF-pilot and ticking-bomb examples are different. We are prepared to authorize a standing instruction to USAF pilots to shoot planes down in such circumstances. But we are not prepared to issue a licence to torture.

Our reluctance to license the practice of torture stems, in part, from the wider harmful consequences of doing so, including, as we have noted, the risk that it may increase the frequency of torture, as well as furnishing propaganda for the terrorist cause. But it also reflects our concern over the internal qualities of torture.

We train soldiers to kill so that they can defend the safety of our state. We even train them to conduct bayonet practice, an activity that, like torture, is of its nature 'up close and personal'. So why is training them to torture judged worse, when the pain and suffering caused by coercive interrogation is less harmful than being shot or bayoneted to death? Part of the answer is that, while training soldiers to kill or wield a bayonet can be corrupting, it is not inherently so. It can, for example, lead to soldiers dehumanizing the enemy. That is why the training has to be conducted with great care, particularly for the multifaceted modern battlefield, where, as we noted in Chapter 6, soldiers may need rapidly to adapt their behaviour as tasks change from those of conflict to peaceful reconstruction. The misbehaviour of soldiers who fail adequately to make that transition is likely to reflect poor training. Training to bayonet or to kill, if improperly done, can be corrupting and so lead to subsequent misbehaviour. But such training is not necessarily corrupting. Training people to torture, on the other hand is a *necessarily morally corrosive activity*. It is training them in a practice that is inherently vicious, where success is judged by the pupil's skills in the humiliation and degradation of his victim. It is this that helps explain our moral antipathy to torture, even where beneficial consequences might result from its employment.

We honour soldiers and policemen, despite or even because of their lethal skills. But we look askance at a special interrogator. If we were introduced at a dinner party to a fellow guest who was a police marksman, trained to shoot and, if necessary, kill, we would have no qualms in welcoming him to the dinner table. We might even admire his courage in carrying out a job that is dangerous but necessary to protect the public, not least from terrorist attacks. But suppose that the dinner guest is not a police marksman but a special interrogator, trained and adept in the skills of the torturer. Our reaction would be likely to be rather different. Indeed, we might be only too pleased when the dinner party was over.

It is Dershowitz's failure to recognize the corrosive nature of the practice of torture that is the fundamental flaw in his position. For his argument gains such plausibility as it has only from attending solely to the external effects of torture, ignoring the internal qualities and nature of both the act and the practice of torture. In philosophical examples the torturer arrives by magic just at the moment we need him; and he departs, conveniently, shortly thereafter. We never encounter him at the dinner table. We confront the torturer only in the individual act of torture. But we hear nothing of what needed to precede this, the selection process and training required to ensure that the interrogation is effective, nor what follows in terms of the corrosive effects of torture, on the character not only of the special interrogator but also of those, including doctors, who provide the necessary support for his activities. For torture to be successfully implemented, it needs to be established as an institutionalized practice. To succeed in his craft, the special interrogator needs to become, in the exercise of his official duties, a man of vice, rather than of virtue.

The aim of morality is to enable us to live well together in communities. In deciding whether to legalize the practice of torture we need, therefore, to consider whether to do so would contribute to human welfare, would promote our flourishing as humans. This requires attending not just to consequences but to the mental states and character of the agent. For these different factors—variegated but consistent—together make up our concept of human flourishing, reflecting our status as intentional beings, beings who care not just what happens to us but how others think and feel about us and we about them.

We need, accordingly, to examine not only the external effects of licensing torture but also the mental states of the torturer and how torture affects the moral character of all those involved in its practice. We need to consider whether we wish to belong to a society that selects, employs, pays, and trains people to torture, despite the corrupting effect this has on both its practitioners and its victims. We need also to consider how institutionalizing the practice of torture will affect the self-image of the military or other officials who are required to perform these grisly tasks. As we noted in Chapter 6, the military are called upon by society to perform tasks that in civilian life would be illegal. It is crucial for both the internal self-respect of the military and our external pride as a nation in their achievements that they are able to distinguish themselves from assassins or murderers and view themselves rather as virtuous warriors in a noble tradition of service to the state. It is hard to reconcile any such noble vision of the profession of arms with the practice of torture.

Torture is not the simple, quick, and clinical act that Dershowitz envisages but, as the Interrogation Log of Detainee 063 evidences, a protracted, painful, and messy process, which is degrading for all those involved, both the victim and the torturer. It affects all those who participate in the process, even those at the periphery. This includes the doctors who, in a perverse interpretation of their Hippocratic Oath, use their medical skills not to save lives but to undertake regular checks of a detainee's continued fitness for torture. Our refusal to license torture thus ultimately reflects our judgement that its practice would not promote and, indeed, would appear at odds with our concept of human flourishing.

Conclusion

It is, therefore, profoundly mistaken to conclude from the ticking-bomb examples that the practice of torture should be legalized. The examples show that it is possible to conceive of exceptional circumstances in which an individual act of torture might be justified if this were the only way to prevent disastrous consequences. But the concatenation of circumstances that would enable such a conclusion to be drawn is extremely unlikely. If such a remote possibility should occur, we might hope that our political leaders would be prepared to face the consequences of breaking the law if this were the only way to save a multitude of lives; and that, if they really had thereby saved so many lives, a jury might be prepared to accept such a plea of necessity in mitigation. It would, however, be unwise to frame laws to cater for such a remote possibility when the legalization of a practice of torture would have the manifest and grave drawbacks that we have noted. Torture is morally wrong, and there are good reasons why its practice is and should remain illegal. It was, therefore, a wise decision of President Obama, on taking office, formally to ban on 22 January 2009 the coercive interrogation techniques, including water-boarding, that had been employed under the previous administration at Guantanamo Bay and elsewhere.

After the terrorist attacks of 9/11 it was claimed that the West had entered a new and dangerous phase of its history. It was argued that the extreme times justified extreme measures—whether special interrogation techniques to uncover terrorist plots or pre-emptive military action to forestall them. But these responses were misguided, leading respectively to the ill-treatment of detainees at Guantanamo Bay and the prosecution of a war in Iraq that, as we shall examine in the next chapter, provoked widespread criticism. Liberal democracies in the past have faced dangerous times and, indeed, more dangerous times, without resort to special interrogation or such military pre-emption. It is important that a liberal democracy in defending itself against a terrorist or other threat does not do so in a way that jeopardizes the values that it is defending. Among these values are the laws and constraints on war embodied in the just war tradition.

TEN

Gulf Wars

B ritish and American forces have invaded Iraq twice since the 1990s. The first operation in 1991 was generally, although not universally, regarded as a just war. The second in 2003 led to far more bitter controversy.

The just war criteria prescribe that a war will be just if undertaken: with competent authority, for a just cause, with right intention, as a last resort, and if the harm judged likely to result is not disproportionate to the good to be achieved, taking into account the probability of success; while in its conduct the principle of proportion and non-combatant immunity should be complied with; and the war should end in the establishment of a just peace. For a war to be just, all these conditions must be met. Let us consider how each of these wars fares against the criteria.

The First Gulf War

Military operations in the First Gulf War began on 16 January 1991. Under US leadership, the campaign was conducted by a broadly based coalition, including both Arab and non-Arab players. The objective was to liberate Kuwait, which Saddam had invaded on 2 August 1990.

The declared reason for the war was the defence of Kuwait against external aggression, in accordance with the inherent right of individual and collective defence if an armed attack occurs as provided for under Article 51 of the UN Charter. Self-defence is regarded as the paradigmatic just cause within the just war tradition. There was thus a just cause for the war.

Some opponents of the war argued that there were other hidden motives, such as the quest for oil, that were more important, so that, even if there were just cause, the war was undertaken without right intention. This was, however, a minority view. Most agreed with the conclusions of the historians of the war:

> There seems little doubt that Bush was influenced most of all by the need to uphold the principle of non-aggression and the analogy with the failure of appeasement in the 1930s . . . When he spoke to Congressmen the day he took his decision on doubling forces, he reported that he had been reading Martin Gilbert's lengthy history of the Second World War.[1]

As well as being legitimized under the self-defence provisions of Article 51, military operations were specifically authorized by the United Nations Security Council Resolution 678, passed on 22 November 1990. This provided that, in the event of Iraq's failure to withdraw from Kuwait by 15 January 1991 as required by previous UN resolutions, member states, cooperating with the Government of Kuwait, were authorized 'to use all necessary means to uphold and implement' these resolutions and 'to restore international peace and security in the area'.

The operations were undertaken for a just cause, with right intention, and with competent authority. There was much debate whether they were undertaken as a last resort or whether more time should have been given for sanctions and/or diplomacy to work.[2] With the lengthy pause between the invasion of Kuwait on 2 August and the start of coalition operations on 16 January, it can hardly be claimed that force was resorted to with undue haste. The last-resort condition is, in any case, a logical rather than a temporal condition: what is important is whether other means are realistically available to resolve the dispute. It is far from clear that means other than force were available in 1990–1 to reverse Saddam's aggression.

Diplomacy had continued up to the last moment, with the UN Secretary General, Perez de Cuellar's, unsuccessful trip to Baghdad on 11–14 January 1991. This culminated in his memorable quip: 'You need two to tango. I wanted to dance but I did not find any nice lady for dancing with.'[3] Those who argued that more time should have been given for sanctions to work failed to provide a convincing explanation how sanctions were supposed to achieve their objective and to do so in a way that did itself not breach the just war requirement to minimize civilian casualties. For, while the harm caused by sanctions to the civilian population was only too evident, there was no clear mechanism for converting the resulting popular discontent into effective pressure to bear on a ruthless dictator who held all the reins of power and was not subject to any democratic constraints. The subsequent failure of twelve years of sanctions to induce Saddam to comply with UN resolutions testified only too palpably to the doubtful efficacy of this tool. It could be fairly maintained that war was embarked on only as a last resort.

The next requirement is that the harm judged likely to result from the war is not disproportionate to the good to be achieved, taking into account the probability of success. Military operations were concluded on 28 February, with the liberation of Kuwait successfully accomplished. Coalition deaths were 240 (many killed from friendly fire and accidents). It is estimated that Iraqi casualties were 30,000 dead, of which 2,000–3,000 were civilians.[4] The objective of reversing Iraqi aggression and thereby upholding international law was fulfilled at an overall cost that, however regrettable, was not disproportionate. The principle of proportion was satisfied.

The *jus in bello* conditions—the second application of the principle of proportion to individual military actions and of the principle of non-combatant immunity—were, in general, also satisfied. Considerable efforts were made to minimize civilian casualties, including through use of the new precision weapons then becoming available. The force used was, on the whole, proportionate to the objectives of the individual military operations undertaken. One possible exception, over which there was much subsequent debate, was whether the damage caused to the civilian infrastructure by the intensive air campaign that preceded the ground assault was excessive to the objective of preventing Saddam using that infrastructure in support of his military campaign. In retrospect, knowing how little resistance was encountered, some of the damage to economic infrastructure caused appears excessive. At the time, however, it had been expected that Iraqi forces would offer more resistance than they did.

Finally, did the campaign lead to the establishment of a just peace? The answer is not in Iraq itself. That unhappy country faced twelve more years of oppression by Saddam, including in the immediate aftermath of the war his brutal suppression of uprisings by the Shi'ites in the south and the Kurds in the north. But the removal of Saddam had never been the objective of the military operations nor licensed by the United Nations. The objective had been to liberate Kuwait. That objective was achieved, with a just peace established within Kuwait and the further aggression that had been feared in the region, particularly against Saudi Arabia, prevented.

While there were some lapses, overall, the coalition operations to liberate Kuwait in their origin, conduct, and conclusion satisfied the just war criteria. On balance, the First Gulf War was a just war.

The Second Gulf War

At the conclusion of the First Gulf War in 1991, the UN Security Council passed Resolution 687 agreeing to the suspension of military activities in return for Saddam's destruction of all his stocks of chemical and biological weapons, all ballistic missiles with a range greater than 150 kilometres, and the termination of his nuclear programme. To encourage his compliance, a range of economic and military sanctions were imposed and a UN Special Commission on Disarmament (UNSCOM) was established to verify that the stocks had been destroyed. UNSCOM successfully supervised the destruction of large quantities of stocks of chemical and biological weapons and the termination of his nuclear programme. But Saddam's cooperation with UNSCOM was, at best, partial and was withdrawn altogether in 1998, following which UNSCOM was withdrawn. At the time of its withdrawal UNSCOM was unable to certify that the provisions of UNSCR 687 had been met.

The effectiveness of the sanctions imposed on Iraq was decidedly mixed. Constraints on the imports of military goods helped impede, if they could not altogether prevent, Saddam's rearmament programme. But the broader economic sanctions had little impact except to cause considerable suffering among the Iraqi people, whilst the UN oil-for-food programme intended to alleviate that suffering was frustrated in achieving its objectives by diversion of supplies and corrupt profiteering by the regime. It was, as we have noted, always unclear how popular discontent brought about by the sanctions was to be translated into effective political pressure against a ruthless dictator.

From 1998 to 2002 no weapons inspection was undertaken. Concern mounted during this period that Saddam might be reconstituting his programme for weapons of mass destruction (WMD). Concern over WMD proliferation was heightened following the demonstration of the damage that could be caused by terrorist attacks on civilian centres on 11 September 2001.

On 9 November 2002 a further UN resolution was passed—Resolution 1441—declaring Iraq to be in 'material breach' of UNSCR 678 and requiring the Iraqi government to prove that it no longer possessed weapons of mass destruction and to cooperate with the United Nations Monitoring, Verification and Inspection Commission (UNMOVIC)—the successor inspection regime to UNSCOM. The Resolution allowed a 'final opportunity' for such cooperation following which 'serious consequences' would ensue if Iraq failed to demonstrate that it had met its disarmament obligations. UNMOVIC arrived in Iraq on 28 November. Iraq cooperated with UNMOVIC. But the cooperation was still partial, and, as Hans Blix, the former Swedish diplomat who was Executive Chairman of UNMOVIC, reported to the UN on 7 March, still fell short of full disclosure. This failed to satisfy the US and UK governments. Operation 'Iraqi Freedom' was launched on 20 March 2003, this time with a much reduced coalition of predominantly US and, as the junior partner, UK forces and no Arab participants. After twenty-one days the campaign was concluded on 9 April with the capture of Baghdad and the much publicized toppling of Saddam's statue to the evident delight of the Baghdad crowds. The campaign had been, in the judgement of the distinguished British military historian John Keegan, 'brief and brilliant'.[5]

Unfortunately, however, this campaign turned out to be only the start, rather than the conclusion, of military operations. The coalition forces, authorized to maintain law and order in Iraq by UN Resolution 1483 passed on 22 May, found this an increasingly difficult task, as they encountered a growing insurgency campaign. The start of this was marked most spectacularly by the al-Qaeda car-bomb attacks in Baghdad on the Jordanian Embassy on 7 August 2003 and on the UN Headquarters on 19 August. The latter attack was particularly devastating, killing twenty-one, including the UN Special representative, Sergio Viera de Mello, and leading to the UN withdrawal of its operations from Iraq. In 2010—seven years later— a counter-insurgency campaign is still being waged and substantial US forces remain in support of the democratically elected Iraqi government.

The decision to embark on military action in 2003 provoked far more political controversy than the First Gulf War. This has been evidenced in the UK by the number of inquiries commissioned by the British government, including the Hutton and Butler inquiries in 2004 and the wide-ranging inquiry being undertaken in 2010 under the chairmanship of Sir John Chilcot. Our concern is, however, with the narrower issue of the morality of the conflict. In particular, how does the Second Gulf War fare against the just war criteria? Let us consider each of these conditions in turn, starting first with those that need to be met before war is undertaken.

Jus ad bellum

Just cause

Different reasons were adduced at different times for the war by the British
and US governments. Indeed, in the months preceding the war it sometimes appeared that so many reasons were adduced, particularly by the US
government, that they could be open to the charge of not providing a clear
rationale for military action. In war, as one just war commentator remarked,
'you have to call your shot, as in billiards'.[6] If too many reasons are
proffered, the just cause for action is left unclear. Clarity over the grounds
for embarking on an enterprise as momentous as war is crucial. So what
were the grounds for embarking on military action in March 2003?

The declared basis for the military operation common to both the US and
British governments was set out in the British government's published war
aims. This stated: 'the prime objective remains to rid Iraq of its weapons of
mass destruction and the associated programmes and means of delivery,
including prohibited ballistic missiles, as set out in relevant United Nations
Security Council Resolutions.'[7] Military operations were being undertaken
to enforce UN Resolutions. Regime change was not the primary objective
of the military action. But, in view of the regime's refusal to comply with
the demands of the UN Security Council, the overthrow of the regime was
judged to be a necessary means to achieve the objective of disarming Iraq of
its WMD and so removing the threat that Saddam posed to peace and
security in the region. Unlike the First Gulf War, the Second Gulf War was
not, in the British government's view, undertaken for self-defence. Nor was
it considered that Iraq had a strategic capability directly to threaten the UK
or USA. The primary concern was rather over the threat that Saddam posed
to peace and security in the region. The action was undertaken to enforce
Saddam's disarmament obligations under successive UN Resolutions and so
remove that threat.

The US government shared that objective. But it added two significant
supplementary reasons for action. Regime change in Iraq had been an
objective of US foreign policy since President Clinton had signed the
bipartisan Iraq Liberation Act of 1998. Such change had initially been
sought by lending support, largely rhetorical and financial, to Iraqi opposition and human-rights groups. But, as the concern over WMD had
mounted after the 9/11 attacks, so had support for military action to disarm

Saddam grown, with regime change perceived as a necessary means to achieve this. The tyrannical nature of Saddam's regime strengthened the concern over his possession of WMD. It also, in the US government's view, furnished humanitarian grounds for taking military action. Saddam was a tyrant whose overthrow would end the brutal oppression of his people. The military operation was accordingly named Operation 'Iraqi Freedom'. In his eve-of-war TV address to the nation, President Bush offered to the Iraqi people: 'We will tear down the apparatus of terror, and we will help you to build a new Iraq that is prosperous and free.'[8]

Overthrowing tyranny is a laudable aim, but does it furnish just cause for war? Both international law and the just war tradition have tended to adopt a cautious approach in answering this question. For, while the benefits of regime change are uncertain, the harm caused by military action is only too evident. Just war thinking would not rule out regime change, but it does insist that the grounds for this need to be compelling, for example, to put an end to a humanitarian catastrophe. Such humanitarian grounds had been the basis for coalition operations in Iraq in 1991 to protect the Kurds in 'safe havens' from attacks by Saddam's forces. But no such humanitarian catastrophe was taking place in 2003, just the steady brutal oppression of his people by a ruthless dictator. The British government accordingly did not seek to base the case for war on humanitarian grounds. The relief of the Iraqi people from oppression would, it was hoped, be a welcome outcome of the military action. But its primary objective was to remove the threat posed by Saddam's weapons of mass destruction.

The next and by far the most significant difference between the US and UK governments reflected their different assessments of how immediate and direct was the threat posed by Saddam's possession of WMD.

Concern over WMD proliferation had increased sharply on both sides of the Atlantic after the 9/11 attacks. Those attacks had demonstrated the scale of destruction that could be wrought by a determined group of terrorists, undeterred by fear of alienating public support or by considerations of personal survival. Moreover, while that damage had been caused by conventional attacks, this had merely served to heighten concern over how much greater would be the destruction that a determined terrorist group could wreak if weapons of mass destruction were employed. As Prime Minister Blair explained to the Butler inquiry: 'What has changed is not the pace of Saddam Hussein's WMD programmes but our tolerance of them post 11th September.'[9] He underlined this claim subsequently to the Chilcot inquiry: 'the crucial thing after September 11 was that the calculus of risk changed.'[10]

The 9/11 attack reinforced existing concerns over the threat that Saddam's WMD capability presented to regional peace and security with the additional fear that one day the weapons might end up in the hands of determined terrorists, so presenting a more direct threat to US and UK interests. Such fear was hardly allayed by the uncovering during this period of the extensive illegal nuclear proliferation network run by Pakistan's top nuclear scientist, A. Q. Khan, whose exploits we explored in Chapter 8. These broader concerns were legitimately invoked by both the US and UK governments to strengthen the case for UN enforcement action to counter WMD proliferation. But the UK government accepted that these wider concerns did not of themselves furnish grounds for military action in self-defence so long as the fear of the linkage between Saddam's weapons and terrorism remained a worrying but still uncertain possibility.[11] But what if such links were already being forged?

That was what the US government argued was happening. They claimed that there was not merely a risk that Saddam's WMD might one day end up in the hands of terrorists but that such links between al-Qaeda and Saddam's regime were already taking place. In his television broadcast to the nation on the eve of war President Bush stated: 'Iraq has aided, trained and harboured terrorists, including operatives of Al Qaeda. The danger is clear. Using chemical, biological or, one day, nuclear weapons, obtained with the help of Iraq, the terrorists could fulfil their stated ambitions and kill thousands or hundreds of thousands of innocent people in our country or any other.'[12]

So, in the US view, action against Iraq could be justified not only as enforcement action on behalf of the UN but also on the basis of its new strategic doctrine of pre-emption, as an extended form of self-defence— attacking the terrorist enemy before he attacks you. Such action in self-defence, it was argued, did not require specific UN authorization.

As we have examined in Chapter 9, the general approach of the just war tradition is to restrict the scope for pre-emptive action by underlining the need to weigh the certain ill effects of war against the uncertain benefits of military action. Whether pre-emptive action is ever permissible is a complex judgement depending on the gravity and likelihood of the threat to be countered and the assessed balance of good over harm thereby achieved. Pre-emptive action may be permissible where there is a direct, immediate, and grave threat. But where the threat, however serious, is more remote and, crucially, less certain, this may be insufficient to justify military action, and other ways of countering it are to be preferred. So, if the fear was that Saddam's WMD might one day end up in terrorist hands, that would not of itself justify military action in self-defence. But if the terrorists had already acquired such weapons, the gravity and likelihood of the threat might be deemed sufficient to justify military action. Bush appeared to be suggesting that there was just such a direct and grave threat.

But did Saddam's WMD present such a threat? The British government's view was that they did not. There had been contacts between al-Qaeda and Saddam's regime, but the UK intelligence experts had concluded that there was 'no evidence that these contacts led to practical cooperation; we judge it unlikely because of mutual mistrust'.[13] That mistrust reflected the very different outlook of a secular Baathist regime from that of the state-less religious fundamentalists of al-Qaeda. The 9/11 attacks had legitimately increased concern over WMD proliferation. But the risk that Saddam's weapons would fall into terrorist hands was still uncertain and not on its own a justifiable basis for war in self-defence.

The US government proffered more reasons for the war than did the British and arguably too many reasons, given the requirement for clarity in the stated rationale for war. There was merit in the more cautious and measured approach of the British government, which sought to justify war solely on the need to enforce the UN resolutions requiring Saddam to get rid of his weapons of mass destruction and so remove the threat he posed to regional peace and security. Concern over WMD proliferation was the shared basis for war of both the US and UK governments. But did Saddam possess weapons of mass destruction?

Saddam's disappearing WMD

We now know, from the publication of the final report of the Iraq Survey Group on 30 September 2004, that Iraq did not have weapons of mass destruction. Saddam had had them and had them in abundance prior to and at the time of the First Gulf War. But the Iraq Survey Group concluded: 'Iraq, by the mid-1990s, was essentially free of militarily significant WMD stocks', although Saddam retained a strategic ambition and capability to reacquire them, once the sanctions regime had ended.[14] We need to consider whether the fact that there were no weapons of mass destruction automatically invalidates the disarmament objective of the coalition as a just cause.

Mr Blair argued in evidence to the Chilcot inquiry on 29 January 2010 that the fact that there were no weapons of mass destruction mattered less than the fact that Saddam 'retained absolutely the intent and intellectual know-how to restart a nuclear and chemical weapons programme when weapons inspectors were out and the sanctions were changed'.[15] We should, he counselled, not be asking the March 2003 question but the 2010 question: what kind of threat would we be facing now if no action had been taken against Saddam in 2003. Saddam's strategic intent and capability to reacquire the weapons was a legitimate cause for concern. But it seems doubtful that there would have been much support in 2003 for a case for war based on what might happen in 2010. For, if our concern in 2003 had been based solely on Saddam's strategic intent, rather than actual possession, it would always have been open to argue that there was time for other options to be deployed to prevent him fulfilling his strategic intent, including rigorous arms inspections and better targeted (so-called smart) sanctions. The requirement of last resort would not have been met. What gave the case for military action in 2003 its force and urgency was the belief that Saddam did actually possess the weapons. So we still need to answer the question whether the fact that he did not possess these weapons invalidates the disarmament objective?

The answer is that it does not necessarily do so if there were reasonable and soundly based grounds for believing that Saddam had such weapons. So were there such reasonable grounds?

As the senior defence official within the UK Cabinet Office in 1997–9, I was responsible, among other duties, for coordinating government policy on Iraq, with access to all the intelligence material and the UN weapons inspectors' reports. I believed Saddam had retained some chemical and biological weapons. So why did I, along with other senior officials and politicians, believe this?

The first reason is that this was what all the experts advised, not just in the UK and USA but in all other Western countries. This was the view not just of the intelligence analysts but also of academic commentators and of the UN weapons inspectors themselves. Even Hans Blix, the Executive Chairman of UNMOVIC whose cautious approach was criticized by the US and UK governments, believed this: 'My gut feeling, which I kept to myself, suggested to me that Iraq was still engaged in prohibited activities and retained prohibited items, and that it had the documents to prove it.'[16]

Saddam had undoubtedly had biological and chemical weapons and had used chemical weapons: against Iranian forces in 1984 and his own Kurdish people in 1988. In the aftermath of the Gulf War it was discovered that his stocks of chemical and biological weapons had been significantly higher than intelligence had suggested prior to the war and that his nuclear programme had been much further advanced than had been thought. This was subsequently confirmed by Husayn Kamil, Saddam's son-in-law, who had been in charge of WMD programmes, when he defected to the West in 1995. There were thus good grounds for concern that Saddam might have retained some chemical and biological weapons and might even be seeking to reconstitute his nuclear programme.

One of the main reasons for supposing that, while substantial stocks had been destroyed under UNSCOM's supervision, Saddam had illegally re- tained some chemical and biological weapons was that he behaved as if he had done so. For he had consistently failed to cooperate fully with the UN weapon inspectors, denying them access to sites, cancelling inspections at the last minute, and, in general, playing what looked like an elaborate cat- and-mouse game of hide-and-seek with the inspectors. Some non-cooper- ation could be presented as a reaction to over-zealous activities of the inspectors, particularly when they sought to search the many extensive premises labelled as Saddam's 'palaces', intrusive inspections that he claimed affronted his sense of dignity and challenged Iraqi sovereignty. But that did not explain his consistent and prolonged pattern of non-cooperation. Moreover, Saddam had finally withdrawn cooperation altogether in 1998. It was difficult to understand why, if he had nothing to hide, he did not cooperate fully with the inspectors to secure an end to their intrusive activities and the removal of sanctions rather than stringing them along. He behaved as if he had weapons of mass destruction, so we believed he did.

There appeared to be good grounds for supposing he had retained some chemical and biological weapons. Yet, as it turned out, he had not. So why did the experts all get it so wrong?

Part of the answer is provided by the Butler Report, commissioned by the UK government to look into failings of the intelligence community. This notes that the intelligence analysts, having underestimated Saddam's capa- bility at the time of the First Gulf War, were determined not to make that mistake again. They were thus 'inclined towards over-cautious or worst case estimates'.[17] Such worst-case planning explains why the analysts overestimated Iraqi stock holdings, so in turn fuelling the suspicions of the weapons inspectors, whom the intelligence analysts briefed, that there were further stockpiles still unaccounted for. But it does not fully explain why there was such a near universal belief that he had weapons of mass destruction. For that we need to look for a more fundamental error of intelligence.

Butler notes in his opening chapter that one of the defects to which intelligence-gathering is prone is 'mirror imaging'.[18] This is the belief that one's own practices and values are universal. But Butler curiously fails to apply this to the particular case of Iraq. 'Mirror imaging' is a crucial part of the explanation for what went wrong. It was assumed that Saddam had the weapons because he behaved as if he had them. After all, no sane Western democratic leader would behave like that, so incurring the penalties of immensely damaging economic sanctions against his people and the threat of military action. The risks would be deemed to outweigh any possible benefits. But Saddam was not a Western democratic leader. He was an Arab despot, with an Arabic sense of pride and shame. He cared little for the penalties that sanctions brought upon his people and was not democratically accountable to the people whose suffering he caused. A Western democratic leader could not survive, behaving as he did. But a ruthless Arab dictator could or, at least, he could for twelve years. The mistake we had made was to apply the canons of Western rationality and democracy in a non-Western, non-democratic context.

What we had failed to reckon on was that Saddam was engaged in a gigantic—and to his mind very clever—game of bluff, destroying weapons stocks to get the inspectors off his back, while pretending he had them in order to deter perceived internal and external threats to his regime, particularly the threat from Iran. It may also have flattered his vanity that he thereby became the centre of attention of the world's superpower. This game of bluff was finally uncovered by the Iraq Survey Group, which concluded that: 'In order to counter these threats, Saddam continued with his public posture of retaining the WMD capability. This led to a difficult balancing act between the need to disarm to achieve sanctions relief while at the same time retaining a strategic deterrence. The regime never resolved the contradictions inherent in this approach.'[19] Those contradictions led ultimately to Saddam's overthrow. His game of bluff had proved decidedly both a more dangerous and a less clever stratagem than he had supposed.

The belief that Saddam had weapons of mass destruction was not unreasonable, but for these reasons was mistaken. But was such a belief the real
reason why military action was undertaken?

Right intention

It is not enough to have a just cause; the military action must be undertaken
for the sake of the just cause and so be undertaken with right intention.
Many opponents of the war thought that the disarming of Iraq was only a
pretext and that there must have been other more sinister reasons for
military action.

Political motivations are typically complex. But, as we explored in
Chapter 4, what is important in assessing right intention is what intention
is dominant. Other motives may be at work that, provided they are not
themselves wicked or inconsistent with the primary intention, will not
invalidate the primary motivation.

One reason successive US governments, both Democrat and Republican,
found Saddam's behaviour so objectionable, was that the USA, along with
key allies such as the UK, had spent substantial sums and, more importantly,
sacrificed the lives of their soldiers, to reverse Saddam's aggression in the
First Gulf War. Yet, despite the investment of such 'blood and treasure',
Saddam was still openly defying the West: cocking a snook at the world's
sole surviving superpower. Saddam had even directed an unsuccessful plot
to assassinate President Bush senior on his visit to Kuwait in April 1993.
Imperial Britain in the nineteenth century had similarly found it difficult to
accept open defiance of its will from small-time dictators. Such imperial
offence was undoubtedly a factor in putting and keeping Saddam near the
top of the US foreign-policy agenda. Meanwhile, the UK government
thought it important to maintain solidarity with the USA, particularly in
the wake of the 9/11 attacks, an alliance in which Mr Blair declared he
believed 'passionately'.[20] But these considerations do not mean that the
concern over Saddam's WMD capability, sharpened by the events of 9/11,
was not genuine. What they do illustrate is that political motivation is often
complex and mixed.

Conspiracy theories on the real underlying motive for the war do,
nonetheless, abound. It was suggested that Bush and Blair had entered
into a secret pact to go to war regardless of the United Nations at their
meeting in the President's ranch at Crawford, Texas, in April 2002. Such a
secret deal has, however, been forcefully denied by Mr Blair, while the

eleven months of patient diplomacy at the UN that followed attest to the seriousness with which the UN route was regarded by both governments and, in particular, the UK government.[21]

It was also argued that the Iraq adventure was driven by neoconservative imperial ambitions to establish a long-term, substantial military presence in the Middle East.[22] Some US neoconservatives may have had such military ambitions. Some certainly saw the military operation as an opportunity to install a friendly government in Iraq, so shaping the overall balance of the Middle East in a way that suited US interests. But there is little evidence to suggest that prior to the war the USA was planning for a long-term occupation. On the contrary, the overwhelming evidence is that the ambitions of those who had responsibility for the military operations from the US President downwards were very different. Far from planning for the long haul, they were planning for a rapid exit, once the initial military campaign had been completed, and were only dragged, willy-nilly, into a long-term occupation by the way subsequent events unfurled. Prior to the war the US Defense Secretary, Donald Rumsfeld, frequently and publicly warned against any action that would 'tie our forces down indefinitely'.[23] In line with his instructions, the US CENTCOM Commander, General Tommy Franks, issued guidelines to his staff on 16 April 2003, only days after the main operation had been concluded, to prepare for a rapid run-down and to reduce US troops in Iraq to about 30,000 by September.[24] Planning for a rapid exit after a regime had been overthrown had its own serious shortcomings, as we shall examine shortly. But it hardly supports claims that the USA had always planned for a long-term occupation.

It was also argued that the intelligence dossier published by the UK government in September 2002 had presented misleading claims about Saddam's WMD capability that furnished evidence that the UK government had lied about Saddam's WMD capability. This latter charge was not, however, substantiated by the careful examination of the Butler Committee, which concluded that the dossier was, in general, an accurate reflection of the underlying intelligence material. There were, however, two important exceptions. First the dossier had failed to make clear the limited extent of the intelligence underlying some of its judgements, reflecting the West's difficulty in penetrating such an alien and hostile dictatorial regime as that of Saddam.[25] The dossier also failed to make clear that its claim, much seized on by some of the British media, that Iraq had plans to deploy some of its chemical and biological weapons in 45 minutes related to tactical, not strategic, weapons and referred to the time needed to move such weapons from forward-deployed storage sites to pre-designated missile units.[26] Both of these were, as Butler conceded, culpable omissions. Indeed, the lack of qualification to the dossier's 45-minute claim and the government's subsequent failure to correct the wilder speculation that this generated in the media made it appear as if the government were seeking to exaggerate the immediacy, directness, and gravity of the threat posed by Saddam's capability.

The dossier's defects were serious. But they did not furnish evidence for supposing that the government's basic claim that Saddam possessed a significant WMD capability was itself a deception nor that its concern over this was not genuine. For the reasons already adduced, it is more accurate to say that the intelligence analysts were deceiving themselves rather than that they, or the politicians who drew on their assessments, were deliberately deceiving the public.

The motivations of the US and UK governments in the drive towards war were undoubtedly mixed, with considerations of realpolitik jostling uneasily with higher-minded concerns. Criticism can also be levelled at the way the case for war was presented, including the lack of qualifications in the UK dossier and, even more, the unjustified linkage made by the US government between Saddam's regime and al-Qaeda terrorists, both of which tended to make the threat appear more direct, immediate, and serious than it was.

But none of this provides grounds for doubting that both governments genuinely believed that Saddam had a WMD capability, were concerned over the threat that this presented to peace and security in the region and more widely, and that this concern was their primary motivation for undertaking military action. Concern over Iraq's WMD capability was also shared by other members of the UN Security Council, which in its Resolution 1441 had declared Iraq to be in material breach of its disarmament obligations. That belief was mistaken but not unreasonable. So the objective of disarming Iraq of its WMD capability in enforcement of UN Resolutions could have constituted a just cause for military action. There are, however, two important qualifications.

First, as we have frequently stressed, the just war criteria are designed to make it difficult to go to war. War inevitably causes suffering, and so it is important to have strong grounds for believing that the benefits of military action will outweigh the disbenefits. This is a particularly challenging condition to meet where action is taken against a threat that is not actual or imminent. The military action taken against Saddam was designed to counter the threat to the peace and security of the region posed by his possession and possible use of WMD. However seriously the threat was viewed, it was not at that stage actual or imminent. For military action to be justified, there needed to be strong evidence both of the gravity and likelihood of the threat and that action to counter it would bring about more good than harm. The evidential bar is set high by the just war criteria, not arbitrarily, but by the grim logic of war, where the suffering caused is certain, while the gains, particularly from action against non-imminent threats, are less certain.

We shall consider whether sufficient steps were taken to ensure that war would not cause more harm than good in assessing the application of the principle of proportion. But was there strong enough evidence of the threatened harm that the military action was designed to avert? To meet this condition it was not enough to have a reasonable belief that Saddam had WMD. That belief needed to be based on very strong evidence of both the gravity and the likelihood of the threatened harm. If the justification for a military operation was based only on evidence furnished by intelligence, governments needed to be sure of the strength and reliability of the evidence. Given the limited extent of the intelligence material on which the judgements of Saddam's capability were based—'sporadic and patchy' in the words of the *Butler Report*[27]—it is not clear that the high evidential standards set by the just war criteria were met.

The second and related difficulty is that, since the military action to disarm Iraq of its WMD capability was being undertaken to enforce UN Security Council Resolutions, it was important that the US and UK governments had the required competent authority to act on behalf of the UN. This was, however, disputed.

Competent authority

The British Attorney General, Lord Goldsmith, argued that the coalition had competent authority. Member states had been authorized to use force by the 1990 UN Resolution 678. That authorization had been suspended but not terminated by Resolution 687 at the end of the First Gulf War and had been revived in 2002 by UNSCR 1441, which had found Iraq to be in material breach of its obligations to disarm.[28]

This was an elegant legal argument, although its validity was disputed by other lawyers, including those within the UK Foreign Office.[29] But, whatever its legal merits, the weakness of such an approach from the standpoint of the just war tradition is that to justify such a momentous decision as embarking on war on behalf of the UN required more than an argument to show that force had been authorized by the UN in the past. It needed evidence that such military enforcement action was still the avowed wish of the international community. That was more difficult to establish.

I argued in Chapter 4 that explicit UN authorization is not always essential where, as with NATO operations in Kosovo, a grave and urgent humanitarian crisis is occurring and there is other clear evidence of substantial international backing. Neither of these conditions was, however, met in this case. Moreover, the fact that the avowed justification for the action was to enforce UN resolutions underlined the particular importance in this case of explicit UN backing. This was why the British government had been rightly keen to secure a second resolution explicitly authorizing the use of force. The failure to secure a majority in the UN Security Council to support that second resolution was itself evidence of the lack of international consensus for military action. This, in turn, cast doubt on the claim that the US and UK governments had the required competent authority.

Moreover, one of the main reasons for the reluctance of the international community to lend such support for a second resolution was a belief that military action was being undertaken too soon and not as a last resort.

Last resort

It was argued that Resolution 1441, while declaring Iraq in material breach of its disarmament obligations, had given Saddam a final chance to prove otherwise. The UNMOVIC inspectors had arrived in Iraq only on 28 November 2002 and had not yet had time to complete their work. These concerns were voiced at the Wehrkunde security conference in February 2003, when the German Foreign Minister, Joschka Fischer, challenged the US Defense Secretary, Donald Rumsfeld: 'Why now?...Are we in a situation where we should resort to force now?'[30]

The counter-argument was that Saddam had had twelve years to demonstrate his compliance and failed to do so. He had had time enough. This was a telling point. But the UNMOVIC inspectors had begun to report a greater degree of Iraqi cooperation. On 7 March, Hans Blix, presenting his third report, stated that the Iraqis were cooperating more fully than in the past,

although still not to the point of full disclosure. His colleague from the
International Atomic Energy Agency, Mohamed El Baradei, added that
there was no evidence that Iraq had reconstituted its nuclear programme.[31]
In view of the more positive findings of UNMOVIC, it is arguable that the
inspectors should have been given more time.

There were genuine concerns whether military action was being undertaken as a last resort, and, in view of these, there was a reluctance to support
a second resolution authorizing force. This, in turn, cast doubt on whether
the condition of competent authority was met and so reinforced the
concern that there was not a just cause for action. Doubt over whether
each of these conditions individually was met did not amount to a knock-
down argument against war. But the doubts taken together mutually reinforced each other and so strengthened the overall concern that there was
not a sufficient just cause.

A year after the end of the war, Prime Minister Blair gave a speech in his
Sedgefield constituency in March 2004 in which he argued that international law should be amended to broaden the scope for what constitutes
a just cause. The implication was that the lawyers had boxed him into going
to war on the too narrow grounds of WMD disarmament when other
stronger grounds were available. He asked:

> It may well be that under international law as presently constituted, a regime
> can systematically brutalise and oppress its people and there is nothing anyone
> can do, when dialogue, diplomacy and even sanctions fail, unless it comes
> within the definition of a humanitarian catastrophe (though the 300,000
> remains in mass graves already found in Iraq might be thought by some to
> be something of a catastrophe). That may be the law, but should it be?[32]

That is a reasonable question, since international law, like domestic law,
needs to be subject to regular scrutiny to ensure its continuing validity and
relevance. But just war teaching insists that any change, particularly a
change that would make it easier for states to make war, would need strong
arguments in its favour. We shall consider in Chapter 11 the case for
extending the moral and legal grounds for intervention for humanitarian
reasons. But the difficulty with Blair's suggestion in 2004 that the removal of
a brutal and oppressive regime, such as Saddam's, should be regarded as a
legitimate cause for war is twofold.

First, as Blair conceded in his speech, this had not been the avowed aim of
the UK government when the war was undertaken, even though it had

been of the US government. The just war tradition looks unkindly on the expansion of war aims as wars run into difficulties. Second, and more fundamental, is the concern we have already noted that the benefits of regime change are uncertain, whereas the disadvantages of military action are only too evident. Just war thinking accordingly insists that, for military action to change a regime to be justified, there would need to be very compelling reasons—for example, to put an end to a humanitarian catastrophe, or to eliminate a grave threat, actual or imminent, posed by a tyrant's wielding WMD. But, without WMD and with no humanitarian catastrophe taking place—only the steady brutal oppression of his people by a ruthless dictator—the case for military action is weakened. For, in the absence of such compelling grounds, the just war tradition, mindful of the risks involved, does not consider regime change undertaken for its own sake or simply to exchange a good for a bad ruler to constitute a just cause.

It is, moreover, perhaps the single most serious charge against those who planned the Second Gulf War that they massively underestimated the disbenefits of military action.

Principle of proportion

For the next requirement of the just war tradition is that, before war is embarked upon, a careful assessment should be undertaken of the consequences of military action to ensure that the harm likely to be caused is not disproportionate to the good achieved, taking into account the probability of success.

Judged against the initial military campaign—what John Keegan called the 21-day conflict—this condition was met. Keegan himself provides a judicious assessment of the outcome of that campaign:

> The toll of coalition fatalities was nevertheless surprisingly light, 122 American, 33 British. Of the British dead, six had been killed in action, the others in accident or by 'friendly fire'. A higher proportion of Americans were killed in combat but, again, most were victims of accident and some of attack by their own aircraft ... The number of Iraqi dead has not yet been counted. Since there were no great battles in the war, it is unlikely that casualties in the Iraqi armed forces were high ... The total of their dead will probably never be known but must have amounted to several thousand. The number of civilian dead was much lower, thanks to the careful precision of coalition air attack on populated areas.[33]

Casualties were considerably lower than in the First Gulf War, partly reflecting the fact that it had not been necessary to mount a prolonged air campaign in advance of operations on the ground. Against the limited casualties could be set the removal of the threat to regional peace and security achieved by the overthrow of Saddam's regime and the opportunity this furnished to disarm Iraq of its WMD. There was evident relief and joy among the Iraqi people that the years of Saddam's oppression had been ended.

So it looked in April 2003. In 2010—seven years on—the balance sheet looks rather different. No weapons of mass destruction were found. Meanwhile, the casualties, military and civilian, have continued to mount. On 29 June 2010 US military deaths (including accidents) had risen to 4,413, British to 179, and other coalition forces to 137.[34] The Iraq Body Count conservatively estimated civilian deaths at between 97,000 and 106,000.[35] In January 2009 (the last date for which estimates are available), two million refugees and asylum-seekers had fled the country, although many may have since returned.

Most of these casualties are not the result of coalition military action but stem from the devastating attacks that the Iraqis are inflicting on one another, as Sunnis and Shia struggle for power and al-Qaeda and other insurgent groups fuel the civil strife. The overall totals also mask significant recent improvements. Casualty levels have been much reduced following the successful US 'surge operations' mounted from February 2007. These operations, directed by General David Petraeus, combined higher US and Iraqi force levels with much more effective counter-insurgency tactics and doctrine, as enshrined in the new US counter-insurgency manual that Petraeus had himself commissioned.[36] US military casualties, which had peaked at 137 a month in November 2004, were down to 8 in June 2010. Likewise, monthly civilian casualties, which had peaked at 3,709 in October 2006, were down to 204 in June 2010. Substantial political progress has also been achieved, with successive Iraqi governments democratically elected in December 2005 and March 2010, albeit with a protracted process of coalition formation. Successful local government elections were held in January 2009.

These improvements are significant. But the cost of getting there has been high and, in particular, much higher than anticipated by those planning the invasion. Coalition leaders could not reasonably be expected to have forecast before military action was taken the precise casualty levels that would ensue. But the coalition leaders are rightly to be criticized for failing to have given sufficient consideration to what would be the effects of regime change and for not having formulated robust plans for promptly re-establishing civil governance in the wake of the regime change. Just as they had undertaken worst-case assessments of Saddam's WMD capability, so they had undertaken best-case assessments of what would happen after the regime had been changed. As Lieutenant General Joseph Kellogg, a senior member of the staff of the US Joint Chiefs of Staff, explained: 'I was there for all the planning. I saw it all. There was no real plan. The thought was, you didn't need it. The assumption was that everything would be fine after the war, that they would be happy they got rid of Saddam.'[37]

In the velvet revolutions of Central and Eastern Europe after the collapse of Soviet power, regime change had been greeted by cheering peaceful crowds and the subsequent transition to democracy achieved without significant violence. Such it was fondly supposed would be the experience after the liberation of Iraq. As one American soldier recalled: 'I imagined Iraqi women would be greeting us with flowers in our gun tubes and holding up babes to be kissed.'[38]

The UK government, with its own imperial experience of the difficulties of ruling Iraq during its League of Nations mandate from 1918 to 1932, might have been expected to take a less rose-tinted view. After the war there were suggestions that the failure of post-war planning had been a US fault, against which the UK had repeatedly warned. But, whatever warnings may have been given, there is little evidence that post-war planning had been a major British priority or concern prior to the invasion. Nor was it according to Major General Tim Cross, the British officer designated to liaise with the Americans on post-war planning. He had counselled the Prime Minister shortly before military action was taken that, while we would win the military campaign, he 'did not believe that we are ready for post-war Iraq'.[39] Indeed, one of the most striking facts disclosed by the Butler Report is that 'intelligence on Iraqi political issues was designated as being Third Order'—in other words, low priority—despite the importance of such information for post-war planning in circumstances 'where the UK is likely to become involved in national reconstruction and institution-building'.[40] Such lack of interest in political intelligence hardly suggests that post-war planning was a high priority of the UK government. Following extensive interviews with officials and diplomats, the British journalist Jonathan Steele concluded:

Analysing the likely consequences of having Western armies occupy one of
the major Arab states should have been a crucial element in judging whether it
was in the British interest (let alone that of the Iraqis) to launch an invasion.
Yet such analysis was simply absent. Ministers never asked for it. Officials
never offered it. This failure to ask the right questions on the eve of a war was
arguably the biggest foreign policy blunder in recent British history since
Suez.[41]

Steele's judgement that no analysis was undertaken may be too harsh. But
such analysis was certainly accorded insufficient priority and, in so far as it was
done, was carried out very late in the day.[42] The British diplomat Hilary
Synnott, who served as the Regional Coordinator for southern Iraq from July
2003 to January 2004, explained in more pragmatic terms why there was so
little planning. The Ministry of Defence was busy planning the war 'and
taking the lead from the US expectation that the main post-conflict challenge
would be humanitarian relief, it was this aspect, rather than the administration
of a failed state, which was the main area of attention'.[43] The FCO, short-
staffed and preoccupied with trying to secure a second UN resolution, 'were
even less engaged in post-conflict planning'.[44] The Department for International Development (DFID), which formally should have been responsible
for such planning, was in the charge of a Secretary of State, Clare Short, who
bitterly opposed the war. 'Consistent with such a rejection of any inevitability
of conflict, DFID undertook little or no planning for possible post-conflict
humanitarian or reconstruction work.'[45] Indeed, as DFID's evidence to the
Chilcot inquiry subsequently underlined, its primary concern had been to try
to ensure that the UN took the lead in any post-conflict reconstruction.[46]

Regime change was regarded as a necessary means to achieve the objective of a disarmed Iraq. But little analysis was undertaken by the coalition
governments of how a Western occupation would be greeted in an independent Arab state. Apart from planning for humanitarian relief operations,
there was little planning in either the USA or UK for what would need to
be done, after the regime had been changed, to ensure continuity of civil
governance, to maintain law and order, and to effect a peaceful transition to
democracy in a state with no democratic experience and tradition from
which to draw. This was a major defect of war-planning. Coalition forces
were accordingly ill prepared to deal with the breakdown of law and order
that followed regime change and the subsequent onset of a violent insurgency against the occupation.

As casualties have mounted in the years since 2003, it has become increasingly difficult to maintain that more good than harm was produced by military action, however evil and oppressive the Saddam regime had undoubtedly been. Moreover, however the balance sheet is scored, what is clear is that the careful assessment of consequences required by the just war tradition before a war is embarked on was not undertaken. Nor was there adequate planning to ensure the prompt restoration of peaceful conditions after military operations and the establishment of a just peace. Both the just war requirements of proportion and *jus post bellum* were accordingly not met.

Jus in bello

As well as an assessment of the overall balance of good and ill before war is undertaken, the just war tradition requires that, in the conduct of a war, the harm judged likely to result from individual military actions should not be disproportionate to the good achieved; and that non-combatant casualties should be minimized. So how did coalition operations fare against these criteria?

Proportion

In the twenty-six-day conflict, the use of force was proportionate. But in the years of ensuing counter-insurgency operations since then there have been occasions when the force used was excessive. Such lapses were particularly apparent during the first year, when coalition, and particularly US, forces struggled to cope with an increasingly violent insurgency campaign, which they had not expected and for which they were neither prepared nor trained. Following their bitter experiences in the Vietnam conflict, the US military had, as we noted in Chapter 8, shredded their counter-insurgency training manuals. It was not until a year after the invasion—on 5 April 2004—that the US commanders issued a first counter-insurgency campaign plan.[47] It was not until 2006 that a new counter-insurgency training manual was produced.

There were criticisms of the way US forces responded in the autumn of 2003 to the growing insurgency with a heavy-handed campaign of large-scale and indiscriminate arrests of civilian suspects.[48] Particular concerns were voiced over the amount of force used in the US operation to secure Fallujah in April 2004. Following the murder and dismemberment of four

US Blackwater contractors, a full-scale divisional assault was hastily launched by the US Marines against the insurgents occupying Fallujah on 5 April 2004 in order to secure the city and bring the murderers to justice. The intensity of the assault provoked criticism even within the coalition and was rapidly brought to a halt on 9 April before its objectives had been achieved. A second, more carefully planned, battle for Fallujah was fought in November 2004 and achieved more success in securing the city. Following the first battle, an internal memorandum within the British Foreign Office observed: 'Heavy-handed US military tactics in Fallujah and Najaf some weeks ago have fuelled both Sunni and Shi'ite opposition to the coalition, and lost us much public support inside Iraq.'[49]

Non-combatant immunity

In the twenty-six-day conflict considerable efforts were successfully made to minimize civilian casualties, which were limited. The published UK war aims made clear that 'every effort will be made to minimise civilian casualties and damage to essential economic infrastructure'.[50] The injunction to reduce damage to civilian infrastructure was a direct response to the criticism recorded earlier that economic infrastructure had been excessively damaged in the First Gulf War.

These objectives have continued during the ensuing years since 2003 and have, in general, been met. Civilian casualties in this period have, however, been high, although the bulk of these have been caused by insurgent action and civil disorder. But there have been serious lapses by coalition forces, especially in the first year of the occupation, as ill-trained troops struggled to cope with the counter-insurgency and the consequent large numbers of civilian detainees. In the autumn of 2003 and early 2004 there were a number of serious cases of abuse of civilian detainees by both US and UK forces.

The most notorious of these were the torture and sexual humiliation of detainees in Abu Ghraib prison. As the US Army report on the abuses noted with disdain: 'Between October and December 2003, at the Abu Ghraib Confinement Facility, numerous incidents of sadistic, blatant and wanton criminal abuses were inflicted on several detainees.'[51] These were in clear breach of Article 3 of the 1949 Geneva Convention banning 'outrages on personal dignity, in particular humiliating and degrading treatment'.

Nor was the British Army immune from such lapses. As we examined in Chapter 6, there were a number of cases of abuse by British soldiers in the autumn of 2003 and early 2004 of Iraqi civilians who had been detained during the looting and breakdown of order that took place following the overthrow of Saddam's regime. These included the unlawful death in custody of Baha Mousa and the ill-treatment of eight other Iraqis in Basra in September 2003. The British Army report concluded that these abuses, and their subsequent cover-up, reflected a serious failure in the ethical conduct of the soldiers involved.[52]

Such abuses by both British and US soldiers were condemned in their own right because the ill-treatment meted out to civilian detainees contravened both the just war requirement to minimize harm to civilians and the specific Geneva conventions prohibiting ill-treatment of detainees. Such failings at the tactical level also had adverse strategic consequences because the behaviour was in conflict with the avowed humanitarian objectives of the coalition mission. The British Army Report soberly observed: 'there is no doubt that such behaviour is particularly damaging when committed by the British Army, in the 21st Century, on operations where we were meant to be improving the lot of the Iraqi people, under the immediate gaze of the world's media.'[53]

As we argued in Chapter 6, such lapses in behaviour underline the need for better education and training for the military at all levels, from the most senior to the most junior, not just in the principles of the just war but also in its daily practice through habituation in the virtues. Virtuous conduct needs to become—through example, training, and exercise—second nature to the soldiers, as deeply engrained as habits of action as are the drills with which they wield their weapons.

Gulf Wars: The Verdict

In this chapter we have considered and compared the two Gulf Wars. Our conclusion is that, overall, the First Gulf War complied with the criteria of the just war and can be judged a just war.

The Second Gulf War was, like most wars, fought from a mixture of motives. But, in the main, the reasons for undertaking the war were honourable and the concerns over WMD proliferation in general and Saddam's contribution to this in particular were genuinely held. It is too easy to present the coalition leaders as wicked men. On the contrary, the tragedy of the Iraq conflict is that those responsible were trying to make the world a better and safer place and were supported by military forces that have exhibited, on the whole, remarkable restraint in challenging conditions and enormous courage, dedication, and fortitude. But, as the just war doctrine, forged from painful experience over the centuries, teaches, noble aspirations are not enough. War is so serious and deadly an occupation that the just war tradition sets the tests for a just war at a high level. Against those high standards, the Second Gulf War is found to be wanting.

The war failed fully to meet any of the criteria that need to be satisfied before a war is undertaken. There were doubts whether the operation was undertaken with competent authority and as a last resort. These doubts, in turn, fuelled the concerns that there was not sufficient just cause. The justice of a cause does not guarantee that a war is just, but a war cannot be just without just cause. The requirement of just cause, as we noted in Chapter 4, has a logical primacy over other conditions. It sets the terms by which most of them are satisfied, including specifying the good against which the harmful consequences of war needs to be measured in applying the principle of proportion. The conditions of just cause and proportion are thus closely interlinked and together set the key boundaries by which the justice of a decision to go to war is measured: just cause specifying the good to be achieved and proportion assessing whether the harm caused will outweigh the good.

In so far as there were doubts about the justice of the cause for military action in 2003, these, in turn, reinforced concerns over whether the principle of proportion could be met. This condition requires that more good than harm should result from military action. But there were doubts over the good to be achieved. There were also concerns over the harm war would bring about. For, crucially, no adequate assessment was undertaken before military action was authorized to ensure that the harm likely to result would not be disproportionate to the good achieved. Nor were there robust plans to ensure the establishment of a just peace after the initial military campaign had been concluded. Finally, in the conduct of military operations, the principles of proportion and discrimination have, in general, been met, but there have been some serious lapses.

The doubts over whether individual conditions were met were grounds for concern. The charge against the Second Gulf War is not, however, that it fell somewhat short of a number of conditions, but rather that such individual failures, when taken together, mutually reinforced each other, so building up cumulatively to support the conclusion that the war was undertaken, in particular, without sufficient just cause and without adequate planning to ensure a just outcome. It thus failed the two key tests that have to be met before a war can be justly undertaken, designed to ensure that military action is initiated only if more good than harm will result.

Our political leaders may have had noble objectives in embarking on military action. But moral fervour is not enough to ensure right decisions are taken. Moral reasoning, as we have frequently underlined, needs to be guided by the judicious exercise of the virtues and, above all, the cool application of practical wisdom, that 'habit of sound judgment about practical situations' that enables us to discern when, where, and how moral principles are to be applied to complex moral dilemmas in a way that ensures human welfare is promoted and suffering minimized. Moreover, our political leaders are required—according to Aquinas, as we noted in Chapter 6— to exercise the very highest form of practical wisdom, which is called statesmanship. It was such statesmanship that was signally lacking in the decision to embark on military action in 2003. Overall, the Second Gulf War is thus judged to be an unjust war.

A just peace?

The invasion of Iraq was unjust. But does it follow that military operations should be terminated forthwith and all coalition forces withdrawn as quickly as possible?

That is the view of many who opposed the war. For example, the British journalist Jonathan Steele, writing in 2007–8 at a time when the insurgency was still in full spate, concluded his savage critique of the Iraq War with the demand for early troop withdrawals: 'Even at this late stage, nearly five years after the invasion, the announcement of readiness to withdraw all US troops within a matter of months would give a vital boost to Iraq's processes of national reconciliation.'[54]

From the fact that the war was unjust it does not, however, follow that all the coalition troops engaged in Iraq should be immediately withdrawn. Or, as David Kilcullen, the Australian counter-insurgency adviser to General Petraeus, more colourfully remarked: 'Just because you invade a country stupidly doesn't mean you have to leave it stupidly.'[55] Just war commentators sometimes write as if the just war criteria need to be applied only twice: once, before war is undertaken; and then in the course of its conduct. The just war conditions are, however, not static but dynamic criteria. They need to be regularly applied and reapplied, before, during, and after a war. A war begun justly may become unjust if in its prosecution the balance of harm exceeds the good to be achieved. Conversely, a war begun unjustly can be fought justly. From an unjust war it may be possible to fashion a just peace. These distinctions are important, since we need to motivate those engaged even in an unjust war to exercise ethical restraint. Moreover, the very injustice of an unjust war may impose a particular obligation on those responsible to help restore a just peace.

So, before any major strategic decision, such as the withdrawal of all troops and the ending of military operations, is taken, the just war criteria need to be reapplied. So how would the coalition operations in Iraq in 2010 be rated against the just war criteria?

There is a just cause for the operations: to restore a just peace. There is also a particular obligation on those who fractured the peace to help to restore it. After the conclusion of the initial military campaign, the coalition forces were authorized to restore security and stability in Iraq under UN Security Resolution 1483 unanimously passed on 22 May 2003 and renewed annually thereafter. The forces are operating in support of the democratically elected Iraqi government, under bilateral security agreements that replaced the UN mandate from the end of 2008. The operations have a legitimacy that the invasion lacked. There is just cause for the operations and, since they are being undertaken for the sake of that cause, just intention. There is also competent authority.

The next criterion of last resort requires that there is no available alternative means to the use of military force to restore law and order to Iraq. The restoration of peace is a complex task requiring a comprehensive approach, drawing from an array of tools—political, diplomatic, and economic, as well as military. But so long as a violent insurgency campaign continues to be waged by al-Qaeda and other insurgent groups, military forces will continue to be an essential component of the counter-insurgency campaign.

The aim is for this task to be taken over fully and as quickly as possible by Iraqi forces. Substantial progress towards this goal has been achieved. This is demonstrated by the successful operations of Iraqi forces to secure Basra and Baghdad in 2008 and the progressive handover of security responsibility to the Iraqi forces, including on 1 September 2008 the responsibility for Anbar province, once the centre of the Sunni insurgency. In accordance with the bilateral security agreement, US forces were withdrawn from the cities on

30 June 2009, as Iraqi forces progressively take over their tasks. President Obama announced on 27 February 2009 that US combat troops would be withdrawn by August 2010 and the last combat unit duly left on 19 August. The remaining 50,000 US troops are planned to leave by the end of 2011.[56] The UK combat mission ended on 30 April 2009 and UK forces were withdrawn in July 2009. The improving security situation should permit an orderly transfer of responsibility to Iraqi forces by the end of 2011. The end of coalition operations are in sight. But the judgement of the security experts, and, most importantly, of the Iraq government itself, is that Iraqi forces are not yet ready to take on this task entirely on their own.

The final *jus ad bellum* condition is for a careful assessment to be made to ensure that more good than harm will be achieved, taking into account the probability of success. It was this test more than any other that the war-planners failed to pass, basing their judgements of what would happen after invasion on ill-founded best-case assessments. This test needs to be applied carefully before a decision is taken to withdraw all combat troops.

Opponents of the war, such as Jonathan Steele, claimed that withdrawal, even as the insurgency still raged, would give a vital boost to national reconciliation but provided no evidence to support this. Nor did he do so to support his claim that, once withdrawal is announced, 'only then will the resistance make a deal to refrain from attacks on US troops as they pull out'.[57] Such restraint seems unlikely from terrorists who began their insurgency campaign in Iraq on 7 August 2003 with the demolition of the UN headquarters in Baghdad. It seems rather more likely that the reverse will be the case. The responsible military commanders certainly take a far more cautious view. General David Petraeus, in reporting to Congress in April 2008 the considerable progress made by the surge operations, warned that that progress was 'fragile and reversible'; and that 'withdrawing too many forces too quickly could jeopardize the progress of the past year'.[58] He also counselled that premature withdrawal would risk provoking wider instability and civil strife, putting many thousands of lives at risk: 'a failed state in Iraq would pose serious consequences for the greater fight against Al Qaeda, for regional stability, for the already existing humanitarian crisis in Iraq, and for the effort to counter malign Iranian influence.'[59] In the years since that report further significant progress has been achieved and the success of the surge operations consolidated. But just when the counter-insurgency campaign is achieving some success, it would seem perverse to put this at risk by terminating operations. Immediate withdrawal would be likely to cause greater harm than good and so fails the first application of the principle of proportion. Such action would also hardly contribute to the establishment of a just peace.

The final conditions that need to be satisfied are the application of the principle of proportion in the conduct of war, together with that of non-combatant immunity. Although there were breaches of these principles, particularly in the first year of the occupation, coalition forces have learnt in the succeeding years how to operate an effective counter-insurgency campaign. A key contribution to the success of this is the need, now recognized both in principle and in practice and enshrined in the *Counterinsurgency Field Manual*, for the forces to operate with restraint and discrimination.

Conclusion

The invasion of Iraq in 2003 was unjust. But the ensuing operations to restore peace and security to that troubled land are just. Those opponents of the war who, even at the height of the insurgency, called for the immediate withdrawal of all troops against an arbitrary, fixed timetable unrelated to conditions on the ground were guilty of the same ill-founded optimism over the consequences of their actions as were those who failed adequately to plan for the war in the first place. Such action would have risked heaping on the injustice of the war the injustice of a failure to restore peace. Just war teaching would counsel that we should rather seek to atone for an unjust war by doing all we can to restore a just peace. Moreover, the success of the surge operations has at last opened up the prospect that such a just peace can be attained and an orderly transfer of responsibility achieved to a democratically elected Iraqi government.

ELEVEN
Humanitarian Intervention

We have so far focused primarily on self-defence as a just cause for military action: the right of a state to defend the lives and way of life of its citizens when these are threatened by external aggression. We need now to consider what happens when a people is being massively oppressed by its own government, engaged in large-scale killings or ethnic cleansing; or, if the government, while not itself the oppressor, fails to protect its people from slaughter or ethnic cleansing being undertaken by others within the boundaries of the state. Does a government have a right, even a duty, to save the lives, not just of its own citizens, but also the citizens of other states? Are we obliged to save the lives of strangers? If we are, what means are we entitled to employ to achieve this?

Humanitarian intervention may take a variety of forms, ranging from the provision of aid through to the use of military force. The force may be employed with or without the consent of the government of the state in which the intervention is taking place; and with or without the sanction of the United Nations. The form of humanitarian intervention that has provoked the most controversy in recent years is whether a state can legitimately intervene in the affairs of another state, if necessary using military force, in order to save the lives of its citizens, without the consent of that state. Is there a right of humanitarian intervention, even when it is non-consensual?

The just war vision of international society

It is, as we noted in Chapter 3, a key feature of morality that it extends its claims progressively further out through ever-widening concentric circles of the communities to which we belong: from the family, to the school, to the village, to a regiment, to a city, to our country, and so outwards towards the international community. The final step—the recognition of the claims of the international community—has taken time to establish and has seemed to some a step too far. Indeed, even the early just war theorists saw the just war principles as a set of rules to govern the behaviour of Christian princes in their dealings with each other. It took the genius of Vitoria, writing in the University of Salamanca in the early sixteenth century, to recognize that the just war principles were not the rules of a closed Christian club but were universal moral principles, based on reason, that necessarily apply to anyone, anywhere, at any time. The solemn assembly of the faculty of the University of Salamanca who convened in 1520 and formally voted, on the basis of these principles, that the Spanish conquest of Central and Southern America was unjust represented a high point of the medieval just war tradition.[1]

Consistent with this universalizing logic, Vitoria also recognized that it was not possible to justify an arbitrary distinction between one's own citizens and those of other lands. As the Parable of the Good Samaritan teaches, the Christian injunction to love our neighbour applies, wherever there is a neighbour who is suffering and in need of help. So Vitoria argued: 'The barbarians are all our neighbours, and therefore anyone, and especially princes, may defend them from such tyranny and oppression.' The 'defence of the innocent against tyranny' was just cause for war: 'I assert that in lawful defence of the innocent from unjust death, even without the pope's authority, the Spaniards may prohibit the barbarians from practising any nefarious custom or rite.'[2] Military action could be undertaken, if necessary, to prevent the suffering of the innocent—for example, as a result of human sacrifice or cannibalism.

Grotius, writing some years later in 1625, generalized these precepts into a broad principle of humanitarian intervention:

> Kings, and those who possess rights on a par with kings, have the right of demanding punishment not only on account of injuries committed against themselves or their subjects, but also on account of injuries which do not directly affect them but grossly violate the laws of nature or of nations in regard to any person whatsoever.[3]

As the just war theory reached its zenith in the sixteenth and early seventeenth centuries, its moral principles were deemed to apply universally to the relations between all states and to offer protection to all people. The doctrine embodied a generous and altruistic vision of the purposes for which military force could be used: not just to protect one's own citizens but also to prevent the suffering of the innocent, wherever they were. But, just as the universal pull of morality was being rediscovered in statecraft, so it was about to be lost there. For the world was about to change.

The norm of non-intervention

The Treaty of Westphalia, signed in 1648, not only ended the Thirty Years War and the territorial aggrandising ambitions of the imperial Habsburgs. It also put an end to Pope Innocent X's grand vision of a unified Christendom. Henceforward Europe was a continent of horizontally organized states. States became the central actors on the world stage, whose rights and duties it became the role of international law to define and to defend. In this fragmented and increasingly secular world of nation states, the Christian just war doctrine fell into oblivion. The relations between states were deemed governed primarily by realpolitik rather than by morality. The need to assuage the suffering caused by war was not altogether lost to sight. But, when in the late nineteenth and early twentieth centuries laws were introduced to constrain the warlike behaviour of states, these were regarded as not so much embodying universal moral principles as being rather more limited bargains struck between sovereign states, initially with the main emphasis on ameliorating the conditions of their soldiery. The first three Geneva Conventions (adopted respectively in 1864, 1906, and 1929) offered soldiers, in exchange for acting under certain rules, including the wearing of military uniforms and insignia, respectful treatment when wounded, sick, or prisoners of war. It was not until the Fourth Convention in 1949, to which additional protocols were added in 1977, that attention broadened to attend to the plight of civilians in war, and then only after the conclusion of a war in which both sides had made civilians the object of devastating area bombing attacks.

Following the conclusion of the Treaty of Westphalia, the doctrine developed over the succeeding centuries of the absolute supremacy of the rights of states and the inviolability of state boundaries, however arbitrarily drawn and whatever wickedness was perpetrated behind them. This doctrine, as we traced in Chapter 4, reached its apogee in the 1945 UN Charter, which prohibited intervention.

Article 2(4) declares: 'All member states shall refrain in their international relations from the threat or use of force against the territorial integrity or political independence of any State.' Only two exceptions are allowed: 'the inherent right of individual or collective self-defence if an armed attack occurs' as provided under Article 51; and military measures authorized by the Security Council under chapter VII in response to 'any threat to the peace, breach of the peace or act of aggression'. States have no legal right of humanitarian intervention recognized by the UN charter. On the contrary, Article 2.7 specifically prohibits interventions 'in matters which are essentially within the jurisdiction of any State'.

Following two calamitous world wars, state borders were proclaimed to be inviolable. The predominant theory in international relations became realism, for whose advocates, as we saw in Chapter 1, state boundaries were judged to be not just political but also moral boundaries beyond which the international realm was deemed to be a moral-free zone. Even a fierce critic of realism such as the political philosopher Michael Walzer eloquently defended a presumption against intervention:

> The boundaries that exist at any moment in time are likely to be arbitrary, poorly drawn, the products of ancient wars. The mapmakers are likely to have been ignorant, drunken, or corrupt. Nevertheless, these lines establish a habitable world. Within that world, men and women (let us assume) are safe from attack; once the lines are crossed, safety is gone . . . it is only common sense, then, to attach great importance to boundaries. Rights in the world have value only if they also have dimension.[4]

The universality of human rights was proclaimed in the Universal Declaration of Human Rights adopted by the UN General Assembly in 1948 and genocide was outlawed in the 1948 Genocide Convention. But no means was established to enforce these decrees. The protection of human rights was not judged lawful grounds for military action. For most of the second half of the twentieth century a norm of non-intervention reigned supreme. There were interventions, like that of the USA in Vietnam. Some interventions were undertaken for humanitarian reasons or, at least, had humanitarian outcomes. But so absolute was the norm against humanitarian intervention that, even when exceptions occurred, they were explained away. Despite evidence to the contrary, the international community resolutely refused to recognize humanitarian interventions.

In 1971 India invaded East Pakistan to prevent the massacre of the Bengali people by the West Pakistan Army. The Indian government initially sought to justify its action on humanitarian grounds. But when this evoked no sympathy in the Security Council, it quickly switched to a claim that it was acting in self-defence. This included a strained extension of the concept of self-defence to cover defence against 'refugee aggression' from the masses fleeing into India from East Pakistan.[5] The reluctance of the international community to sanction military action for humanitarian reasons led the Indian Ambassador to berate his fellow members of the Security Council: 'What ... has happened to our conventions on human rights, self-determination, and so on?'[6] 'Why', he asked, were members 'shy about speaking about human rights ... What has happened to the justice part (of the UN Charter)?'[7] His appeals fell on deaf ears.

In 1979 Vietnam invaded Cambodia and toppled the Pol Pot regime that had slaughtered 1.7 million of its own people and was threatening the lives of many more. Further genocide was successfully stopped. Later in the same year Tanzania invaded Uganda to put an end to the brutal oppression of the Amin regime. Both Vietnam and Tanzania sought to defend their actions as undertaken in self-defence. The international community, grateful to see the end of the Amin regime, turned a blind eye to the Tanzanian intervention, which was not even discussed in the Security Council. But the Security Council roundly condemned the Vietnamese intervention, viewing it through the distorting prism of the Cold War, as an illegitimate extension of territorial influence by a Russian satellite state, rather than a humanitarian action that saved many hundreds of thousands of lives.

The norm of non-intervention not only fitted with the prevailing theory of state sovereignty. It also accorded with the prudence induced by the nuclear stalemate between the rival superpowers. During the long years of the Cold War the doctrine of the inviolability of boundaries went largely unchallenged. Superpower rivalry meant there was little prospect of the Security Council agreeing to collective action under Chapter VII, while the risk of nuclear escalation induced a cautious prudence in inter-state behaviour.

With the ending of the Cold War the unanimous international condemnation of Saddam's invasion of Kuwait in 1990 appeared to offer hope that the UN might recover its capacity for effective action. As we explored in Chapter 8, the thawing of the bipolar glacier also released ethnic rivalries and tensions leading to mayhem and massacre within Europe itself. Human rights were massively under threat not in a distant continent but right in the heart of Europe. Meanwhile, globalization meant that news channels carried instant detailed reports of atrocities virtually wherever they occurred in the world.

An emerging norm for intervention?

When I first argued in the early 1990s that such human-rights abuses justified military action to prevent them, mine was a lonely voice.[8] Such views were also unwelcome within the UK Ministry of Defence where I was working. The then Conservative administration was desperately seeking to avoid entanglement in what was perceived as a hopeless Balkans imbroglio of warring states and factions within Bosnia. It is often assumed by critics of humanitarian intervention that governments and their military advisers are naturally predisposed to intervene and have to be restrained from doing so by public opinion. In my experience the reverse is more likely to be true. There was a deep reluctance in the early 1990s on the part of all Western governments to intervene to prevent mass slaughter, even when this was taking place within their own continent of Europe. What shifted government behaviour was in large measure a public outcry for action to be taken.

For, as the 1990s advanced, the moral clamour for intervention, fuelled by media reports of atrocities, gradually grew with increasing intensity. More people were no longer prepared to accept that state boundaries should represent impenetrable barriers behind which torture and genocide should be freely allowed to take place. By the end of the decade, even hard-nosed international-relations theorists were beginning to question some of the presumptions of political realism and to recognize that the concept of a state invented at Westphalia was neither the permanent feature of the human condition nor yet the boundary of human moral endeavour that their theory presupposed.[9] Shifting opinion began, albeit gradually and haltingly, to be reflected in the changing practice of governments.

In 1994 the international community failed to intervene to prevent the genocide in Rwanda when over 800,000 Tutsis were murdered at the instigation of the Hutu-dominated government. The genocide was not carried out by a sophisticated military machine deploying the latest equipment and technology. Most of the killings were done by mobs wielding machetes. A subsequent study by the Carnegie Commission on Preventing Deadly Conflict concluded that a brigade-level intervention by sophisticated Western forces could have prevented the genocide.[10] But the USA, still smarting from the loss of eighteen rangers in their botched intervention the previous year in Somalia, and with support from the UK in the UN Security Council, turned its face against intervention. Reluctant to accept the responsibilities that the UN Convention on Genocide imposes on its signatories once genocide is declared, they instead sought to argue that what was taking place was not genocide but inter-tribal civil war.[11] In 1995 UN peacekeepers failed to prevent the massacre of over 8,000 Bosnians at Srebrenica.

But in 1999 NATO launched military operations to persuade the Serbian government to desist from ethnic cleansing of the Kosovar Albanians in what was openly justified as a humanitarian operation. At the height of the NATO campaign, on 22 April 1999, Prime Minister Blair set out his 'Doctrine of the International Community' in a speech to the Chicago Economic Club, confidently proclaiming: 'We are all internationalists now whether we like it or not . . . We cannot turn our backs on conflicts and the violation of human rights if we still want to be secure.'[12]

In 2004 world leaders meeting in New York on the tenth anniversary of the Rwanda massacre vowed never to allow this to happen again. Summing up the prevailing international mood, Tony Blair declared: 'If Rwanda happened again today as it did in 1994 when a million people were slaughtered in cold blood we would have a moral duty to act there also.'[13]

The moral clamour has not just changed the political rhetoric and agenda but has also elicited important shifts in international legal thinking. Successive British Attorney Generals have argued for a right of intervention in the face of imminent or actual humanitarian catastrophe. This doctrine, developed in response to the humanitarian catastrophe facing the Kurds in northern Iraq in 1991, was most clearly explained in public by Baroness Symons as a justification for the NATO operations in Kosovo. Speaking in the House of Lords on 6 May 1999, she said:

> There is no general doctrine of humanitarian necessity in international law. Cases have nonetheless arisen (as in northern Iraq in 1991) when, in the light of all the circumstances, a limited use of force was justifiable in support of purposes laid down by the Security Council but without the Council's express authorisation when that was the only means to avert an immediate and overwhelming humanitarian catastrophe.[14]

The British interpretation of the legal position was far from universally shared. But at the start of the new millennium there were two important reports by international commissions that marked a significant change in international thinking.

The 2001 International Commission on Intervention and State Sovereignty, sponsored by the Canadian government, called on the international community to recognize its 'international responsibility to protect'. This new concept reflected the idea that 'sovereign states have a responsibility to protect their own citizens from avoidable catastrophe—from mass murder and rape, from starvation—but that when they are unwilling or unable to do so that responsibility must be borne by the broader community of states'.[15] The principle of non-intervention accordingly yields to an 'international responsibility to protect'.[16] Sovereignty brings with it not just rights but responsibilities. A state that fails to fulfil its responsibility to protect its own people may forfeit its right to non-intervention. There would be a just cause for military intervention where there is:

> serious and irreparable harm occurring to human beings or imminently likely to occur of the following kind:
>
> A. *large-scale loss of life*, actual or apprehended, with genocidal intent or not, which is the product of deliberate state action, or state neglect or inability to act, or a failed state situation; or
> B. *large-scale 'ethnic cleansing'*, actual or apprehended, whether carried out by killing, forced expulsion, acts of terror or rape.[17]

These conclusions were echoed in the December 2004 report by the UN Secretary General's High Level Panel. This report endorsed what it called

> the emerging norm of a responsibility to protect citizens from large scale violence that is held, first and foremost, by national authorities. When a State fails to protect its citizens, the international community then has a further responsibility to act, through humanitarian operations, monitoring missions and diplomatic pressure—and with force, if necessary, though as a last resort.[18]

The threat must be serious, involving 'genocide and other large-scale killing, ethnic cleansing or serious violations of international humanitarian law, actual or imminently apprehended'.[19] The responsibility of a state to protect its own people and, if it fails to do so, for the international community to act was subsequently endorsed at the UN Summit on 14–16 September 2005. The declaration, endorsed by Heads of State and Government, states:

Each individual state has the responsibility to protect its population from genocide, war crimes, ethnic cleansing and crimes against humanity...We are prepared to take collective action, in a timely and decisive manner, through the Security Council, in accordance with the Charter, including Chapter VII, on a case-by-case basis and in cooperation with relevant regional organisations as appropriate, should peaceful means be inadequate and national authorities manifestly fail to protect their populations from genocide, war crimes, ethnic cleansing and crimes against humanity.[20]

However qualified and convoluted was the language, the declaration's acceptance of an international responsibility to protect is clear and significant. As Prime Minister Tony Blair noted: 'For the first time at this summit we are agreed that states do not have the right to do what they will within their own borders.'[21]

So by 2005 it looked as if the long and intense debate that had raged during the 1990s about humanitarian intervention had finally been won by the interventionists. Humanitarian intervention had at last been sanctioned by the international community. Or had it?

A retreat from humanitarian intervention?

The language of the Summit declaration is more hedged in with caveats than that of the two preceding high-level reports. The occasions for action are no longer 'large-scale killings, actual or apprehended' or 'large-scale ethnic cleansing' but the more circumscribed 'genocide, war crimes, ethnic cleansing and crimes against humanity'. Moreover, responsibility devolves to the international community to act not when states are 'unable or unwilling' to protect their populations from such scourges but when they 'manifestly fail' to do so. There is also no mention of the 'precautionary principles', based on the just war criteria, that were included in both the preceding high-level international reports designed to guide when and how interventions may take place.[22] The inclusion of such criteria was opposed on somewhat inconsistent grounds by, on the one hand, the USA fearing it would constrain its freedom of action and, on the other, by Russia and China fearful it might encourage action bypassing the Security Council.[23]

The International Commission had conceded that, if the UN Security Council failed to act responsibly, states would act on their own initiative and that it was a real question whether more harm was thereby done, 'in the damage to the international order if the Security Council is bypassed or in the damage to that order if human beings are slaughtered while the Security Council stands by'.[24] By contrast, the Summit declaration, while conceding that non-consensual action may be necessary, offers no such solace to those espousing unilateral humanitarian intervention. The only action contemplated is collective action through the Security Council and even this is to be considered on a 'case-by-case basis'.

More importantly, whatever fine words remained in the Summit declaration, the international community has subsequently shown little appetite for humanitarian intervention. The NATO action in Kosovo remains the only recent example of a successful humanitarian intervention, undertaken without the consent of the state involved. Indeed, it was ironic that, even as the UN held its special ceremony in 2004 to commemorate the tenth anniversary of the Rwanda genocide, reports were reaching New York of large-scale killings taking place in Darfur, the Western providence of Sudan. The world had ignored the civil war that had been raging in Sudan for nearly twenty years between the Muslim North and Christian South, claiming two million lives. But with the tragedy of Rwanda so fresh in the memory there were grounds for hoping that the brutal oppression in Darfur would attract the attention and action of the world.

Human-rights violations had started in early 2003 when an uprising by the Muslim African population in Darfur had been violently suppressed by the Muslim Khartoum government, assisted by the notorious *Janjaweed* militia. By the spring of 2004 the scale of human-rights violations had escalated dramatically. In June 2004 the African Union sent 10 monitors to the region followed by a 300-strong protection force.

Throughout the autumn of 2004 the UN debated the crisis on a number of occasions. No action was, however, agreed, not even a modest proposal to impose a no-fly zone. China, a large importer of oil from Sudan, threatened its veto. The USA and the UK, while expressing concern, were preoccupied with Iraq. It was not until July 2007 that the UN finally agreed a Security Council Resolution, UNSCR 1769, authorizing deployment of a new joint UN/African Union peacekeeping force of 26,000 troops and police to replace the ill-equipped and under-resourced African Union force. But the obduracy and prevarications of the Sudanese government and the tardiness of donor nations delayed the effective deployment of the force. By December 2009 only 19,900 troops and police had been deployed to keep peace in a territory the size of France. By then an estimated 300,000 had died, a third brutally murdered and the rest dying from hunger and disease caused by the conflict. Over two million displaced persons had fled to neighbouring Chad and in 2010 remain there too frightened to return to their homes.

Despite all the glowing rhetoric on the tenth anniversary of Rwanda, the world had once more failed to intervene effectively. As Kofi Annan summed it up on a BBC *Panorama* programme on 3 July 2005: 'We were slow, hesitant, uncaring and we had learnt nothing from Rwanda.'[25]

Prospects for humanitarian intervention elsewhere look similarly bleak. Indeed, even a modest proposal to bring pressure to bear on the regime of President Mugabe, which was brutally terrorizing and murdering the people in Zimbabwe, failed to secure Security Council support. The US-drafted Security Council Resolution, imposing an arms embargo, travel ban, and limited financial sanctions targeted at individual members of the regime, was vetoed by Russia and China on 11 July 2008. They argued that the UN was not entitled to intervene in the internal affairs of states, the same grounds they had invoked earlier against intervention in Sudan and Kosovo. It was as if the 2005 UN Summit had never taken place, as if the concept of an international responsibility to protect had never been endorsed. Liberal interventionism began to appear as a brief and illusory episode of moral concern in an enduring narrative of statist realpolitik.

So, what has gone wrong? Did the liberal interventionists win the argument but lose the war?

Rewinning the argument for intervention

Prospects for humanitarian intervention are perhaps not quite as gloomy as this analysis suggests. Some military operations being undertaken in 2010 have a humanitarian dimension, such as US and NATO operations in Afghanistan. These were initially undertaken in 2001 in self-defence but have in the years since then also acquired a significant and openly (if intermittently) acknowledged humanitarian component. Nonetheless, there is a current reluctance to mount further operations, such as in Kosovo, with a primarily humanitarian objective.

A major cause of this reluctance has been the concerns aroused by the US-led intervention in Iraq. This intervention, as discussed in the previous chapter, provoked widespread criticism in the international community. It has also had two consequences for the wider debate on humanitarian intervention. First, there has been the practical consequence that the two countries best equipped to undertake military interventions, the USA and the UK, have been heavily engaged in Iraq and Afghanistan, and so have had few forces to spare for elsewhere, such as Darfur. But secondly, and most importantly, the Iraq intervention in 2003 reinforced the concerns already felt by many smaller countries that any right of humanitarian intervention would be abused by the great powers, who would be tempted to cloak military actions undertaken for reasons of realpolitik in the guise of humanitarian motives. These concerns were further fuelled by the US government's arrogation to itself of a right of pre-emptive military action in its new doctrine of pre-emption, whose defects we examined in Chapter 9. The fear is that humanitarian intervention may be misused to mask a new form of Western colonial imperialism.

These concerns are genuinely felt. They explain some of the qualifications that crept into the 2005 Summit Declaration from the pellucid prose of the preceding high-level reports. They also explain, in part, why the doctrine of the inviolability of state borders held sway for so long. But the reasons why the UN summit modified the doctrine of the inviolability of state borders remain valid. Sovereignty entails responsibilities, as well as rights, including the responsibility of a government to protect its people. If a government fails to exercise that right, the international community, operating in the first instance through the UN Security Council, has a responsibility to do so itself.

The doctrine of the impermeability of state boundaries was rightly rejected by the 2005 UN Summit. There is, therefore, no justification for using the injustice of the Iraq intervention as a pretext for reinstating the doctrine. Nor should it be used to try to undermine the case for humanitarian intervention where, as in Darfur, gross abuses of human rights are taking place. For the Iraq intervention was not a humanitarian intervention. It is illogical to suggest that, because one intervention, not itself undertaken for humanitarian reasons, was unjust, all humanitarian interventions are unjust.

Moreover, the shift in international thinking in favour of humanitarian intervention does not, as some had feared, mark the end of the stability and order of the international system of sovereign states. What is proposed is not the abolition of state sovereignty but rather some rebalancing of the rights of states to grant greater recognition to the rights of individuals. State sovereignty remains important. But it is no longer accorded the absolute status that it had been accorded by the UN Charter. The choice posed by some opponents of intervention between order and justice is an unreal one. It is possible to have both. The case for humanitarian intervention remains as strong as ever.

If the international community is to recover its confidence in humanitarian intervention, it is, however, essential that the criteria for a just intervention should be clearly defined and agreed in advance and rigorously and consistently applied in practice. An ethical foreign policy needs to be underpinned by robust and soundly based ethical reasoning. The just war criteria are not, as some have suggested, optional extras that can be readily dispensed with.[26] They furnish essential guidance for governments and the international community to determine when interventions may legitimately be undertaken; and when they may not. They impose crucial constraints on the behaviour of states, including their ability to take pre-emptive action. They provide the basis not only for criticizing the United Nations for its failure to intervene, for example, in Rwanda, but also for criticizing interventions by states that fail to meet the criteria, such as that in Iraq. They are a crucial restraint on the abuse of power by states. For that reason, it was hardly surprising that some states, wishing to avoid such restraint, opposed the public espousal of criteria in the UN Summit declaration. But such lack of scruple on the part of some states hardly furnishes a justification for supposing that the international community can or should seek to manage without them. On the contrary, the just war criteria are indispensable guides to the morality of the actions of states, and necessary constraints on their behaviour.

For just war doctrine insists that it is not enough for there to be a just cause. All the just war conditions must be met. A humanitarian intervention will be just only if undertaken: with competent authority, for a just cause, with right intention, as a last resort, and if the harm judged likely to result is not disproportionate to the good to be achieved, taking into account the prospects of success; while in its conduct the principles of proportion and non-combatant immunity should be complied with; and the intervention should end in the establishment of a just peace.

Applying the just war criteria

Let us consider how each of these principles should be applied to a humanitarian intervention.

Jus ad bellum

Competent authority

Within the classic just war tradition competent authority belongs to governments. The requirement, accordingly, precludes bellicose actions by private
individuals. In recent years just war commentators have sought to extend this
to a requirement for UN authorization of interventions other than for self-
defence. The point was well made in 1984 by Hedley Bull: 'Ultimately, we
have a rule of non-intervention because unilateral intervention threatens the
harmony and concord of the society of sovereign states. If, however, an
intervention itself expresses the collective will of the society of states, it may
be carried out without bringing that harmony and concord into jeopardy.'[27]

UN authorization is, therefore, highly desirable and would be sufficient to
establish competent authority. As the International Commission on Intervention and State Sovereignty noted: 'There is no better or more appropriate
body than the UN Security Council to authorize military intervention for
humanitarian purposes.'[28] There are compelling reasons why a government
contemplating military action should seek explicit authorization from the UN
for military operations. But the Security Council is composed of sovereign
states that may not always act from the best of motives. The key question is
whether UN authorization is always necessary. The answer, as we suggested
in Chapter 4, is that there may be a graduating scale, depending on the degree
of international consensus and the gravity and urgency of the crisis to be
averted. So the NATO humanitarian intervention in Kosovo, while lacking
the authority of a UN Security Council resolution because of fears it would
be vetoed by Russia or China, could, nonetheless, be deemed to be justified,
since it commanded substantial international support and the humanitarian
crisis was grave and urgent. Moreover, at the extreme, the gravity and
urgency of a humanitarian crisis may be so great as to require intervention
even where international consensus is lacking. The then Secretary General of
the United Nations, Kofi Annan, publicly mused on such difficult cases in an
address to the UN General Assembly on 20 September 1999. Recalling the

events of Rwanda, he asked: 'If, in those dark days and hours leading up to the 1994 genocide, a coalition of states had been prepared to act in defence of the Tutsi population but did not receive prompt Council authorization, should such a coalition have stood aside as the horror unfolded?'[29] The implication was that they should not.

Last Resort

The requirement that military action should be undertaken only as a last resort does not mean that war should be resorted to only temporally last after all other options have been tried and failed. Indeed, postponing a humanitarian intervention until last in time may be a recipe for disaster, as the lapse in time may allow the humanitarian crisis to worsen and make military intervention more difficult.

The last-resort condition requires rather that war should be—not temporally but logically—last, preferred only if other options are judged unlikely to succeed. Since the use of force is likely to involve the infliction of harm, it is important that other options, including political and diplomatic measures, are carefully considered. But force may not always be avoidable. In determining whether the last-resort condition is met, much depends on what is deemed to be the cause for military action and how urgent is the need for intervention. If the grounds for a military operation are humanitarian—for example, to prevent large-scale killings being carried out by a brutal dictator—the need for action may, indeed, be sooner rather than later.

Just cause

The next requirement is that there is a just cause for the sake of which the military action is undertaken. The grounds for humanitarian intervention are specified in the Summit declaration as 'genocide, war crimes, ethnic cleansing and crimes against humanity'. These would certainly constitute grounds for intervention, even without the consent of the state in which intervention is taking place. Indeed, if the state is itself implicated in such crimes, its consent is most unlikely to be forthcoming. In defining what constitutes a just cause for humanitarian intervention, it is important that we should not make it too easy for states to intervene. There are strong reasons against intervention, and the principle of non-intervention should be lifted only when the threat to human rights is sufficiently dire.

On the other hand, it is important to avoid a cliff-edge approach of waiting to see whether the deaths and suffering taking place in a foreign calamity really amount to a humanitarian catastrophe before contemplating intervention. If the barrier is set too high or too steep, the risk remains of any intervention being too little, too late, or even not happening at all. Indeed, it is arguable that this is just what happened in Rwanda in 1994. As the days and weeks went by and only a few thousand more Tutsis were slaughtered, the international community argued among itself whether this really constituted genocide requiring intervention; or whether, as the USA argued, the killings were rather attributable to renewed fighting in the civil war. If the bar is set too high, interventions are likely never to take place or to take place too late. There would, therefore, be merit in broadening the narrow grounds for intervention specified in the Summit declaration at least to cover 'the large-scale killing' envisaged in the two preceding high-level panel reports.

Right intention

It is not enough for there to be a just cause. Just war teaching also insists that the military action must be undertaken for the sake of that cause, undertaken with what the tradition calls right intention. An imperial adventure masked under a humanitarian cloak would be forbidden.

Proportion

Even if a just cause exists, military action cannot be justified unless it is judged likely to bring about more good than harm, taking into account the prospects for success. This balancing of consequences is a hard condition to meet. For it involves difficult decisions made in conditions of uncertainty and fine judgements about the likely outcome of military action. Yet such judgements, however difficult, must be made. For military action, even undertaken for humanitarian purposes, can be justified only if more good than harm is judged likely to result.

Jus in bello

The just war tradition requires that the conditions of proportion and discrimination are met in the conduct of military operations. The former requires that, for each individual military operation, the military force used should be proportionate to the objectives to be achieved. The principle of discrimination requires that non-combatant casualties should be minimized. Both these conditions need to be met in the conduct of humanitarian interventions. Indeed, since the objective of humanitarian intervention is to protect innocent lives, the need to avoid any action that could put these at risk is paramount. Failure to protect civilians at the tactical level can undermine the strategic—humanitarian—objectives of a mission.

Jus post bellum

The just war tradition always recognized that it is not enough for a war to begin justly and to be conducted justly but that it must also end justly. Within the classic development of the tradition that requirement is implicit in other principles. It is, however, particularly helpful in assessing humanitarian interventions to separate out *jus post bellum* as a condition in order to give it greater prominence. For where the international community intervenes in a failed state or to stop a government massively oppressing its own people, some political reconstitution, including regime change, is likely to be a necessary constituent of any *post-bellum* settlement. Without political reconstitution, the oppression that gave rise to the intervention is likely to recur.

Some interventions may be quick in-and-out rescue operations, like the UK intervention in Sierra Leone in 2000 that, with a relatively small but highly effective force, successfully removed the rebel threats to President Kabbah's incipient democracy. Moreover, the state that intervenes may not necessarily be the state committed to nation-building, since a division of labour such as that between NATO and the UN and European Union in Kosovo may be appropriate. But intervention is seldom an easy option, and an intervening state needs, in Prime Minister Tony Blair's cautionary words during the Kosovo conflict, to 'be prepared for the long term'.[30] A state contemplating intervention must include the *post-bellum* settlement in the overall balance of consequences to be assessed. It must also crucially have a carefully thought-out plan for dealing with *post-bellum* conditions to ensure that the military intervention ends justly.

The just war criteria all have to be satisfied before military action can be justified. They provide a powerful constraint against military action and reassurance for those concerned that, if humanitarian intervention is licensed, interventions might be undertaken too readily. But just war teaching also insists that, if the lives of many innocents are at stake, interventions should not be undertaken too reluctantly. If all the just war criteria are met, it is morally permissible to intervene militarily in the affairs of another state. Indeed, we may have not just a right to intervene but also, on occasion, a duty to do so.

Is there a duty to intervene?

This may seem a step too far. For, if we have a duty to intervene, how do we avoid becoming responsible for curing all the ills of the world? How do we avoid a slide towards an ethic of universal responsibility that is both exhausting and impractical? The realist solved this dilemma by setting the limit of responsibility at the boundary of the state. That limit is too arbitrary. But if our responsibility extends beyond the boundary of the state, where does it stop? For what suffering in the world are we responsible?

If consequences are all that matter, it may be difficult to set limits. For the consequences of the actions of the machete-wielding Hutus, and of the inaction of those governments who failed to intervene, were the same: the deaths of many hundreds of thousands of Rwandans. But it is absurd to suppose that the governments who failed to intervene and those committing the genocide bear equal responsibility. It may, therefore, be suggested that we should distinguish between those ills in the world that we intend and for which we have full responsibility; and those that we do not intend but merely allow to happen. No Western state intended the deaths of the Tutsis macheted to death in Rwanda, so no Western state was responsible for those deaths. Even if we had a right to intervene, it did not follow that we had a duty to do so. But lack of intention appears then to furnish too easy a way to evade moral responsibility. There is an important distinction between what we intend and what we do not intend to do. But it is not just the consequences we intend for which we can be held responsible. Lack of intention does not necessarily excuse our failure to prevent genocide taking place. So how are we to decide for what evils in the world we are to be held responsible?

Virtuous consequentialism suggests that ethical reasoning should be guided—and moral responsibility apportioned—by a judicious balancing of both the agent's mental states and capabilities and the consequences of his agency. Such judgements require the careful exercise of practical wisdom. We assess the moral quality of an action or inaction not, as the absolutist suggests, by applying a simple cut-off procedure determined by the presence or absence of intentions; nor, as the consequentialist proposes, by attending only to consequences. We deploy rather a graduating scale on which we assess degrees of mental responsibility, judged by the extent to which the consequences are within the agent's control and consented to by him; and weigh these up together with the assessed balance of good and ill to be achieved, taking into account both the nature and the probability of the consequences. Where the consequences are within the agent's control and intended by him, full responsibility rests with the agent. But where great harm may result, mere lack of intention would not excuse an act, or an omission to act, whose consequences we foresaw, could have prevented, and, by failing to prevent, could be judged to have consented to. At the other end of the spectrum of responsibility, where we have no knowledge or control over events, we bear no moral blame. In between these extremes there will be variations in moral responsibility, depending on the degree of consent and control and the gravity of the consequences, with responsibility reducing as the causal chain lengthens and becomes gappier and our control and consent diminish.

So, for what suffering in the world can we be held responsible? Virtuous consequentialism answers that it is suffering of which we are fully aware, that through our action we could prevent; and that, if we do nothing to prevent, we can be deemed to have consented to. In assessing moral responsibility for the deaths of strangers, what matters is: on the one hand, how far we have knowledge of what is happening, have control or influence over the events, and, through our action or failure to act, may be deemed to have consented to the deaths; and, on the other hand, the seriousness and gravity of the consequences of our agency.

Where there are major abuses of human rights—mass killings or ethnic cleansing—the consequences are, *ex hypothesi,* of extreme gravity. If we know what is happening and can do something to prevent it but do not do so, we can be judged to have consented to its occurrence. In such circum-stances, and assuming all the just war criteria are met, it is reasonable to conclude that we have not just a right but a responsibility to intervene. We have, in that sense, a duty to save the lives of the innocent.

But, if that is so, to whom does this duty fall? In the wake of the genocide in Rwanda, Kofi Annan argued that everyone has a duty to prevent geno-cide. 'Why', he asked, 'did no-one intervene? The question should not be addressed only to the United Nations, or even its member states . . . Each of us as an individual has to take his or her share of responsibility.'[31] That is true. But a duty that falls to everyone is a duty too widely extended to have real practical impact. The UN High Level Panel report talks about the responsibility falling to the 'international community'. But who in the international community? The preferred answer is the UN. But the UN Security Council, dominated by sovereign states pursuing their own interests, may not always be willing or able to act. Moreover, even where the Security Council authorizes military action, the UN still has to rely upon states to furnish the forces, since it has no military forces of its own.

But which states? If it is always a few self-selecting powerful Western states, such as the USA and the UK, they risk becoming oppressed with 'intervention fatigue' and their forces overstretched, particularly since an intervening state may need to stay after the intervention to assist in rebuilding the state. Such a 'coalition of the willing' or an 'alliance of democracies'[32] may also be open to the charge of 'humanitarian imperialism', to the accusation that the humanitarian interventions mask a new form of Western colonial expansionism.

So which states? Moral responsibility presupposes capability: if we ought to do something, this presupposes we can do it. The answer is, therefore, those states best placed and able to help. This is not just a matter of having the resources and capability to intervene. It may also be a matter of having particular knowledge or influence over the situation, through geographical or historical association, cultural ties or political or military alliance. So the state best placed to help may be a neighbour, as with Tanzania's intervention in Uganda. It may be a regional organization, such as the African Union in Darfur or NATO in Kosovo. It may be a former colonial power such as the UK, which successfully intervened at the request of the threatened democratic government in Sierra Leone.

Such considerations may provide practical guidance to help us choose between humanitarian interventions and to set some practical limits to our responsibilities. But the demands of ethics can still be very challenging. For, suppose the scale of suffering in a distant land is very great and widely reported in the media. Suppose, further, that we have the capability to do something to relieve that suffering successfully. The conditions of knowledge, consent, and control are fulfilled. Let us suppose all the criteria of the just war are met. In those circumstances, it may be difficult to resist calls for intervention in far away countries, to which our only link is shared humanity. For, as Michael Walzer notes: 'Whenever the filthy work can be stopped, it should be stopped. And if not by us, the supposedly decent people of the world, then by whom?'[33]

Conclusion: a return to the just war vision

The just war criteria set clear limits to when force can justifiably be used and so constrain the actions of states. Against those criteria, the 2003 Iraq intervention stands condemned. But the just war tradition also recognizes that the use of force may sometimes be not merely morally permissible but required. The filthy work of mass killing and ethnic cleansing needs to be stopped. The concerns raised by the Iraq intervention should not be used as an excuse to inhibit the international community from acting, where this would be licensed by the just war criteria, to prevent gross abuses of human rights, where and when they occur.

But the Iraq intervention is only part of the explanation for the reluctance of the international community to accept its newly defined responsibilities. A deeper reason is that noted at the outset of this chapter: that the sway of morality in international affairs remains fragile. For some states, like some individuals, remain hesitant to take the final step of extending the claims of morality to the international community. There are amoral states, just as there are amoral individuals like Thrasymachus. All states, just like individuals, operate from a mixture of motives, with moral considerations not always accorded the weight that they should be. Just as individuals do not always live up to the moral standards to which they aspire, neither do states. But in neither case does that invalidate the moral standards.

It has been an aim of this book to insist that the international realm is not a moral-free zone. The UN Summit's recognition of an international responsibility to protect was an important victory for morality. It was a belated rediscovery in the twenty-first century of the altruism and universality of the just war principles as taught by Vitoria in the sixteenth century. It is crucial that the concessions rewon for morality in 2005 are not lost. But the hold of morality in the international realm is precarious. It needs to be constantly guarded, protected, and promoted by concerned members of the international community, by 'us the supposedly decent people of the world'. Just as within states moral rules, such as the prohibition on murder, are reinforced with the force of law, so too do enforcement mechanisms need to be strengthened in the international realm through the vigorous working of institutions, such as the International Criminal Court, whose operations we shall explore in the next chapter. For without vigilance in support of the universal claims of morality, another genocide like Rwanda will occur and the world will, once again, as it did in 1994, stand idly by while millions are slaughtered. The injured stranger whom we were called upon to help in the Gospel story lay on the road to Jericho. Today she could be huddled with her family in a hut in Darfur, fearfully awaiting the arrival of the *Janjaweed*.

TWELVE

Making War Just

If you could hear, at every jolt, the blood
Come gargling from the froth-corrupted lungs
Bitten as the cud
Of vile, incurable sores on innocent tongues,
My friend, you would not tell with such high zest
To children ardent for some desperate glory,
The old Lie: *Dulce et decorum est*
Pro patria mori.

Wilfred Owen, 'Dulce et Decorum Est'

CAPTAIN: We go to gain a little patch of ground
That hath in it no profit but the name

Hamlet, Act IV, sc. 4

The Ypres cloth hall

In the centre of the small Belgian market town of Ypres there is a magnificent medieval cloth hall. Inside the hall there is an exhibition, enlivened with the latest technology, called *In Flanders Fields*. This vividly tells the story of the First World War battles that took place only a few kilometres from the town within that small corner of Belgium to which the allies desperately clung, known as the Ypres Salient. Sadly, no longer on display, from the technologically unembellished exhibition that used to be in the hall, is a series of faded photographic prints of the cloth hall itself. These showed, frame by frame, the dismal progress of the cloth hall during the war: from medieval Gothic splendour to a pile of rubble. The present building is not original but a painstaking reconstruction of the medieval building that was completely destroyed during the war.

No one set out to destroy the cloth hall. It was not, like Coventry Cathedral, bombed. Nor was it subject to deliberate assault. It was just that Ypres was only 5 kilometres from the front line where the British and German trenches faced each other. The intensity of the artillery barrages that each side hurled at the other across the trenches was such that an abundance of stray shrapnel gradually reduced the cloth hall to a pile of rubble. Its destruction was an accident of war. The demolition was collateral damage from the nearby fighting within the Ypres Salient, in which for four years each side struggled to wrest territory from the other. The amount gained usually turned out to be no more than 'a little patch of ground'—a few metres or, at most, kilometres of shell-pocked waste land. Over half a million men on both sides died within the Salient. The names of nearly 55,000 British and Commonwealth soldiers who fell there, listed as missing in action, are inscribed on the Menin Gate memorial on the outskirts of Ypres. Every evening at 8 p.m. a last post is sounded to commemorate those who died.

It is impossible to visit Ypres without coming away with an abiding sense of both the horror and the futility of war. But, if war is so horrific and futile, why do we tolerate it? Should not the primary goal of all political endeavour be the abolition of war?

The abolition of war

The abolition of war has long been an aspiration of mankind. A few years before the First World—in 1899 and 1907—statesmen and diplomats had been invited by Tsar Nicholas II to conferences in The Hague to discuss the abolition of war and the establishment of an international court for the settlement of disputes by arbitration. Such arbitration had been adumbrated by the sixteenth-century just war thinker Francisco Suarez, who had counselled princes in cases where the justice of their claims were finely balanced to 'submit the matter to the decision of good men'.[1] Long before that, in the eighth century BC, the prophet Isaiah had looked forward to a time of peace when the lamb could lie down with the lion.[2]

But the path to peace is strewn with obstacles. The Hague convention did nothing to prevent the First World War, and a follow-up conference planned to take place in 1915 had to be abandoned because of the war. As Martin Luther acerbically remarked of Isaiah's prophecy, if the lion lies down with the lamb, the lambs are likely to need regular replacement.[3]

Despite all the protestations at the end of the First World War that it had been a war to end all wars, twenty-one years later Europe was once again convulsed with war. Britain once more, and with great reluctance, took up arms, initially alone with its Commonwealth dominions, but later joined by a growing coalition of allies led by the United States and Soviet Union, to defeat the monstrous tyrannies of fascism. This was a war that, however horrific, few regarded as futile and most deemed to be both necessary and just.

In his 1998 Reith lectures, the British military historian John Keegan noted that the rides of three of the four horsemen of the Apocalypse, and particularly famine and pestilence, had been halted and even turned back in the previous ninety years. But war still rode on and had been the scourge of the twentieth century, particularly through the global wars of the first half of that century. Keegan, nonetheless, expressed the hope that 'the worst of war is now behind us and that mankind, with vigilance and resolution, will henceforth be able to conduct the affairs of the world in a way that allows war a diminishing part'.[4]

For many, including Keegan, hopes of abolishing, or at least reducing the incidence of, war have rested on the extension of international law and the strengthening of international institutions.[5] Some have looked towards the establishment of a world government. A better world order was the aim of those who established the League of Nations Society in 1915. The League of Nations failed, lacking universal membership and an effective enforcement mechanism. But it was hoped that the United Nations, set up in 1945 after the Second World War, could address these defects by providing a universal forum and more effective mechanisms for promoting peace by the collective action of sovereign states. The United Nations was not designed as an incipient world government. But many have hoped that its institutions could be developed so that it might eventually become the basis for world government.[6] Within states, violence has been controlled by the rule of law, enforced by agents of the state entrusted with a monopoly on the organized use of force. Just so, it is hoped that, internationally, violence could be constrained by the international rule of law, enforced by a world government wielding a monopoly on the use of force.[7] War could then be banned.

But could it? Liberal philosophers, their consciences appalled by the horrors of war, have fondly supposed that there is some simple, easy solution that, if only all men of good will cooperated together to implement, could remove the threat of war. For Tom Paine the solution lay in the promotion of democracy; for Bentham in the abolition of colonial ambitions and secret diplomacy; while John Stuart Mill held that commerce would rapidly render war obsolete.[8] In the twentieth and twenty-first centuries hopes have rested, with more justification, on the strengthening of international institutions. In all these areas can progress be made. But so long as the causes of war—including the Thucydidean triad of 'security, honour and self-interest' noted in Chapter 1—still persist, even the superimposition of strengthened international structures on the world as it is would not of itself succeed in abolishing war. For the world would remain riven by political, religious, cultural, and tribal rivalries, and marred by gross inequalities in the distribution of the earth's resources. The grounds, and hence occasions, for conflict would still abound.

The challenge presented by war might simply mutate. To enforce peace in such a troubled world, a world government would need to be entrusted with massive coercive power, including a monopoly on nuclear force. Our concern might then be that such a powerful world government, remote from the people whose destiny it controlled, might degenerate into a 'soulless despotism', as Kant feared in his pamphlet on *Perpetual Peace*.[9] Far from abolishing wars, its 'police' actions might be as brutal as any inter-state wars. The name of war might have been banned, but its reality would persist.

Fears that an all-powerful world government could itself become tyrannical explain the reluctance of sovereign states to yield a monopoly of force, including nuclear force, to such a body. They also explain, in part, their reluctance even to adopt the more modest step of assigning military forces permanently to the United Nations. Sixty-five years since its inception, the United Nations still has no standing forces and needs to beg and plead for the assignment of forces from sovereign states each time a crisis arises.

So, is the abolition of war unattainable? Such a conclusion would be a counsel of despair. But we need to recognize that there is no single, simple solution to war. The establishment of perpetual peace will be achieved only with difficulty, step by halting step, and with constant and unremitting effort. It will necessitate not just a massive strengthening of international structures, underpinned by ever closer political and economic ties between states, but also a wide range of other actions to reduce the causes of war, including a more just distribution of the earth's resources. We should continue to strive towards such a goal. But its attainment remains a distant and utopian objective. In the meantime, the pressing priority is to reduce the incidence and ravages of war by ensuring that war is embarked on only when it is just, and that wars are fought and end justly. Our aim is *to make war just and to make only just war.* To achieve this we need to address three closely interrelated challenges: political, military, and to society as a whole. Let us consider each of these in turn.

The political challenge: making only just war

Philosophers for much of the twentieth century taught that morality, whose domain they conceived as primarily our personal lives, lacked rational foundation. Realists have accordingly proclaimed that the realm of politics, particularly international politics, is a morality-free zone. Others have conceded a role for morality in the public realm but have argued that moral standards and the nature of moral reasoning are different in the public and private realms. One of the aims of this book has been to demonstrate that such views arc ill-founded. Morality applies equally to the private and the public spheres and in both areas is amenable to rational criticism. The nature of moral reasoning—which we have suggested is appropriately characterized as virtuous consequentialism—is the same in both. Politicians and public officials can be held to account against the same moral principles and deploying the same moral reasoning as we use in our private lives.

In no area is there a more pressing need to hold politicians morally to account than in the area of war. The challenge is to ensure that our political leaders go to war only when it is just, and conduct and conclude wars justly. So how can this be achieved?

The just war tradition teaches that a war is just only if it is undertaken with competent authority, for a just cause, with right intention, as a last resort, and with more good than harm judged likely to result, taking into account the probability of success; while in its conduct individual applications of force should be both proportionate and discriminate, minimizing non-combatant casualties; and the war should end in the establishment of a just peace.

The principles furnish a series of tests, all of which need to be passed, if a war is to be just. But the principles do not provide simple or ready-made answers to the difficult questions of peace and war. Just war teaching is not an answering machine that we can dial up to obtain an instant assessment of whether a particular conflict is or is not just.[10] The principles provide rather a way of structuring our thinking about war. They ensure we ask the right

questions; seek the appropriate evidence; probe in the right areas. But
difficult and complex judgements still remain to be made.

The rules of war are sometimes viewed as just *ad hoc* agreements between
states, bargains struck between would-be belligerents, to limit the violence
of war. Such a view motivated many of the participants in the inter-state
conferences that led to The Hague and Geneva conventions. There is a role
for such *ad hoc* bargaining. It has yielded valuable agreements, not least those
protecting the rights of prisoners of war and detainees. But it is not the only
approach required. It is not the approach of the just war tradition.

The just war principles are not an arbitrary and *ad hoc* set of principles,
whose validity derives only from the field of war. They are, indeed, the rules
of war and apply to war. But they are rationally based moral principles,
justified on the same basis and in the same way as the broader moral
principles that we follow elsewhere in our lives, with which they are
consistent and from which the key just war principles can be deduced.
Self-defence is justified as a just cause for war on analogy with the right of
individual self-defence. Just as individuals have a right to defend themselves,
so too do states. But a just cause does not legitimate action unless the action
is undertaken for the sake of that cause and so undertaken with right
intention, a requirement that prevails elsewhere in our moral reasoning.
The principle of non-combatant immunity has a particular application,
relating to those who are to be protected in war, but it is derived from a
broader principle forbidding the deliberate killing of innocents. The principle of proportion, which has to be applied both before and during war,
requires that war, and individual applications of force in war, should be
undertaken only when more good than harm is judged likely to ensue. This
applies to war a basic principle of moral reasoning that holds within the
private and public realms.

The key just war principles derive from broader moral principles. Moreover, both the just war principles and these broader moral principles are, in
turn, justified at a deeper level on the same basis. The right of self-defence,
like the prohibition on killing the innocent, may itself require further
justification when, for example, moral principles conflict. At a more fundamental level, the basis for the just war principles, and the rights and duties
they enshrine, is to be sought—as with other moral principles—from the
contribution that they make to human welfare and the prevention of
suffering.

In understanding, applying, and implementing the just war principles to resolve the difficult challenges posed by war, we need to draw guidance from the broader ethical framework that we deploy elsewhere to guide our moral deliberations. This framework I have called virtuous consequentialism. The just war principles are not absolute principles that can be simply applied without any regard to consequences. In thinking about war, as in our wider ethical deliberations, we need necessarily to take consequences into account. The just war principles are justified by their beneficial consequences. In applying the principle of proportion before and during war we necessarily have regard to consequences. But consequences are not all that matter. As the principle of right intention underlines, the mental states of the agents involved are also crucial to our ethical assessment.

But that too is not enough. For if we are to have any reasonable prospect of reaching correct ethical conclusions on such difficult issues, amid the heat, fury, and fog of war, all those involved, from the most senior political and military leaders to the most junior service personnel, need to have been trained and well practised in the virtues and, above all, in practical wisdom. Only thus will they be able to confront the difficult practical challenges that they face with the appropriate beliefs, desires, and feelings and have acquired a habit of sound reasoning in practical matters. Only thus can we be assured that our governments' security and foreign policies will be underpinned by appropriately robust ethical reasoning. We need our political leaders to be not consequentialists but virtuous consequentialists, men and women schooled by precept, example, and practice in the virtues. The virtues—lost in recent just war teaching—need to be rediscovered and reintegrated within the just war tradition, as they had been in the thirteenth-century teachings of Aquinas.

In the selection and training of our political leaders, we should require that they are deeply familiar with the principles of the just war. We should also insist that they are men and women of established moral character and, in particular, with a proven track record in that highest form of practical wisdom that belongs to statesmen. Just war counsels should ring out in their Cabinet war rooms. Just war principles should provide the yardstick against which government actions are judged and furnish the currency in which public debate on war and peace is conducted.

In order to help ensure that only just wars are waged, two further practical measures are suggested. First, a government that proposes to go to war or to embark on military action should be required in advance to publish a short white paper setting out the grounds for the military action and how what is proposed meets each of the just war criteria. This document would be presented to Parliament and form the basis for the formal parliamentary approval that the UK government announced in March 2008 that it would seek before committing UK forces into armed conflict.[11]

Before that parliamentary approval is granted, one further step should also be instituted. This is that the ethical case for war, as set out in the white paper, should be assessed by an independent Office of Moral Assessment. Only if the Office endorses the ethical case would a decision to go to war be lawful. The Office of Moral Assessment would furnish independent ethical scrutiny of the executive's actions in relation to war similar to the role in monitoring its fiscal responsibility of the Office for Budget Responsibility, set up by the UK Chancellor of the Exchequer in May 2010 to provide an independent audit of public spending and borrowing.[12]

The true model for the Office of Moral Assessment is, however, to be found within the just war tradition. This is the Council of the Wise that just war teachers urged should always be consulted by a wise prince before he embarks on war. As Vitoria notes:

> The king is not capable of examining the causes of war on his own, and it is likely that he may make mistakes, or rather that he will make mistakes, to the detriment and ruin of the many. So war should not be declared on the sole dictates of the prince, nor even on the opinion of the few, but on the opinion of the many, and of the wise and reliable.[13]

In a parliamentary democracy, Parliament represents the views of 'the many'. The role of the Office of Moral Assessment would be not to usurp that of Parliament but to assist Parliament in reaching its decision, by advising it whether the executive's proposal to go to war complied with the just war criteria. The advisory body should be small and meet only as required. The key qualification for membership would be, as Vitoria suggests, the wisdom of its members. They should be men and women of the highest calibre and deepest experience, with proven track records in the exercise of practical wisdom. The membership might include: a moral philosopher, a theologian, a retired statesman, and a retired general, admiral, or air marshal. The members could be appointed as Privy Counsellors and so be able to have access, as necessary, to confidential and classified material.

Both these proposals may attract vigorous opposition from the executive. It may be argued that to insist that a government's actions comply with formal published criteria would unduly constrain its freedom of action. Such was the objection levelled, as we noted in Chapter 11, by the previous US administration in opposing the proposals of the UN Secretary General, supported by the UK government, to include ethical criteria in the 2005 UN Summit Declaration on the international community's responsibility to protect. The answer to this charge is that the criteria are designed to constrain a government's freedom of action. But no undue constraint is proposed. The only constraint is that governments should behave ethically. No government that wished to behave ethically should have reason to object.

It may also be objected that there is no time for such consultation before decisions on military action are taken and that the requirement for such consultation would risk damaging delay. To achieve its objective, military action may need to be undertaken swiftly and even secretly. We may need to respond to a surprise attack 'launched from the blue'. Military operations, such as a rescue by special forces of hostages kidnapped by terrorists, may require speed and secrecy. But such occasions are of their nature exceptional, for which exceptional procedures should be devised. They should not dictate the procedures to be followed normally and, in particular, not those to be followed on a decision of such public import as whether or not to go to war. The executive, as Vitoria noted, can make mistakes, which in the area of war can be to the detriment and ruin of the many. Proper consultation and debate are crucial to avoid such mistakes. Moreover, where time is critical, the Office of Moral Assessment can be obliged to submit its advice within a fixed and, if necessary, very brief time period to avoid any unnecessary delay.

The military challenge: making war justly

Like our political leaders, so should the military be well versed in the principles of the just war. But they too need to draw on all the resources that virtuous consequentialism insists are required to enable ethically correct decisions to be made. For it is not enough that our service people have a theoretical understanding of the conduct of just war. What matters is that they behave morally. Learning the rules and codes of war is necessary for the ethical behaviour of those involved with war. But rules alone are not sufficient to ensure that the right decisions are taken before, during, and after war. Our service people need moral education so that they know and understand the principles of morality and, in particular, those relating to the conduct of war.

But they also need to be trained so that they have the appropriate traits of character and skills to apply the principles in practice to the diverse challenges and tasks with which they may be faced on an ever-shifting battlefield, even when under pressure and when time is short. We need the training just 'to take over'. Our service people need, therefore, to be schooled, through precept, example, and practice, in the virtues, including the practical wisdom that Aquinas teaches is required of the military. Aquinas taught that such wisdom is required only of generals. But the delegation of responsibility to ever lower levels within the military means that practical wisdom needs to be taught and exercised at all levels.

Our service people are licensed to wield force, including lethal force, on behalf of society. It is crucial that our service people behave morally. Ethical training needs to be afforded high priority within our military establishments. We require our service people to behave justly. But what happens if an order they receive is unjust? Should a service person disobey an order that he or she believes to be unjust?

Determining whether and when it is right to disobey an order is a difficult issue in military life. For it is a fundamental principle governing military conduct that lawful orders should be obeyed. Obedience is a pre-eminent military virtue. It is a virtue valued for both its internal qualities and its external effects. It is crucial to the relationship that bonds together members of a military unit and to the trust that each can place in the other. It is also essential to the effective functioning of a military unit. For the success of a military mission requires that each level in the military hierarchy can be confident that orders will be transmitted and obeyed without delay, even amid the heat and confusion of battle. Lives depend upon obedience. The virtue of obedience is a core value of the British Army, in which its members are daily instructed, trained, and practised.

Obedience is not just crucial within the military but is also fundamental to the relations between the military and the civil authority within a democracy. The obedience of the military to the lawful orders of the civil authority is critical to the effective functioning of democracy. It is a hard-won principle whose importance needs to be daily proclaimed and taught in our military establishments. As Samuel Finer observed in his sombre survey of the role of the military in politics:

There is a common assumption, an unreflecting belief, that it is 'natural' for
the armed forces to obey the civil power...But instead of asking why the
military engage in politics, we ought surely to ask why they ever do otherwise.
For at first sight the political advantages of the military *vis-à-vis* other civilian
groupings are overwhelming. The military possess vastly superior organisation. And they possess arms.[14]

Finer was writing in 1962, when, even within Western Europe, there were
still military dictatorships in Spain and Portugal and there had been a
successful military *coup* in France as recently as 1958 and an unsuccessful
military *putsch* against the Paris government by the French generals in
Algeria in 1961. There has since been an extension and stabilization of
democracy in Europe, not least thanks to the workings of the European
Union. But in Eastern Europe democracy is still a recent and fragile
institution, while elsewhere in the world military takeovers continue with
depressing regularity.

So obedience—both within the military and between the military and
civilian authorities—is extremely important. What happens, then, if the
principle of obedience is in conflict with one or more of the principles of
the just war? Should a serviceman disobey an unjust order?

It has been argued that it is wrong for a serviceman to pit his private
conscience against the welfare of the state. The politician has to take into
account wider considerations—*raisons d'état*. In so doing, as Samuel Huntington observed, 'the statesman may well feel compelled to violate com-
monly accepted morality in order to further the interests of the state'.[15]
Where state welfare is at stake, it may be inappropriate for a service person
to question the orders of the politician. To offer such moral latitude to the
politician is, however, to revert to the world of the realist, for whom the
public realm is either exempt from morality or subject to different moral
constraints from our private lives. Virtuous consequentialism insists rather
that we all belong to the same moral universe: that the same moral considerations apply in both the public and the private spheres.

There may be circumstances where the principle of obedience can be over-
ridden on moral grounds. But, given the fundamental importance of the principle, such overriding would be justified only if grave consequences would
otherwise arise. Disobedience should be an exceptional and extreme expedient.

So, for example, a British officer who believed the 2003 Iraq War was
unjust would not have been justified in disobeying the order to go to war.
The decision to undertake military operations was taken by a democratically

elected government and approved by Parliament. The order was lawful. The participation of an individual serviceman in military operations would not of itself have led to dire consequences. While, as we explored in Chapter 10, there were grounds for doubting the justice of the war, the issues were complex and open to dispute. Given the fundamental importance of the subordination of the military to political authority, there was no basis for disobeying a lawful order from the civil authority. If an officer, nonetheless, felt compelled by his conscience not to fight, the responsible option open to him would have been to resign his commission and leave the service.

This would be to exercise, as an individual, a right to resign on grounds of conscience from military service, accepting whatever financial and other penalties might thereby be incurred. This is very different from the organized resignations *en masse* of the Curragh Mutiny that sent shudders through the British establishment in March 1914. This mutiny arose at the Curragh Camp in southern Ireland. In March 1914, 57 out of 70 British cavalry officers serving in Ireland, including the commanding officer Briga-dier-General Gough, resigned rather than enforce the government's policy of Home Rule for Ireland. This mass resignation was objectionable on two grounds. First, the resignations were not individual acts of conscience so much as an organized protest that, because it was so widespread, threatened the viability of the military operation. Second, and crucially, the officers were not objecting on moral grounds but were rather questioning the political wisdom of the democratically elected government. Their actions struck at the fundamental principle of the accountability of the military to the civil authority. For a service person does not have a right to question orders on political grounds, setting himself up as a rival source of political competence to that of the civil authority.

A service person may, however, as a moral agent, question immoral or unlawful orders. Where compliance with an order would have morally grave consequences, disobedience can be justified. In Chapter 6 we exam-ined the case of the German police reservists who on 13 July 1942 received an order to round up all the Jews in the Polish village of Jozefow and kill all those not of working age. The police reservists would have been justified in refusing to obey the order to massacre Jews, since that order manifestly contravened the laws of war and, in particular, the injunction to minimize harm to civilians. We also consider that Rommel was justified in disobeying Hitler's order on 28 October 1942 that all enemy soldiers encountered behind enemy lines were to be killed at once, rather than taken prisoner.

Rommel was a highly decorated general with great power and responsibility. Of such people much is expected. But how far down the line should we expect soldiers to disobey orders? On 16 March 1968, during the Vietnam War, a company of American soldiers entered the village of My Lai, where enemy combatants were thought to be hiding. No combatant was found, but the soldiers killed 504 civilians—men, women, and children. The officer who led the unit into the village and issued the order to kill civilians was Lieutenant William Calley. He was the only person convicted of offences arising from the massacre, although he claimed he was merely obeying orders from his superior, Captain Medina. None of the enlisted men who carried out the massacre was punished. Should they have been?

More than forty years on, with responsibility devolved to ever lower levels within armed forces that are now, in both the USA and UK, fully professional, it is easier to recognize that not only officers but also ordinary soldiers involved in a massacre of civilians should be held both morally and legally responsible for their actions. Nor in such circumstances would a defence of following orders be acceptable. For an order to kill innocent civilians is, as the army judge at the Calley trial noted, one that 'a man of ordinary sense and understanding would, under the circumstances, know to be unlawful'.[16] The enlisted men should have disobeyed the order.

Nonetheless, we accept that, in general, officers, because of their probable greater knowledge and control over events, bear a particular moral responsibility. Indeed, this recognition can give rise to the contrary concern voiced, for example, over the prosecution of only junior personnel following the abuses during the Iraq conflict at Abu Ghraib and Basra. This is concern that it should be not just the lowest ranks who are charged with breaching the codes of war. Responsibility should be traced to where it rests higher up the military and, if appropriate, the political chain as well.

We expect our political leaders and service people, at all levels, to behave justly in the conduct of war. Where they do not and offences are committed, they should be punished. Responsibility for the application of legal sanctions rests, in the first instance, with the judicial system of the state in whose service they are employed. But, where the crimes are particularly grave, or the state itself is implicated in their commission, referral can now be made to the International Criminal Court (ICC). The ICC was established on a permanent basis on 1 July 2002 after ratification by sixty countries, including the United Kingdom.

The court has jurisdiction over the crimes of most concern to the international community—in 2010 genocide, crimes against humanity, and war crimes. National justice systems are expected to prosecute such cases. But the court will do so, 'if national justice systems do not carry out such proceedings or when they claim to do so but in reality are unwilling or unable to carry out such proceedings genuinely'.[17] This division of responsibilities—known as the principle of complementarity—is designed to protect the sovereignty of states. The court may also exercise jurisdiction only over such international crimes if they are committed on the territory of a state party or by one of its nationals. Such restrictions do not, however, apply if the case is referred to the court by the UN Security Council, whose resolutions are binding on all UN member states. The prosecutor can initiate investigations where cases are referred to him by a state party or by the UN Security Council. He can also do so on his own initiative on the basis of information received from reliable sources and subject to the agreement of a Pre-Trial Chamber composed of three independent judges.

The ICC came into being amid controversy, with the US government, in particular, having initially championed its cause, declining to join because of fears that its operations would encroach upon US sovereignty.[18] Some of these fears would appear unfounded, since the principle of complementarity is designed to protect the sovereignty of national judicial systems. But there are genuine concerns that the power of the prosecutor to initiate investigations independent of the UN Security Council will need to be exercised with considerable care to avoid conflicts with the Council's wider responsibility for peace and security. The potential for conflict in this area was illustrated by the concerns raised over the timing of the prosecutor's efforts to initiate proceedings in July 2008 against Omar al-Bashir, the President of Sudan, just when the UN Security Council was seeking to engage the President in the peace settlement process for Darfur.[19] He was subsequently formally charged with war crimes and crimes against humanity and an arrest warrant issued on 4 March 2009.

The ICC is as yet an imperfect and largely untried instrument. Broadening of its membership will be essential if the court is to be fully effective. Further evolution of its responsibilities and mode of operation will be required and may help allay the concerns of those states that have so far declined to ratify the Rome statute. But, whatever its current imperfections, the establishment of the ICC is an important moral and political gain. No such court has ever existed before. None was available in the First or Second

World Wars. At the conclusion of the Second World War, the Nuremberg Tribunal had to be specially set up to try those who had committed crimes during the war. Similarly, during the violent upheavals of the 1990s *ad hoc* international tribunals had to be established to deal with the genocide of Rwanda and the ethnic cleansing in former Yugoslavia. Without a permanent international court, there is no means of enforcing moral constraints internationally, where states are unable or unwilling to do so, except through the establishment of *ad hoc* courts. *Ad hoc* courts can, however, smack of victors' justice, the criticism made of the Nuremberg trials. Since they are also set up to administer justice only after a war crime has been committed, they provide little or no prior disincentive to its commission. The establishment of a permanent international criminal court represents a significant step forward in the extension of legal and moral constraints to the realm of international affairs.

The wider challenge: making society just

We need to improve the way we select, teach, and train not only our political leaders and their senior civilian and military advisers but also our service people at all levels to ensure that all those involved with war behave justly. This will present a major challenge. But such reforms will not succeed unless they are supported and reinforced by a change in the outlook of society as a whole. Political thought was led astray by those moral philosophers who focused morality primarily on the realm of the personal; and who conceded to morality little basis other than in personal preference and choice. Morality should rather be viewed as a seamless web extending from the personal to the public spheres; and, in both areas, the subject of rational support, discourse, and criticism. We need, as a society, to recover our confidence that morality is rational and teachable; and our belief in the crucial importance of moral wisdom to both our private and our public lives.

Such recovery of our moral self-confidence is desirable in its own right. It is also necessary if we are to meet the many wider challenges currently facing Western society, including those arising from the collapse of banking systems brought about, in part, by the moral failings, including the greed and selfishness, of their operators. There are also two particular reasons why such a recovery is needed if we are to ensure the just conduct of war.

Samuel Huntington once argued that the military tradition of service and discipline had much to teach wider American society: 'That the disciplined order of West Point has more to offer than the garish individualism of Main Street.'[20] So it does. For the importance that the military has continued to attach to the virtues, when elsewhere they have largely fallen out of fashion, is a lesson from which society as a whole can benefit. But it is impractical for the military to operate as a moral community within a society that is itself morally sceptical or indifferent. We cannot expect moral leadership to be shown by our officers when they themselves have received inadequate ethical education and training within the communities from which they are drawn. An ethical military needs the support and guidance of the wider community. Moreover, a society that attaches insufficient importance to the moral education and training of its citizens will not be able to produce and nurture the practically wise and virtuous politicians and military and civilian leaders whom we need if just decisions are to be taken on the crucial choices between peace and war.

We are, as moral beings, appalled by the horror of war. The abolition of war must, therefore, be our ultimate objective. But, for the foreseeable future, war looks likely to remain with us; and the use of force to continue to be necessary to constrain the actions and ambitions of evil men. Our immediate objective should be to diminish the suffering caused by war, by reducing the incidence of war and its ravages when it occurs. We need to ensure, as far as is in our power, that war is undertaken only when it is just, when it is conducted justly, and when it leads to the establishment of a just peace.

With the ending of the strategic certainties and moral clarity of the Cold-War period, we have entered a challenging period of confusion and change. Wars are now undertaken more from choice than from the necessity of territorial defence. The need for moral clarity over when, where, and how to start, conduct, and conclude war has never been greater. The just war tradition provides not only a robust but an indispensable guide for addressing the security challenges of the twenty-first century.

Notes

INTRODUCTION

1. David Fisher, *Morality and the Bomb* (London: Croom Helm; New York: St Martin's Press, 1985).
2. Michael Walzer, *Just and Unjust Wars: A Moral Argument with Historical Illustrations* (London: Allen Lane, 1978).
3. Lord Layard, quoted in an interview with Stuart Jeffries, 'Will this Man Make you Happy?' *Guardian*, G2, 24 June 2008, 15.
4. Nicholas Rengger, 'The Just War Tradition in the Twenty-First Century', *International Affairs*, 78/2 (Apr. 2002), 362.
5. General Sir Richard Dannatt, 'Foreword', in Charles Reed and David Ryall (eds.), *The Price of Peace: Just War in the Twenty-First Century* (Cambridge: Cambridge University Press, 2007), p. xiv.
6. Fisher, *Morality and the Bomb*. See also David Fisher, 'Can Deterrence Be Just in the Twenty-First Century? ', in Brian Wicker and Hugh Beach (eds.), *Britain's Bomb: What Next?* (London: SCM Press, 2006).

CHAPTER 1: WAR WITHOUT MORALITY

1. Theodore Draper, 'Nuclear Temptations', *New York Review of Books*, 30/21–22 (Jan. 1984).
2. *The Concise Oxford Dictionary of Current English*, ed. H. W. and F. G. Fowler (London: Oxford University Press, 1961).
3. Thucydides, *The Peloponnesian War*, bk. 5, chs. 84–111, The Melian Dialogue. The quotation is from chapter 89. The translation used here and elsewhere (except where indicated otherwise) is that of Rex Warner (Harmondsworth: Penguin Books, 1977).
4. Thucydides, 5, 105.
5. Thucydides, 5, 111.
6. Thucydides, 5, 111.
7. Thucydides, 5, 116.
8. Thucydides, 3, 83, 1.
9. Thucydides, 3, 82, 4.

10. Dionysius, *Thucydides*, 39, quoted by F. M. Cornford, *Thucydides Mythistoricus* (London: Edward Arnold, 1907), 176. A less colourful but helpful study of Thucydides' pessimism is Peter R. Pouncey, *The Necessities of War: A Study of Thucydides' Pessimism* (New York: Columbia University Press, 1980).

11. Walzer, *Just and Unjust Wars*, 5.

12. Thucydides, 1, 2–23.

13. Thucydides, 1, 8, 4.

14. Thucydides, 1, 76, 2. The motives, in Greek *time*, *deos*, and *opheleia*, are better translated as 'honour, fear and self-interest'.

15. Thucydides, 2, 41, 1.

16. Thucydides 2, 43, 1. Warner's translation is 'the greatness of Athens' but Thucydides' word *dynamis* is better translated, as I have done in the text, as 'power'.

17. Thucydides, 4, 61, 5.

18. Thucydides, 7, 77, 4.

19. Thucydides, 3, 40, 7–8.

20. Thucydides, 3, 44, 7.

21. Thucydides, 3, 49, 6.

22. Thucydides, 2, 65, 7.

23. Thucydides, 2, 51, 5–6.

24. Thomas Hobbes, *Leviathan* (1651; London: Dent, Everyman Library, 1953), ch. 13, p. 65.

25. George Kennan, *American Diplomacy 1900–1950* (London: Secker & Warburg, 1952), 82.

26. Hans J. Morgenthau, *Politics among Nations* (New York: Alfred A Knopf, 1973), 5.

27. Hans J. Morgenthau, *Scientific Man* (Chicago: Chicago University Press, 1946), 194–5.

28. Morgenthau, *Politics among Nations*, 9.

29. Hedley Bull, *The Anarchical Society* (Houndsmill: Palgrave, 2002).

30. Kenneth N. Waltz, *Man, the State and War* (New York: Columbia University Press, 2001), 227.

31. John J. Mearsheimer, *The Tragedy of Great Power Politics* (New York: W.W. Norton, 2001), 3.

32. Mearsheimer, *Tragedy of Great Power Politics*, 11.

33. Christopher Meyer, *Getting our Way: 500 Years of Adventure and Intrigue: The Inside Story of British Diplomacy* (London: Weidenfeld & Nicolson, 2009); see especially ch. 8, 'Hobbes Rules, OK'.

34. These criticisms of realism are discussed in William C. Wohlforth, 'Realism and the End of the Cold War,' *International Security*, 19/3 (1994), 91–129.

35. Kenneth N. Waltz, 'The Origins of War in Neorealist Theory', in Robert I. Rotberg and Theodore K. Rabb (eds.), *The Origin and Prevention of Major Wars* (Cambridge: Cambridge University Press, 1989).

36. Mearsheimer, *Tragedy of Great Power Politics*, 25.
37. Morgenthau, *Politics among Nations*, 12.
38. Morgenthau, *Politics among Nations*, 247.
39. Quoted in Mearsheimer, *Tragedy of Great Power Politics*, 31.
40. Thucydides, 5, 89, translation by Benjamin Jowett (Oxford: Clarendon Press, 1900).
41. Bull, *Anarchical Society*, 131.
42. Bull, *Anarchical Society*, 8.
43. Michael Walzer, *Spheres of Justice: A Defence of Pluralism and Equality* (Oxford: Basil Blackwell, 1985), 65.
44. William Tecumseh Sherman, *Memoirs of General W. T. Sherman* (New York: Literary Classics of the United States, 1990), 602.
45. Quoted in B. H. Liddell Hart, *Sherman: Soldier, Realist, American* (New York: Da Capo Press, 1993), 426.
46. Sherman, *Memoirs*, 593.
47. Sherman, *Memoirs*, 594.
48. Sherman, *Memoirs*, 598.
49. Sherman, *Memoirs*, 601.
50. Sherman, *Memoirs*, 585.
51. Liddell Hart, *Sherman*, 430.
52. Quoted in Angus Calder, *The People's War: Britain 1939–1945* (London: Cape, 1969), 229.
53. Walzer, *Just and Unjust Wars*, 231.
54. Walzer, *Just and Unjust Wars*, ch. 16, 'Supreme Emergency', and ch. 17, 'Nuclear Deterrence'.

CHAPTER 2: 'WHOSE JUSTICE? WHICH RATIONALITY?'

1. The title is from Alasdair MacIntyre, *Whose Justice? Which Rationality?* (London: Duckworth, 1988).
2. Simon Blackburn, *Being Good: A Short Introduction to Ethics* (Oxford: Oxford University Press, 2001), 19.
3. J. S. Mill, *On Liberty* (1859), ch. 3, in Stefan Collini (ed.), *J. S. Mill: On Liberty and Other Writings* (Cambridge: Cambridge University Press, 2000), 57.
4. Mill, *On Liberty*, ch. 1, p. 13.
5. Walzer, *Spheres of Justice*, 6.
6. Walzer, *Spheres of Justice*, 313–16.
7. Isaiah Berlin, *The Proper Study of Mankind*, ed. Henry Hardy and Roger Hausheer (London: Chatto & Windus, 1997), 5.
8. Berlin, *Proper Study of Mankind*, 237.
9. Berlin, *Proper Study of Mankind*, 12–13.

10. Timothy Garton Ash, 'What Young British Muslims Say Can Be Shocking: Some of it is also True', *Guardian*, 10 Aug. 2006.

11. Mick Hume, quoted by David Martin Jones and M. L. R. Smith, 'Language and Atrocity in Cool Britannia', *International Affairs*, 82/6 (Nov. 2006), 1092.

12. G. E. Moore, *Principia Ethica* (Cambridge: Cambridge University Press, 1903; repr. 1971), 189.

13. A. J. Ayer, *Language, Truth and Logic* (London: Gollancz, 1936).

14. C. L. Stevenson, *Ethics and Language* (New Haven: Yale University Press, 1945).

15. R. M. Hare, *The Language of Morals* (Oxford: Oxford University Press, 1952).

16. Bernard Williams, *Ethics and the Limits of Philosophy* (London: Fontana Press, 1985), 35.

17. Although Hume does not use these precise words, the non-deducibility of an 'ought' from an 'is' is the usual interpretation of the discussion in David Hume, *A Treatise of Human Nature*, ed. L. A. Selby Biggs and P. H. Nidditch (Oxford: Oxford University Press, 1978), bk. iii, pt. 1, sect. 1, pp. 469–70.

18. Bernard Williams, 'Replies', in J. E. J. Altham and R. Harrison (eds.), *World, Mind and Ethics* (Cambridge: Cambridge University Press, 1995), 199.

19. Williams, *Ethics and the Limits of Philosophy*, 153.

20. Blackburn, *Being Good*, 111.

21. Michael Walzer, 'Moral Minimalism', in *Thick and Thin: Moral Arguments at Home and Abroad* (Notre Dame, IN: University of Notre Dame, 1994), 18.

22. Richard Layard, *Happiness: Lessons from a New Science* (London: Allen Lane, Penguin Books, 2005), ch. 9, 'Does Economics Have a Clue?'

23. Lionel Robbins, *On the Nature and Significance of Economic Science* (London: Macmillan, 1932), 132, 134.

24. Layard, *Happiness*, ch. 3, 'Are we Getting Happier?', 29–30.

25. See, e.g., John Rawls, *Political Liberalism* (New York: Columbia University Press, 1996), pp. xviii–xx, xxii. For a critique of Rawls's attempt to divorce politics from moral values, see Michael J. Sandel, *Liberalism and the Limits of Justice* (1982; 2nd edn., New York and Cambridge: Cambridge University Press, 1998).

26. Richard Rorty, *Contingency, Irony and Solidarity* (Cambridge: Cambridge University Press, 1989), 67.

27. Rorty, *Contingency, Irony and Solidarity*, 61.

28. Layard, interview with Jeffries, 'Will this Man Make you Happy?', *Guardian*, G2, 24 June 2008, 15.

29. Dannatt, 'Foreword', in Reed and Ryall (eds.), *Price of Peace*, p. xiv.

30. National Conference of US Catholic Bishops, 'The Challenge of Peace: God's Promise and our Response', Pastoral Letter on War and Peace, in Philip J. Murnion (ed.), *Catholics and Nuclear War* (London: Geoffrey Chapman, 1983), para. 93, p. 278.

31. A view defended by H. L. A. Hart, *Law, Liberty and Morality* (London: Oxford University Press, 1963). A different view was taken by Lord Devlin, *The Enforcement of Morals* (Oxford: Oxford University Press, 1959).

32. J. S. Mill, *Utilitarianism* (1863), ch. 2, in Alan Ryan (ed.), *John Stuart Mill and Jeremy Bentham: Utilitarianism and Other Essays* (London: Penguin Books, 1987), 281.

33. Mill, *On Liberty*, ch. 4, p. 76.

34. Michael J. Sandel, *Justice: What's the Right Thing to Do?* (London and New York: Allen Lane, 2009), 243.

35. *Countering International Terrorism: The United Kingdom's Strategy, July 2006*, Cm. 6888 (Norwich: HMSO, 2006), 2. The need to challenge values even if they 'fall short of supporting violence' is affirmed in the updated strategy, *The United Kingdom's Strategy for Countering International Terrorism, March 2009*, Cm. 7547, para. 0.38, p. 13.

36. Roger Scruton, *The West and the Rest* (London and New York: Continuum, 2002), 161.

37. Gilbert Harman, 'Moral Relativism', in Gilbert Harman and Judith Jarvis Thomson, *Moral Relativism and Moral Objectivity* (Oxford: Blackwell, 1996), 11.

38. Mary Midgely, 'Towards an Ethic of Global Responsibility', in Tim Dunne and Nicholas J. Wheeler (eds.), *Human Rights in Global Politics* (Cambridge: Cambridge University Press, 1999), 160.

39. The overlap between Christian and Islamic teaching on war, in general, and terrorism, in particular, is explored in David Fisher and Brian Wicker (eds.), *Just War on Terror? A Christian and Muslim Response* (Aldershot: Ashgate, 2010). There is a survey of mainstream Islamic teaching, reaffirming the prohibition on killing the innocent, in John Kelsey, 'Arguments concerning Resistance in Contemporary Islam', in Richard Sorabji and David Rodin (eds.), *The Ethics of War: Shared Problems in Different Traditions* (Aldershot: Ashgate, 2006), ch. 4, especially pp. 77–84. The common ground between the traditions was also examined by a group of Islamic and Christian scholars, including the present author, in Harfiyah Abdel Haleem, Oliver Ramsbotham, Saba Risaluddin, and Brian Wicker (eds.), *The Crescent and the Cross: Muslim and Christian Approaches to War and Peace* (Houndmills and London: Macmillan, 1998).

40. Aristotle, *Nicomachean Ethics*, 1123^b2 and 1124^b9–10.

41. Leo Strauss, letter to Karl Lowith, 20 Aug. 1946, trans. in *Independent Journal of Philosophy*, 4 (1983), quoted in Robert Faulkner, *The Case for Greatness* (New Haven and London: Yale University Press, 2007), 29.

42. Harman, 'Moral Relativism', 11.

43. Harman, 'Moral Relativism', 62.

44. Thomas Mann, *Nietzsche's Philosophy in the Light of Recent Events* (Washington: Library of Congress, 1947), 35.

45. Richard Rorty, *Achieving our Country: Leftist Thought in Twentieth-Century America* (Cambridge, MA: Harvard University Press, 1998).

CHAPTER 3: VIRTUES AND CONSEQUENCES

1. A point noted by Julia Annas, *The Morality of Happiness* (Oxford: Oxford University Press, 1993), 431.
2. Layard, *Happiness*, 125.
3. For a robust defence of consequentialism see, e.g., the essay by J. J. C. Smart in J. J. C. Smart and Bernard Williams, *Utilitarianism for and Against* (Cambridge: Cambridge University Press, 1973).
4. G. E. M. Anscombe, 'Modern Moral Philosophy', *Philosophy*, 35 (1958), repr. in Anscombe, *Collected Philosophical Papers* (Oxford: Basil Blackwell, 1981), iii. 26–42; and in Roger Crisp and Michael Slote (eds.), *Virtue Ethics* (Oxford: Oxford University Press, 1997), 26–44.
5. Anscombe, 'Modern Moral Philosophy', in Crisp and Slote (eds.), *Virtue Ethics*, 37.
6. Peter Geach, *The Virtues* (Cambridge: Cambridge University Press, 1977), 106.
7. John Finnis, *Fundamentals of Ethics* (Oxford: Clarendon Press, 1983), 87.
8. The more judicious formulation is that offered by Jeremy Bentham in the 'Note by the Author' added in July 1822 to *An Introduction to the Principles of Morals* (London: 1789; Oxford: Clarendon Press, 1907). What Bentham meant by the principle of utility is discussed by B. Parekh, 'Bentham's Justification of the Principle of Utility', in B. Parekh (ed.), *Jeremy Bentham: Ten Critical Essays* (London: Frank Cass, 1974).
9. The 'Superbowl' dilemma is discussed by Jean Porter, 'Basic Goods and the Human Good in Recent Catholic Moral Theology', *Thomist*, 57/1 (Jan. 1993), 39.
10. Geach, *Virtues*, 107.
11. 'Bedrock' is the term used for the basic rules of morality by Elizabeth Anscombe, 'War and Murder', repr. in Richard A. Wasserstrom, *War and Morality* (Belmont, CA: Wadsworth, 1970), 50.
12. Smart, in Smart and Williams, *Utilitarianism*, 42.
13. Smart, in Smart and Williams, *Utilitarianism*, 25.
14. P. F. Strawson, 'Freedom and Resentment', in Strawson (ed.), *Studies in the Philosophy of Thought and Action* (Oxford: Oxford University Press, 1968), 75.
15. For an account of the 'Haditha killings', see Thomas E. Ricks, *The Gamble: General Petraeus and the Untold Story of the American Surge in Iraq, 2006–8* (London and New York: Allen Lane, 2009), 1–8.
16. The revival of interest in Aristotelian ethics has been led by Alasdair MacIntyre, with his fully developed Thomist position set out in *Dependent Rational Animals* (Chicago and La Salle, IL: Open Court, 1999). Similar Thomist views are found in Herbert McCabe, *The Good Life* (London: Continuum, 2005). The first modern exposition of the virtues, combining both deontology and Thomism, was Geach, *Virtues*. The leading secular exponent has been Philippa

Foot, whose mature reflections are in *Natural Goodness* (Oxford: Clarendon Press, 2001). Other works on virtue ethics are in the Bibliography (see Hursthouse 1995, 1999; Crisp 1997, 2003).

17. Aristotle, *Nicomachean Ethics*, 1142^b32–3. The translation is by J. A. K. Thomson, *The Ethics of Aristotle* (London: Penguin Books, 1966), 184.

18. Aristotle, *Nicomachean Ethics*, 1140^a26–28; Thomson, *Ethics*, 176.

19. Williams, *Ethics and the Limits of Philosophy*, 153.

20. Quoted by McCabe, *Good Life*, 40.

21. Aristotle, *Nicomachean Ethics*, 1105^a32: for acts to be counted as virtuous they have to be 'chosen for their own sake'.

22. Aristotle, *Nicomachean Ethics*, 1098^a16; cf. 1102^a5.

23. Aristotle, *Nicomachean Ethics*, 1116^a10: 'the brave man chooses to face danger because it is the fine [*kalon*] thing to do.'

24. Plato, *The Republic*, bk. II, sect. 360. The translation is by H. P. D. Lee, *Plato: The Republic* (Harmondsworth: Penguin Books, 1965), 89–90.

25. For a modern attempt to revive Glaucon's argument, see David Fisher, 'Why should I be Just?' *Proceedings of the Aristotelian Society*, 77 (1976), 43–61. For the reasons explained in the text, I no longer subscribe to this view.

26. John Rawls, *A Theory of Justice* (London, Oxford, and New York: Oxford University Press, 1973).

27. Luke 10: 25–37. The quotation is from v. 33 in The New Revised Standard Version.

28. See, e.g., Martha C. Nussbaum, *Frontiers of Justice* (Cambridge, MA, and London: Harvard University Press, 2007), especially ch. 4, 'Mutual Advantage and Global Inequality: The Transnational Social Contract'.

29. Philippa Foot, 'Morality as a System of Hypothetical Imperatives', *Philosophical Review*, 81/3 (July 1952), repr. in Foot, *Virtues and Vices* (Oxford: Basil Blackwell, 1978), 157–73. The reference to Leningrad is on p. 167.

30. This is the basis of virtue according to Matt Ridley in *The Origins of Virtue* (Harmondsworth: Penguin Books, 1997), expounding the theory of Richard Dawkins, *The Selfish Gene* (Oxford: Oxford University Press, 1976).

31. Alasdair MacIntyre, *Three Rival Versions of Moral Enquiry* (London: Duckworth, 1990), 193.

32. Aristotle, *Politics*, 1253^a1.

33. Aristotle, *Nicomachean Ethics*, 1169^b16–19. The translation is by Martha Nussbaum in the frontispiece to *Frontiers of Justice*.

34. Homer, *Odyssey*, 9.112–15. The translation is by Martha Nussbaum in 'Aristotle, Nature and Ethics', in J. E. J. Altham and R. Harrison (eds.), *World, Mind and Ethics* (Cambridge: Cambridge University Press, 1995), 97.

35. MacIntyre, *Dependent Rational Animals*, 108.

36. McCabe, *Good Life*, 55.

37. Williams, *Ethics and the Limits of Philosophy*, 46.

38. Aristotle, *Nicomachean Ethics*, 1101^a16.

39. MacIntyre, *Dependent Rational Animals*, 119.

40. Aristotle, *Nicomachean Ethics*, 115^{a}21–2. The translation is by Martha Nussbaum, 'Non-Relative Virtues: An Aristotelian Approach', in Martha Nussbaum and Amartya Sen (eds.), *The Quality of Life* (Oxford: Clarendon Press, 1993), 242.

CHAPTER 4: THE JUST-WAR TRADITION

1. St Augustine, *Questions on the Heptateuch*, bk. VI, ch. 10, in Gregory Reichberg, Henrik Syse, and Endre Begby (eds.), *The Ethics of War: Classic and Contemporary Readings* (Oxford: Basil Blackwell, 2006), 82.

2. The history of the tradition is well set out in F. H. Russell, *The Just War in the Middle Ages* (Cambridge: Cambridge University Press, 1975); James Turner Johnson, *Ideology, Reason and the Limitation of War* (Princeton: Princeton University Press, 1975), and *Just War Tradition and the Restraint of War* (Princeton: Princeton University Press, 1981).

3. St Thomas Aquinas, *Summa Theologiae*, IIa IIae40: 'On War', art 1, responsio, in *Aquinas: Political Writings*, ed. R. W. Dyson (Cambridge: Cambridge University Press, 2002), 240–1.

4. Francisco de Vitoria, *On the American Indians*, in *Vitoria: Political Writings*, ed. Anthony Pagden and Jeremy Lawrance (Cambridge: Cambridge University Press, 1991), 233–92.

5. The just war tradition was revived in the USA by John C. F. Ford, 'The Morality of Obliteration Bombing', *Theological Studies*, 5 (1944), 261–309, repr. in Wasserstrom, *War and Morality*, 15–41; and Paul Ramsey, *War and the Christian Conscience* (Durham, NC: Duke University Press, 1961), and *The Just War: Force and Political Responsibility* (New York: Scribner, 1968). Just war thinking was deployed by Michael Walzer to furnish a critique of the Vietnam War in *Just and Unjust Wars*. In the UK, the just war tradition was applied to both sides of the nuclear debate in Fisher, *Morality and the Bomb*, and Anthony Kenny, *The Logic of Deterrence* (London: Firethorn Press, 1985), both books originating in a series of seminars delivered jointly by their authors at Oxford University in Hilary Term, 1984. A brief but clear exposition of the principles is in Charles Guthrie and Michael Quinlan, *Just War* (London: Bloomsbury, 2007). Other works are in the Bibliography (see Paskins and Dockrill 1977; Coates 1997; O'Donovan 2003; Orend 2006; Reed and Ryall 2007).

6. This is, for example, a central contention of National Conference of US Catholic Bishops, 'The Challenge of Peace', in Murnion (ed.), *Catholics and Nuclear War*, 272–6.

7. St Augustine, *City of God*, bk. XIX, ch. 7, in *Basic Writings of St Augustine*, ed. Whitney Oates (New York: Random House, 1948).

8. St Augustine, *City of God*, bk XIX, ch. 7, in Reichberg, Syse, and Begby (eds.), *Ethics of War*, 72.

9. Christine de Pisan, *The Book of Fayttes of Armes and of Chivalry*, trans. William Caxton, ed. A. T. P. Byles (London: Oxford University Press, 1932), 1.2.

10. Aquinas, *Summa Theologiae*, IIaIIae 40: 'On War', art. 1. The translation is from *Aquinas: Selected Political Writings*, ed. A. P. D'Entreves (Oxford: Basil Blackwell, 1948).

11. The problem of simultaneous ostensible justice is discussed by Vitoria in *On the Law of War*, 2.2–3, sect. 27, in *Vitoria: Political Writings*, ed. Pagden and Lawrance, 309–13.

12. Such surprise was recalled by a D-Day veteran in a TV documentary commemorating the fiftieth anniversary of the landings, quoted in A. J. Coates, *The Ethics of War* (Manchester and London: Manchester University Press, 1997), 148.

13. Vitoria, *On the Law of War*, 2.4, sect. 32, in *Vitoria: Political Writings*, ed. Pagden and Lawrance, 313.

14. Vitoria, *On the Law of War*, 1.3, sect. 13, in *Vitoria: Political Writings*, ed. Pagden and Lawrance, 302–3.

15. Vitoria, *On the American Indians*, 3.5, sect. 15, in *Vitoria: Political Writings*, ed. Pagden and Lawrance, 288.

16. Hugo Grotius, *On the Law of War and Peace*, bk.II, ch. XX, sect. XL(1), in Reichberg, Syse, and Begby (eds.), *Ethics of War*, 407. The translation is based on that in Grotius, *De jure et pacis*, trans. F. W. Kelsey, *The Classics of International Law*, no. 3, vol. 2 (Oxford: Clarendon Press, 1925).

17. David Rodin, *War and Self-Defence* (Oxford: Clarendon Press, 2002), especially ch. 6, and 'War and Self-Defence', *Ethics and International Affairs*, 18/1 (2004), 63–8.

18. Walzer, *Just and Unjust Wars*, 34.

19. A point made by Jeff McMahan in his review of Rodin's book, 'War as Self-Defence', *Ethics and International Affairs*, 18/1 (2004), 76.

20. Rodin, *War and Self-Defence*, 173.

21. Ronald Lewin, *Rommel as Military Commander* (London: B. T. Batsford, 1968), 294, 311.

22. Nigel Hamilton, *Monty: Master of the Battlefield 1942–1944* (London: Hamish Hamilton, 1983), 7.

23. Aquinas, *Summa Theologiae*, IIaIIae40, in *Aquinas: Political Writings*, ed. Dyson, 241.

24. Augustine, *Epistolae*, 189, quoted with approval by Aquinas, *Summa Theologiae*, IIaIIae40, in *Aquinas: Political Writings*, ed. Dyson, 242.

25. Vitoria, *On the Law of War*, 3.1., sect. 17, in *Vitoria: Political Writings*, ed. Pagden and Lawrance, 315.

26. Rodin, *War and Self-Defence*, 10–11.

27. Other applications of Parmenides' Fallacy, named after the Greek philosopher who held all change to be an illusion, are discussed in Philip Bobbit, *Terror and Consent: The Wars for the Twenty-First Century* (London and New York: Allen Lane, 2008), 208–9, 592 n. 55.

28. Rodin, *War and Self-Defence*, 10.

29. The four levels of military planning are described by General Sir Rupert Smith in *The Utility of Force: The Art of War in the Modern World* (London and New York: Allen Lane, 2005), 12–15.

30. Christine de Pisan, *The Book of Fayttes of Armes and of Chivalry*, 225.

31. So argued by Rodin, *War and Self-Defence*, ch. 8. McMahan argues similarly in 'War as Self-Defence'.

32. Murnion (ed.), *Catholics and Nuclear War*, 282.

33. The case for a separate *jus post bellum* condition is well argued in Brian Orend, *The Morality of War* (Toronto: Broadview Press, 2006), chs. 6 and 7.

34. Vitoria, *On the Law of War*, conclusion, sect. 60, in *Vitoria: Political Writings*, ed. Pagden and Lawrance, 327.

35. Jeff McMahan, 'Just Cause for War', *Ethics and International Affairs*, 19/3 (2005), 1–21.

36. Augustine, *Questions on the Heptateuch*, bk VI, ch. 10, in Reichberg, Syse, and Begby (eds.), *Ethics of War*, 82.

37. Aquinas, *Summa Theologiae*, IIaIIae40, quoting St Paul: Romans 13: 4. The translation used is that of The New English Bible.

38. Vitoria, *On the Law of War*, 1.3, sect. 13, in *Vitoria: Political Writings*, ed. Pagden and Lawrance, 303.

39. Rodin, *War and Self-Defence*, 188.

40. Rodin, *War and Self-Defence*, 188.

41. Rodin, *War and Self-Defence*, 170.

42. *Trials of War Criminals before the Nuremberg Military Tribunals* (Washington: US Government Printing Office, 1950–1), xi. 488–9.

43. St Augustine, *On Free Choice of the Will*, bk. I, chs. 5 and 6, in Reichberg, Syse, and Begby (eds.), *Ethics of War*, 75–7.

44. Grotius, *On The Law of War and Peace*, bk. II, ch. I, sect. XVI, in Reichberg, Syse, and Begby (eds.), *Ethics of War*, 404.

45. Aquinas, *De regimine principum*, bk. I, a treatise on kingship written for the king of Cyprus, in *Aquinas: Political Writings*, ed. Dyson, 44.

CHAPTER 5: IS NON-COMBATANT IMMUNITY ABSOLUTE?

1. The development of the threat to non-combatant immunity by strategic bombing is traced in Stephen A. Garrett, 'Airpower and Non-Combatant Immunity: The Road to Dresden', in Igor Primoratz (ed.), *Civilian Immunity in War* (Oxford: Oxford University Press, 2007), 161–81.

2. 'War amongst the people' is the concept introduced by Smith, *Utility of Force*, part three.
3. Vitoria, *On the Law of War*, 3.1, sect. 37, in *Vitoria: Political Writings*, ed. Pagden and Lawrance, 315.
4. Aquinas, *Summa Theologiae*, IIaIIae64, art. 7: 'Whether it is lawful to kill someone in self-defence', in *Aquinas: Political Writings*, ed. Dyson, 263–4.
5. G. E. M. Anscombe, 'War and Murder', repr. in Wasserstrom, *War and Morality*, 50.
6. The principle of double effect is discussed by David Wiggins, *Ethics: Twelve Lectures in Moral Philosophy* (London: Penguin Books, 2006), ch. 9, with this example quoted on p. 250.
7. These cases are discussed by Philippa Foot, 'Problems of Abortion and the Doctrine of Double Effect', *Oxford Review*, 5 (1967), repr. in Foot, *Virtues and Vices*, 19–33; Jonathan Bennett, 'Whatever the Consequences', *Analysis*, 26 (1965–6), 83–102; Jonathan Glover, *Causing Death and Saving Lives* (London: Allen Lane, 1977), ch. 6; Nigel Biggar, *Aiming to Kill: The Ethics of Suicide and Euthanasia* (London: Darton, Longman and Todd, 2004), ch. 3; T. A. Cavanaugh, *Double-Effect Reasoning: Doing Good and Avoiding Evil* (Oxford and New York: Oxford University Press, 2006), ch. 3.
8. Biggar, *Aiming to Kill*, 85.
9. Biggar, *Aiming to Kill*, 80.
10. Biggar, *Aiming to Kill*, 86.
11. Cavanaugh, *Double-Effect Reasoning*, 101.
12. Cavanaugh, *Double-Effect Reasoning*, 112–13.
13. Cavanaugh, *Double-Effect Reasoning*, 113.
14. Cavanaugh, *Double-Effect Reasoning*, 119.
15. Quoted by H. L. A. Hart, *Punishment and Responsibility* (Oxford: Oxford University Press, 1968), 120.
16. Strawson, 'Freedom and Resentment', 75.
17. Anscombe, 'War and Murder', 50.
18. Geach, *Virtues*, 107.
19. Geach, *Virtues*, 107.
20. Geach, *Virtues*, 108.
21. These are the guidelines drawn up by the Royal Dutch Medical Association for when euthanasia on request is permissible in the Netherlands. They are discussed by J. K. M. Gevers, 'Legal Developments concerning Active Euthanasia on Request in the Netherlands', *Bioethics*, 1 (1987), 156–62. Compliance with the guidelines became mandatory when euthanasia and assisted suicide were legalized in April 2002.
22. Williams, in Smart and Williams, *Utilitarianism*, 98–9.
23. A difficulty noted by Anthony Kenny, 'Philippa Foot on Double Effect', in Rosalind Hursthouse, Gavin Lawrance, and Warren Quinn (eds.), *Virtues and Reasons: Essays in Honour of Philippa Foot* (Oxford: Clarendon Press, 1995), 80.

270

NOTES

24. 'Government House utilitarianism' is the phrase used by Williams, *Ethics and the Limits of Philosophy*, 108.
25. Aeschylus, *Agamemnon*, vv. 205–11:

> The king, the leader, spoke aloud;
> 'A hard fate, to disobey the seer;
> A hard fate, if I must slay my child …
> Here are no ways that do not lead to ill.'

The translation is that of Kenneth Dover, 'The Oresteia', in Dover, *The Greeks* (Oxford: Oxford University Press, 1982), 89.
26. William Ames, 'Conscience, with the Power and Cases thereof', Quest. 6,33, A. 4, quoted by Johnson, *Ideology, Reason and the Limitation of War*, 199.
27. These lessons are set out in the *US Army and Marine Corps Counterinsurgency Field Manual* (Chicago: Chicago University Press, 2007).
28. 'Israel Vows War on Hamas in Gaza', *BBC News*, 30 Dec. 2008, www.news.bbc.co.uk.
29. The rival estimates are discussed in 'Israel Disputes Gaza Death Rates', *BBC News Channel*, 26 Mar. 2009, www.news.bbc.co.uk/1/hi/world/middle_east/7966718.stm.
30. Human Rights Watch, 'Rain of Fire: Israel's Unlawful Use of White Phosphorus in Gaza', report, 25 Mar. 2009, www.hrw.org/en/report/2009/03/25rain-fire.
31. Goldstone Report, *Report of the United Nations Fact-Finding Mission on the Gaza Conflict*, report by Justice Richard Goldstone, 29 Sept. 2009, para. 38, www2.ohchr.org/english/bodies/hrcouncil/docs/1.
32. *US Army and Marine Corps Counterinsurgency Field Manual*, 45.
33. For an account of the NATO campaign, see Dana H. Allin, 'NATO's Balkan Interventions', Adelphi Paper 347 (Oxford: Oxford University Press for IISS, 2002), ch. 3.
34. Human Rights Watch, 'Civilian Deaths in the NATO Air Campaign: The Crisis in Kosovo', report (2000), 1, www.hrw.org/reports/2000/nato/Natbm200-01.htm.
35. General Wesley Clark, 'Remarks to the American Enterprise Institute regarding Military Action in Yugoslavia', 31 Aug. 1999.
36. The shift in US position is traced in Ivo H. Daalder and Michael E O'Hanlon, *Winning Ugly: NATO's War to Save Kosovo* (Washington: Brookings Institution, 2000), 155–61.
37. Human Rights Watch, 'Civilian Deaths in the NATO Air Campaign', 4.
38. General Joseph W. Ralston, vice-chairman of the Joint Chiefs of Staff, noted that civilian casualties were 'estimated at less than 1,500 dead' at the AFA Policy Forum, 'Aerospace Power and the Use of Force', 14 Sept. 1999.
39. Protocol 1 Additional to the Geneva Conventions, 1977, Part IV: Civilian Population, Art. 52.1, states that 'civilian objects shall not be the object of

attack' and Art. 51.2 defines civilian objects as not military objectives that 'make an effective contribution to military action'.

40. Patrick Ball, Wendy Betts, Fritz Scheuren, Jana Dudukovich, and Jana Asher, *Killings and Refugee Flow in Kosovo, March–June 1999: A Report to the International Criminal Tribunal for the Former Yugoslavia*, 3 Jan. 2002 (New York: American Association for the Advancement of Science, 2002), 4.

CHAPTER 6: VIRTUES

1. Alasdair MacIntyre, *After Virtue: A Study in Moral Theory* (London: Duckworth, 1985), 233.
2. Sir John Winthrop Hackett, 'Society and the Soldier: 1914–18', in Malham M. Wakin (ed.), *War, Morality, and the Military Profession* (Boulder, CO: Westview Press, 1979), 81.
3. Aristotle, *Nicomachean Ethics*, bk. 2, ch. 5, 1106^{b}36–1107^{a}2. Translations, except where indicated otherwise, are my own.
4. William James, *The Principles of Psychology* (London: Dover Publications, 1950), i. 127.
5. James, *The Principles of Psychology*, 125.
6. Sir W. David Ross, *Foundations of Ethics: Gifford Lectures, 1935/6* (Oxford: Clarendon Press, 1939), 292.
7. This feature of the virtues was noted by Georg Henrik von Wright, *The Varieties of Goodness* (London: Routledge & Kegan Paul, 1963), ch. VII, pp. 139–42.
8. Discussed by N. J. H. Dent, *The Moral Psychology of the Virtues* (Cambridge: Cambridge University Press, 1984), 15–16.
9. Von Wright, *Varieties of Goodness*, 145.
10. Aristotle, *Nicomachean Ethics*, 1106^{b}21–3.
11. Aristotle, *Nicomachean Ethics*, 1140^{a}26–8.
12. Aristotle, *Nicomachean Ethics*, 1141^{b}13.
13. Aristotle, *Nicomachean Ethics*, 1141^{b}18–22.
14. Geach, *Virtues*, 160.
15. Aristotle, *Nicomachean Ethics*, 1144^{b}30–2.
16. Von Wright, *Varieties of Goodness*, 149.
17. Geach, *Virtues*, 16.
18. Aristotle distinguishes the three kinds of justice in *Nicomachean Ethics*, bk. 2, chs. 1–5. The quotation is from 1129^{b}27–30, trans. Thomson, *Ethics*, 141.
19. Micah 6: 8. The translation is that of The New English Bible.
20. Aquinas, *Summa Theologia*, 2a2ae 50, 1.
21. Aquinas, *Summa Theologia*, 2a2ae 50, 2.

22. Aquinas, *Summa Theologia*, 2a2ae 50, 4. The translation is by Thomas Gilby OP, in *St Thomas Aquinas Summa Theologiae, Volume 36, Prudence* (London: Blackfriars in conjunction with Eyre & Spottiswoode, 1974), 91, 93.

23. Geach, *Virtues*, 150.

24. The values are described by Dannatt, 'Foreword', in Reed and Ryall (eds.), *Price of Peace*, p. xv.

25. Aristotle, *Nicomachean Ethics*, 1115^{b}11.

26. Aristotle, *Nicomachean Ethics*, 1116^{a}11–12.

27. Aquinas, *Summa Theologica* 2a2ae.123, 5. The translation is by Anthony Ross OP and P. G. Walsh, in *St Thomas Aquinas, Summa Theologiae, Volume 42, Courage* (London, Blackfriars in conjunction with Eyre & Spottiswoode, 1966), 19.

28. The activities of these SS units are described by Antony Beevor, *Stalingrad* (London: Penguin Books, 1999), 54 ff.

29. John Baynes, *Morale: A Story of Men and Courage: The Second Scottish Rifles at the Battle of Neuve Chapelle, 1918* (London: Cassell, 1967), 108.

30. Baynes, *Morale*, 254.

31. Christopher R. Browning, *Ordinary Men: Reserve Police Battalion 101 and the Final Solution* (New York: HarperCollins, 1992).

32. Browning, *Ordinary Men*, 77.

33. Aitken Report, *An Investigation into Cases of Deliberate Abuse and Unlawful Killing in Iraq in 2003 and 2004* (London: UK Ministry of Defence, 25 Jan. 2008).

34. Aitken Report, 12.

35. Aitken Report, paras. 41–2, p. 24.

36. Quoted by Peter Maas, 'A Bulletproof Mind', *New York Times Magazine*, 10 Nov. 2002, p. 55.

37. The story of the Marine is told by Mark Osiel, *Obeying Orders: Atrocity, Military Discipline and the Law of War* (New Brunswick: Transaction Publishers, 1999), 23, quoted by Shannon E. French in 'An American Ethicist's Perspective', in Reed and Ryall (eds.), *Price of Peace*, 297–9. See also Shannon E. French, *The Code of the Warrior: Exploring Warrior Values Past and Present* (Lanham, MD: Rowman & Littlefield, 2003), 14. The contribution of Stoic virtues to military character, including anger control, is explored by Nancy Sherman in *Stoic Warriors: The Ancient Philosophy behind the Military Mind* (Oxford and New York: Oxford University Press, 2005), esp. ch. 4, 'A Warrior's Anger'.

38. French, 'An American Ethicist's Perspective', 299.

39. Aitken Report, 1.

40. *Modernising Defence Training: Report of the Defence Training Review* (London: UK Ministry of Defence, 2001), 5.

41. The changes are summarized in the Aitken Report, paras. 15–16 and Annex A, 'Measures to Prevent Abuse on Operations since 2003'.

42. Emma Brockes, 'What Happens in War Happens', an interview with Lynddie England, *Guardian*, 3 Jan. 2009.
43. Dannatt, 'Foreword', in Reed and Ryall (eds.), *Price of Peace*, p. xiv.
44. Mental Health Advisory Team IV, Operation Iraqi Freedom 05–07, Final Report, 17 Nov. 2006, Office of the Surgeon General, Multinational Force Iraq, and Office of the Surgeon General, United States Army Medical Command, quoted by Ricks, *Gamble*, 7–8.

CHAPTER 7: VIRTUOUS CONSEQUENTIALISM

1. Williams, *Ethics and the Limits of Philosophy*, 17
2. Walzer, *Just and Unjust Wars*, p. xvii.
3. A statistic quoted by Blackburn, *Being Good*, 57.
4. The moral equivalence of acts and omissions with identical consequences is propounded by Glover, *Causing Death and Saving Lives*, chs. 7 and 8. See also Jonathan Bennett, *Morality and Consequences: The Tanner Lectures on Human Values, 1981* (Cambridge: Cambridge University Press; Salt Lake City: University of Utah Press, 1981).
5. Feodor Dostoyevsky, *The Brothers Karamazov*, trans. David Magarshack (London: Penguin Books, 1982), 339.
6. Ford, 'Morality of Obliteration Bombing'.
7. Bernard Williams, 'Politics and Moral Character', in Stuart Hampshire (ed.), *Public and Private Morality* (Cambridge: Cambridge University Press, 1978), 56.
8. Stuart Hampshire, 'Public and Private Morality', in Hampshire (ed.), *Public and Private Morality*, 50. The reference to 'love and friendship' is on p. 52.
9. Hampshire, 'Public and Private Morality', 50.
10. Thomas Nagel, 'Ruthlessness in Public Life', in Hampshire (ed.), *Public and Private Morality*, 84.
11. Nagel, 'Ruthlessness in Public Life', 85.
12. Nagel, 'Ruthlessness in Public Life', 85.
13. Nagel, 'Ruthlessness in Public Life', 82.
14. Michael Walzer, 'Political Action: The Problem of Dirty Hands', *Philosophy and Public Affairs*, 2/2 (Winter 1973), 160–80, repr. in Sanford Levinson (ed.), *Torture: A Collection* (Oxford: Oxford University Press, 2004).
15. Bobbitt, *Terror and Consent*, 361.
16. Niccolò Machiavelli, *The Prince*, trans. George Bull (London: Penguin Books, 2003), 50.
17. Hampshire, 'Public and Private Morality', 52.
18. A. T. Mahan, 'The Military Rule of Obedience', *Retrospect and Prospect* (London: Sampson Low, Marston, 1902), 283.

CHAPTER 8: THE PROTEAN NATURE OF WAR

1. Bernard Brodie, 'The Atomic Bomb and American Security', Memorandum no. 18, Yale Institute of International Studies, 1945, repr. in Brodie (ed.), *The Absolute Weapon* (New York: Harcourt, Brace, 1946), 76.
2. President George Bush, State of the Union Speech, 29 Jan. 1991.
3. The words are those used by Chamberlain to describe Czechoslovakia.
4. So related by Smith, *Utility of Force*, 352.
5. UN Department of Peacekeeping Operations website, background to UNPROFOR, http://www.un.org/Depts/dpko/co_mission/unprof_b.htm.
6. Samantha Power, *A Problem from Hell: America and the Age of Genocide* (New York: Basic Books, 2002), describes the massacre in chapter 11.
7. General Sir Rupert Smith has provided his own account of these events in Smith, *Utility of Force*, ch. 9, 'Bosnia: Using Force amongst the People'.
8. Mary Kaldor, *New and Old Wars: Organised Violence in a Global Era* (1999; repr. with a new afterword, Cambridge: Polity Press, 2001).
9. Smith, *Utility of Force*, 403–4.
10. Thucydides, *Peloponnesian War*, trans. Warner, 241.
11. John Keegan, *War and our World: The Reith Lectures 1998* (London: Pimlico, 1999), 72.
12. General Jack Keane on the *Jim Lehrer News Hour*, 18 Apr. 2006, quoted by John A. Nagl, 'Foreword', in *US Army and Marine Corps Counterinsurgency Field Manual* (Chicago: University of Chicago Press, 2007), p. xiv. See also John A. Nagl, *Learning to Eat Soup with a Knife: Counterinsurgency Lessons from Malaya and Vietnam* (Chicago: University of Chicago Press, 2005).
13. The *US Army and Marine Corps Counterinsurgency Field Manual*, with a Foreword by General David H. Petraeus and Lieutenant General James F. Amos, was first issued on 15 Dec. 2006.
14. Rt. Hon. Tony Blair, 'Doctrine of the International Community', 22 Apr. 1999, Hilton Hotel, Chicago, Illinois.
15. Whether or not we are at 'war' with terror has occasioned much debate. Philip Bobbitt argues for 'war' in *Terror and Consent*. The contrary view is taken by Michael Howard in 'Philip Bobbitt's *Terror and Consent*: A Brief Critique', in Fisher and Wicker (eds.), *Just War on Terror?* See also Michael Howard, 'Are we at War? ', *Survival*, 50/4 (Aug.–Sept. 2008), 247–56.
16. The increase in casualties is noted by Brian M. Jenkins, 'Combating Global War on Terrorism', in Peter Katona, Michael B. Intriligator, and John P. Sullivan (eds.), *Countering Terrorism and WMD: Creating a Global Counter-Terrorist Network* (Abingdon and New York: Routledge, 2006), 182.
17. One of the paradoxes of counter-insurgency is that 'the more you protect your force, the less secure you may be' (*US Army and Marine Corps Counterinsurgency Field Manual*, 48).

18. Osama bin Laden, 'Conversation with Terror', interview by Rahimilla Yusufzai, *Time,* 11 Jan. 1999, p. 39.

19. The intelligence operation to uncover and dismantle the Khan network is described in the Butler Report, *The Review of Intelligence on Weapons of Mass Destruction,* Report of a Committee of Privy Counsellors, chaired by Lord Butler of Brockenwell (House of Commons 898, 14 July 2004), ch. 2, paras. 64–75.

20. Kamran Khan and Molly Moore, 'Nuclear Experts Briefed Bin Laden, Pakistanis Say', *Washington Post,* 12 Dec. 2001, p. 1.

21. Bobbitt, *Terror and Consent,* especially ch. 1, 'The New Masque of Terrorism'.

22. World Islamic Front Statement, 22 Feb. 1998. The full text is in the appendix to chapter 4, 'Arguments Concerning Resistance in Contemporary Islam', by Kelsey in Sorabji and Rodin (eds.), *Ethics of War,* 89–91.

23. Osama bin Laden called for all Americans to convert to Islam and submit to God's laws as revealed in Islam in his August 1996 'Declaration of War against the Americans Occupying the Land of the Two Holy Places', in Bruce Lawrence (ed.), *Messages to the World: The Statements of Osama bin Laden* (New York: Verso, 2005). The al-Qaeda leader in Iraq, the late Abu Musab al-Zarqawi, declared a bitter war against the principle of democracy in January 2005, BBC News website, 25 Jan. 2005, http://news.bbc.co.uk/1/hi/world/middle_east/4200783.stm.

24. George W. Bush, *The National Security Strategy of the United States of America,* 17 Sept. 2002, www.whitehouse.gov/nsc/nss.pdf, p. 6.

25. *Guardian,* 7 Mar. 2008, p. 9.

26. The debate of the War Cabinet is described in Ian Kershaw, *Fateful Choices: Ten Decisions that Changed the World, 1940–41* (London: Allen Lane, 2007), 11–54.

27. *US Army and Marine Corps Counterinsurgency Field Manual,* 51.

28. Sarah Sewall, 'Introduction', in *US Army and Marine Corps Counterinsurgency Field Manual* (Chicago: University of Chicago Press, 2007), p. xxii.

29. Smith, *Utility of Force,* 284.

30. As noted by Sewall, 'Introduction', p. xxxi.

31. The statistics for civilian deaths are from Kaldor, *New and Old Wars,* 100.

32. Threats to civilians in current wars are detailed in Hugo Slim, *Killing Civilians* (London: Hurst & Co., 2007).

CHAPTER 9: EXTREME TIMES, EXTREME MEASURES

1. Francis Fukuyama, *The End of History and the Last Man* (New York: Avon Books, 1992).

2. Bobbitt, *Terror and Consent,* 529. In the 2008 hardback edition of *Terror and Consent* Bobbitt tended to use pre-emption and preclusion interchangeably, but

he qualified this in the US paperback edition (2009). He now favours 'preclusion' for military action against grave but non-imminent threats, as he explains in Philip Bobbitt, 'A Reemphasis more than a Reply', in Fisher and Wicker (eds.), *Just War on Terror?* See also in the same volume David Fisher, 'Terror and Pre-emption: Can Military Pre-emption ever be Just? ' for a fuller exposition of my critique of pre-emption.

3. Bobbitt, *Terror and Consent*, 530.
4. Bobbitt, *Terror and Consent*, 138.
5. Bush, *National Security Strategy of the United States of America*, 15.
6. Bobbitt, *Terror and Consent*, 137.
7. Hillary Clinton, confirmation hearing, Senate Foreign Relations Committee, 13 Jan. 2009. President Obama's *National Security Strategy*, May 2010, can be viewed at www.whitehouse.gov/sites/default/files/rss_viewer/national_security_ strategy.pdf.
8. Daniel Webster, the US Secretary of State, in his written response to Lord Ashburton, the British Ambassador, 6 Aug. 1842, in John Bassett Moore, *History and Digest of the International Arbitrations to which the United States has been a Party* (Washington: Government Print Office, 1898), i. 896.
9. Bobbitt, *Terror and Consent*, 531.
10. Osama bin Laden declared war against the USA in August 1996; see his 'Declaration of War against the Americans Occupying the Land of the Two Holy Places', in Lawrence (ed.), *Messages to the World*.
11. A distinction between just pre-emption and unjust prevention is, for example, drawn in the report of the Church of England, General Synod, Board for Social Responsibility, *Iraq: Would Military Action Be Justified? The Church's Contribution to the Debate*, GS Report 1475 (London: Church House, 2002), sects. 54, 46. A more careful analysis of the varied uses of the terms 'preemption' and 'prevention' is in the editors' introduction to Henry Shue and David Rodin (eds.), *Preemption: Military Action and Moral Justification* (Oxford: Oxford University Press, 2007).
12. A point well made by Nigel Biggar, 'Between Development and Doubt: The Recent Career of Just War Doctrine in British Churches', in Reed and Ryall (eds.), *Price of Peace*, 70.
13. Grotius, *On the Law of War and Peace*, bk. II, ch. I, sect. V, in Reichberg, Syse, and Begby (eds.), *Ethics of War*, 403.
14. Grotius, *On the Law of War and Peace*, bk. II, ch. XXII, sect. V, in Reichberg, Syse and Begby (eds.), *Ethics of War*, 410.
15. UNSCR 487, passed unanimously, was 'deeply concerned about the danger to international peace and security created by the premeditated Israeli air attack on Iraqi nuclear installations on 7th June 1981'.
16. Jeff McMahan, 'Preventive War and the Killing of the Innocent', in Sorabji and Rodin (eds.), *Ethics of War*, 186. McMahan argues that preventive war is necessarily indiscriminate because 'it is waged against those who are not, at least

as yet, responsible for an unjust threat' (p. 178). David Rodin similarly argues that
the problem with prevention is that, 'in preventive war, one attacks and kills those
who have not yet committed a wrongful aggression against you' (Shue and Rodin
(eds.), *Preemption*, 164–5).

17. Alberto Gonzales, Counsel to the President, memorandum to President Bush,
    25 Jan. 2002, quoted in Philippe Sands, *Torture Team: Deception, Cruelty and the
    Compromise of Law* (London: Allen Lane, 2008), 222.
18. *Ireland* v. *United Kingdom* (1978) 2 EHRR 25, Judgment of the European Court
    of Human Rights.
19. Sands, *Torture Team*, 14.
20. Testimony of Lieutenant General Randall M. Schmidt, taken 24 Aug. 2005 at
    Davis-Monthan Air Force Base, Arizona, for Department of the Army Inspect-
    or General, Virginia, quoted in Sands, *Torture Team*, 8.
21. Steven Bradbury, Principal Deputy Assistant Attorney General, memorandum
    to John Rizzo, Acting General Counsel, CIA, 30 May 2005, p. 5. This can be
    viewed, together with the other 'torture memos', at www.aclu.org/safefree/
    general/olc_memos.html.
22. The techniques, including the use of 'insects placed in a confinement box', are
    described in the memorandum by Jay Bybee, Assistant Attorney General, to
    the Acting General Counsel of the CIA, 1 Aug. 2002.
23. Mark Tran, 'CIA Admits "Waterboarding" al-Qaida Suspects', www.guard-
    ian.co.uk, 5 Feb. 2008.
24. Bradbury memorandum, 30 May 2005, pp. 8–9.
25. Walzer, 'Political Action: The Problem of Dirty Hands' (1973), repr. in
    Levinson (ed.), *Torture*, 64–5.
26. Alan M. Dershowitz, *Why Terrorism Works* (New Haven and London: Yale
    University Press, 2002), 143–4.
27. Jean Bethke Elshtain, 'Reflection on the Problem of "Dirty Hands"', in
    Levinson (ed.), *Torture*, 78.
28. Dershowitz, *Why Terrorism Works*, 144–5.
29. A point well made by Barrie Paskins, 'Realism and the Just War', *Journal of
    Military Ethics*, 6/2 (2007), 126.
30. Parker Report, *Report of the Committee of Privy Counsellors Appointed to Consider
    Authorised Procedures for the Interrogation of Persons Suspected of Terrorism*, Chairman:
    Lord Parker of Waddington, Cmnd. 4901 (London: HMSO, Mar. 1972), 2.
31. Convention III relative to the Treatment of Prisoners of War, Article 3,
    Geneva, 12 Apr. 1949, International Committee of the Red Cross, Inter-
    national Humanitarian Law, Treaties and Documents. This can be viewed at
    www.icrc.org/ihl.nsf/WebART/375-590006.
32. UN Convention against Torture and Other Cruel, Inhuman and Degrading
    Treatment or Punishment came into force on 26 June 1987. It can be viewed at
    www.un.org/documents/ga/res/39/a39r046.htm.
33. C. S. Lewis, *Voyage to Venus* (London: Pan Books, 1953), 90.

34. Jean Amery, *Par-dela le crime et le chatiment: Essai pour surmonter l'insurmontable* (1966; Arles: Actes Sud, 1994), 79.

35. Walzer, 'Political Action: The Problem of Dirty Hands', in Levinson (ed.), *Torture*.

36. Alan Dershowitz, 'Want to Torture? Get a Warrant', *San Francisco Chronicle*, 22 Jan. 2002. The proposals were developed further in 'Should the Ticking Bomb Terrorist be Tortured? ' in Dershowitz, *Why Terrorism Works*, ch. 4. Dershowitz responded to his critics in 'Tortured Reasoning', in Levinson (ed.), *Torture*, 257–81.

37. Dershowitz, *Why Terrorism Works*, 150

38. Dershowitz, *Why Terrorism Works*, 151.

39. Dershowitz, 'Tortured Reasoning', 273.

40. Dershowitz, 'Tortured Reasoning', 265.

41. Richard A. Prosner, 'Torture, Terrorism and Interrogation', in Levinson (ed.), *Torture*, 296.

42. Parker Report, 3.

43. Dershowitz, 'Tortured Reasoning', 263.

44. Dershowitz, 'Tortured Reasoning', 263.

45. Walzer, 'Political Action: The Problem of Dirty Hands', in Levinson (ed.), *Torture*, 63.

CHAPTER 10: GULF WARS

1. Lawrence Freedman and Efraim Karsh, *The Gulf Conflict 1990–1991* (London: Faber and Faber, 1993), 212.

2. A delay of 'one year' for sanctions to work was, for example, urged by Roger Williamson, *Just War in the Gulf?* (Uppsala: Life and Peace Institute, 1991), 62.

3. Perez de Cuellar, quoted in *Daily Telegraph*, 15 Jan. 1991.

4. Freedman and Karsh, *Gulf Conflict*, 408–9, 329.

5. John Keegan, *The Iraq War* (London: Pimlico, 2005), 218.

6. Orend, *Morality of War*, 49.

7. 'Iraq: Military Campaign Objectives', para. 1. The text is quoted in full as Butler Report, annex C.

8. Micah L. Sifry and Christopher Cerf (eds.), *The Iraq War Reader: History, Documents, Opinions* (New York and London: Simon Schuster International, 2003), 504. The full text, 'President Bush Addresses the Nation', 17 Mar. 2003, can be viewed at www.pbs.org/newshour/bb/white_house/jan-june03/bush_3.17.html.

9. Rt. Hon. Tony Blair's evidence to the Butler Commission, Butler Report, para. 284.

10. Rt. Hon. Tony Blair's evidence to the Chilcot inquiry, 29 Jan. 2010. This and all other quotes from the inquiry can be found at www.iraqinquiry.org.uk/transcripts/oral evidence.
11. Butler Report, para. 266, quotes the conclusion of a British government policy review in March 2002 that there was 'no justification for action against Iraq in self-defence to counter imminent threats of terrorism'.
12. Sifry and Cerf (eds.), *Iraq War Reader*, 503.
13. The conclusion of the Joint Intelligence Committee, 28 Nov. 2001, quoted in Butler Report, para. 481.
14. *Iraq Survey Group Final Report*, 30 Sept. 2004, i. 34, viewed at www.globalsecurity.org/wmd/library/report/2004/isg-final-report.
15. Blair's evidence to Chilcot inquiry, 29 Jan. 2010.
16. Hans Blix, *Disarming Iraq* (London: Bloomsbury, 2004), 112. Academic experts also shared the consensus view that Iraq had WMD; see IISS, 'Iraq's Weapons of Mass Destruction: A Net Assessment', strategic dossier, 9 Sept. 2002.
17. Butler Report, para. 209.
18. Butler Report, para. 56.
19. *Iraq Survey Group Final Report*, 30 Sept. 2004, i. 34.
20. Blair evidence to Chilcot inquiry, 29 Jan. 2010.
21. Blair evidence to Chilcot inquiry, 29 Jan. 2010: 'The only commitment I gave was to deal with Saddam. That was not a covert position, but a public position.'
22. So argued, for example, by Jonathan Steele, *Defeat: Why They Lost Iraq* (London and New York: I. B. Tauris, 2008), ch. V.
23. Quoted by Bob Woodward, *State of Denial* (New York: Simon and Schuster, 2006), 360.
24. Michael Gordon, 'Pre-War Planning for Iraq Painted Very Rosy Picture,' *New York Times,* 16 Feb. 2007.
25. Butler Report, para. 332.
26. Butler Report, paras. 508–9.
27. Butler Report, para. 330.
28. The Attorney General, Lord Goldsmith, set out his findings in a Written Answer in the House of Lords, 17 Mar. 2003. His answer, together with a fuller explanation prepared by the FCO, 'Iraq: Legal Basis for the Use of Force', are quoted in Butler Report, Annex D.
29. Evidence of Sir Michael Wood, Legal Adviser, FCO, and Elizabet Wilmshurst, Deputy Legal adviser, FCO, to the Chilcot inquiry, 26 Jan. 2010.
30. Quoted by Thomas E. Ricks, *Fiasco: The American Military Adventure in Iraq* (London and New York: Allen Lane, 2006), 95.
31. Keegan, *Iraq War*, 118.
32. Rt. Hon. Tony Blair, MP, speech in his Sedgefield constituency, 5 Mar. 2004.
33. Keegan, *Iraq War*, 204–5.

34. The military casualty figures in this and the next paragraph are collated from government sources by the Brookings Institute and published in the Brookings Iraq Index, viewed at www.brookings.edu/iraqindex. The fatalities are total figures, including accidental deaths. Of the 4,413 US military deaths, 3,488 died as a result of hostile incidents. The figures for monthly civilian casualties and refugees are also from the Brookings Iraq Index.

35. The total civilian casualty figures are documented civilian deaths from violence as estimated by the Iraq Body Count on 29 June 2010, www.iraqbodycount. org/database.

36. The tactical success of the surge operation is described in Ricks, *Gamble*.

37. Quoted in Ricks, *Fiasco*, 109–10.

38. Quoted in Tim Pritchard, *Ambush Alley* (New York: Ballantine Books, 2005), 234.

39. Evidence of Major General Tim Cross to Chilcot inquiry, 7 Dec. 2009.

40. Butler Report, para. 459.

41. Steele, *Defeat*, 164.

42. Chatham House was, for example, tasked by the government to run seminars on how to handle post-conflict Iraq, but only during and after the conflict.

43. Hilary Synnott, *Bad Days in Basra* (London and New York: I. B. Tauris, 2008), 136.

44. Synnott, *Bad Days in Basra*, 136.

45. Synnott, *Bad Days in Basra*, 137.

46. Evidence of Sir Suma Chakrabarti, Permanent Secretary, DFID, to Chilcot inquiry, 8 Dec. 2009.

47. Ricks, *Fiasco*, 392.

48. 'The Descent into Abuse', ch. 12, in Ricks, *Fiasco*.

49. The FCO document leaked to the *Sunday Times*, 23 May 2004, is quoted in Steele, *Defeat*, 152.

50. 'Iraq: Military Campaign Objectives', quoted in Butler Report, annex C, para. 5.

51. Report by Major General Antonio Taguba, quoted in Ricks, *Fiasco*, 378.

52. Aitken Report, para. 42.

53. Aitken Report, para. 5.

54. Steele, *Defeat*, 257.

55. David Kilcullen, quoted in Ricks, *Gamble*, 29.

56. Ewan MacAskill, 'Six Years after Iraq Invasion, Obama Sets out his Exit Plan', *Guardian*, 28 Feb. 2009.

57. Steele, *Defeat*, 257.

58. General David H. Petraeus, Commander, Multi-National Force–Iraq, 'Report to Congress on the Situation in Iraq, 8–9 April 2008', 1, 6.

59. Petraeus, 'Report to Congress', 6.

CHAPTER 11: HUMANITARIAN INTERVENTION

1. This heroic moment from the academic world is noted by Michael Walzer in 'The Triumph of Just War Theory', in Walzer, *Arguing about War* (New Haven and London: Yale University Press, 2004), 4, 197 n. 3.

2. Vitoria, *On the American Indians*, 3.5, sect. 15, in Vitoria: Political Writings, ed. Pagden and Lawrance, 288. *De Indis* was published in 1539.

3. Grotius, *On the Law of War and Peace*, bk. II, ch. XX, sect. XL(1), in Reichberg, Syse, and Begby (eds.), *Ethics of War*, 407.

4. Walzer, *Just and Unjust Wars*, 57–8. Walzer has more recently argued in favour of intervention: 'I don't mean to abandon the principle of non-intervention—only to honour its exceptions' (Walzer, *Arguing about War*, 81).

5. UN Security Council Resolution (SCOR), 1606th Meeting, 4 Dec. 1971, 17, quoted in Nicholas J. Wheeler, *Saving Strangers* (Oxford: Oxford University Press, 2002), 61.

6. UN Security Council Resolution (SCOR), 1606th Meeting, 4 Dec. 1971, 32, quoted in Wheeler, *Saving Strangers*. 63.

7. SCOR, 1608th Meeting, 6 Dec. 1971.

8. David Fisher, 'The Ethics of Intervention', *Survival: The IISS Quarterly*, 36/1 (Spring 1994), 51–60. See also David Fisher, 'Some Corner of a Foreign Field' and 'The Ethics of Intervention and Former Yugoslavia', in Roger Williamson (ed.), *Some Corner of a Foreign Field: Intervention and World Order* (Basingstoke: Macmillan; New York: St Martin's Press, 1998), 28–37, 166–73; and David Fisher, 'Humanitarian Intervention', in Reed and Ryall (eds.), *Price of Peace*, 101–17.

9. The new interventionist mood among international-relations scholars is illustrated in the essays in Dunne and Wheeler (eds.), *Human Rights in Global Politics*. The more traditional realist approach is defended in David Chandler, *From Kosovo to Kabul: Human Rights and International Intervention* (London: Pluto Press, 2002).

10. William Shawcross, *Deliver Us from Evil* (London: Bloomsbury Publishing, 2000), 116.

11. Shawcross, *Deliver Us from Evil*, 117.

12. Blair, 'Doctrine of the International Community', 22 Apr. 1999.

13. Prime Minister Rt. Hon. Tony Blair in a TV interview, Oct. 2001, quoted in *BBC Panorama*, 3 July 2005.

14. UK Parliamentary Debates, Lords, 6 May 1999, col. 904 (Baroness Symons), previously issued as a written answer on 16 Nov. 1998.

15. International Commission on Intervention and State Sovereignty, *The Responsibility to Protect* (Ottawa: International Development Research Centre, Dec. 2001), p. viii.

16. International Commission on Intervention and State Sovereignty, *The Responsibility to Protect*, p. xi.

17. International Commission on Intervention and State Sovereignty, *The Responsibility to Protect*, p. xii; see also paras. 4.18 and 4.19, p. 32.
18. UN Secretary General's High Level Panel on Threats, Challenges, and Change, *A More Secure World: Our Shared Responsibility*, report (New York: United Nations, 2004), 4.
19. UN Secretary General's High Level Panel on Threats, Challenges, and Change, *A More Secure World*, 57–8.
20. UN General Assembly 2005, *World Summit Outcome*, 15 Sept. 2005, paras. 138–9.
21. Tony Blair's address to the UN Summit on 14 Sept. 2005, reported in Ian Williams, 'Annan has Paid his Dues', *Guardian*, 20 Sept. 2005.
22. International Commission on Intervention and State Sovereignty, *The Responsibility to Protect*, 32–7; UN Secretary General's High Level Panel on Threats, Challenges, and Change, *A More Secure World*, 57–8.
23. US and Russian/Chinese motives in opposing the inclusion of criteria in the Summit declaration are noted in Alex J. Bellamy, 'The Responsibility to Protect and the Problem of Military Intervention', *International Affairs,* 84/4 (July 2008), 625.
24. International Commission on Intervention and State Sovereignty, *The Responsibility to Protect*, para. 6.37, p. 55.
25. Kofi Annan, BBC *Panorama*, 3 July 2005.
26. So argued by Bellamy, 'The Responsibility to Protect and the Problem of Military Intervention', 624.
27. Hedley Bull, 'Conclusion', in Hedley Bull (ed.), *Intervention in World Politics* (Oxford: Oxford University Press, 1984), 195.
28. International Commission on Intervention and State Sovereignty, *The Responsibility to Protect*, para. 6.14, p. 49.
29. Quoted by Shawcross, *Deliver Us from Evil*, 375.
30. Blair, 'Doctrine of the International Community', 22 Apr. 1999.
31. Kofi Annan, quoted in C. R. Whitney, 'The No Man's Land in the Fight for Human Rights', *New York Times*, 12 Dec. 1999.
32. The need for an alliance of democracies to counter the new terrorist threat has been argued for by, among others, Bobbitt, *Terror and Consent*, 537.
33. Walzer, *Arguing about War*, 81.

CHAPTER 12: MAKING WAR JUST

1. Francisco Suarez, *Disputation XIII: On War*, sect. VI.5, in Reichberg, Syse, and Begby (eds.), *Ethics of War*, 358.
2. Isaiah, 11: 6.
3. Quoted by Jean Bethke Elshtain, *Just War against Terror* (New York: Basic Books, 2005), 46.

4. Keegan, *War and our World*, 1.

5. Keegan, *War and our World*, 72–3.

6. Such is the hope of the World Federalist Movement, founded in 1947 and still active. See G. Clark and L. Sohn, *World Peace through World Law* (Cambridge, MA: Harvard University Press, 1960).

7. An argument first advanced by Charles Castel, the eighteenth-century Abbé de Saint-Pierre, in Abbé de Saint-Pierre, *Projet pour rendre la paix perpetuelle en Europe*, ed. Simone Goyard-Fabre (Paris: Fayard, 1986).

8. The contortions of the liberal conscience in addressing war are magisterially traced in Michael Howard, *War and the Liberal Conscience* (1978; London: Hurst & Co., 2008). For Paine, see pp. 20–1; for Bentham, pp. 24–6; for Mill, p. 29.

9. I. Kant, *Perpetual Peace: A Philosophical Sketch*, in *Kant's Political Writings*, ed. Hans Reiss (Cambridge: Cambridge University Press, 1970), 113.

10. National Conference of US Catholic Bishops, 'The Harvest of Justice is Sown in Peace', Pastoral Letter, 17 Nov. 1993, sect. I B2, notes: 'The just-war tradition is not . . . a set of mechanical criteria that automatically yields a simple answer, but a way of moral reasoning to discern the ethical limits of action.' The letter can be viewed at www.usccb.org/sdwp/harvest.shtml.

11. *The Governance of Britain: Constitutional Renewal,* Cm. 7342-1, volume I, presented to Parliament 25 Mar. 2008 (Norwich: HMSO, 2008). See, in particular, 'War Powers: The Way Forward", 50–7.

12. 'Office for Budget Responsibility: Watchdog Assigned to Stop Chancellors "Fiddling the Figures"', *Guardian,* 18 May 2010, p. 7.

13. Vitoria, *On the Law of War*, 2.2, sect. 24, in *Vitoria: Political Writings*, ed. Pagden and Lawrance, 308.

14. S. E. Finer, *The Man on Horseback: The Role of the Military in Politics* (1962; London: Pinter Publishers, 1988), 4.

15. Samuel P. Huntington, *The Soldier and the State* (Cambridge, MA, and London: Harvard University Press, 1957; repr. 2000), 78.

16. Quoted in Walzer, *Just and Unjust Wars*, 313.

17. The International Criminal Court, 'The ICC at a Glance', p. 1, www.icc-cpi.int/-3k.

18. US objections to the ICC, voiced by both the Clinton and the Bush administrations, are explained by John B. Bellinger, Legal Adviser to the State Department, in 'The United States and the International Criminal Court: Where We've Been and Where We're Going', Remarks to the DePaul University College of Law, Chicago, 25 Apr. 2008, US Department of State, http://www.state.gov.

19. Such concerns were voiced by both the UN Secretary General and the British government. See Alex Duvall Smith, 'Britain Blocks Prosecution of Sudan's Ruler', *Observer*, 14 Sept. 2008.

20. Huntington, *Soldier and the State*, 465.

Bibliography

Aitken Report, *An Investigation into Cases of Deliberate Abuse and Unlawful Killing in Iraq in 2003 and 2004* (London: UK Ministry of Defence, 25 Jan. 2008).

Allin, Dana H., 'NATO's Balkan Interventions', Adelphi Paper 347 (Oxford: Oxford University Press for IISS, 2002).

Altham, J. E. J., and Harrison, R. (eds.), *World, Mind and Ethics* (Cambridge: Cambridge University Press, 1995).

Amery, Jean, *Par-dela le crime et le chatiment: Essai pour surmonter l'insurmontable* (1966; Arles: Actes Sud, 1994).

Annas, Julia, *The Morality of Happiness* (Oxford: Oxford University Press, 1993).

Anscombe, G. E. M., 'War and Murder', repr. in Richard Wasserstrom (ed.), *War and Morality* (Belmont, CA: Wadsworth, 1970).

Anscombe, G. E. M., 'Modern Moral Philosophy', *Philosophy*, 35 (1958), repr. in Anscombe, *Collected Philosophical Papers* (Oxford: Basil Blackwell, 1981), iii. 26–42; and in Roger Crisp and Michael Slote (eds.), *Virtue Ethics* (Oxford: Oxford University Press, 1997), 26–44.

Aquinas, St Thomas, *Aquinas: Political Writings*, ed. R. W. Dyson (Cambridge: Cambridge University Press, 2002).

Aquinas, St Thomas, *Aquinas: Selected Political Writings*, ed. A. P. D'Entreves (Oxford: Basil Blackwell, 1948).

Aquinas, St Thomas, *St Thomas Aquinas, Summa Theologiae, Volume 42, Courage*, trans. Anthony Ross OP and P. G. Walsh (London: Blackfriars in conjunction with Eyre & Spottiswoode, 1966).

Aquinas, St Thomas, *St Thomas Aquinas Summa Theologiae, Volume 36, Prudence*, trans. Thomas Gilby OP (London: Blackfriars in conjunction with Eyre & Spottiswoode, 1974).

Aristotle, *Nicomachean Ethics*, trans. J. A. K. Thomson, in *The Ethics of Aristotle* (London: Penguin Books, 1966).

Ash, Timothy Garton, 'What Young British Muslims Say Can Be Shocking: Some of it is also True', *Guardian*, 10 Aug. 2006.

Augustine, St, selected writings, in Gregory Reichberg, Henrik Syse, and Endre Begby (eds.), *The Ethics of War: Classic and Contemporary Readings* (Oxford: Basil Blackwell, 2006).

Augustine, St, *City of God*, in *Basic Writings of St Augustine*, ed. Whitney Oates (New York: Random House, 1948).

Ayer, A. J., *Language, Truth and Logic* (London; Gollancz, 1936).

Ball, Patrick, Betts, Wendy, Scheuren, Fritz, Dudukovich, Jana, and Asher, Jana, *Killings and Refugee Flow in Kosovo, March–June 1999: A Report to the International Criminal Tribunal for the Former Yugoslavia*, 3 Jan. 2002 (Washington: American Association for the Advancement of Science, 2002); http://shr.aaas.org/kosovo/icty_report.pdf.

Baynes, John, *Morale: A Story of Men and Courage: The Second Scottish Rifles at the Battle of Neuve Chapelle, 1918* (London: Cassell, 1967).

Beevor, Antony, *Stalingrad* (London: Penguin Books, 1999).

Bellamy, Alex J., 'The Responsibility to Protect and the Problem of Military Intervention', *International Affairs*, 84/4 (July 2008), 615–39.

Bellinger, John B., 'The United States and the International Criminal Court: Where We've Been and Where We're Going', Remarks to the DePaul University College of Law, Chicago, 25 Apr. 2008, US Department of State, www.state.gov.

Bennett, Jonathan, *Morality and Consequences: The Tanner Lectures on Human Values, 1981* (Cambridge: Cambridge University Press; Salt Lake City: University of Utah Press, 1981).

Bennett, Jonathan, 'Whatever the Consequences', *Analysis*, 26 (1965–6), 83–102.

Bentham, Jeremy, *An Introduction to the Principles of Morals* (1789; Oxford: Clarendon Press, 1907).

Berlin, Isaiah, *The Proper Study of Mankind*, ed. Henry Hardy and Roger Hausheer (London: Chatto & Windus, 1997).

Biggar, Nigel, *Aiming to Kill: The Ethics of Suicide and Euthanasia* (London: Darton, Longman and Todd, 2004).

Biggar, Nigel, 'Between Development and Doubt: The Recent Career of Just War Doctrine in British Churches', in Charles Reed and David Ryall (eds.), *The Price of Peace: Just War in the Twenty-First Century* (Cambridge: Cambridge University Press, 2007).

Blackburn, Simon, *Being Good: A Short Introduction to Ethics* (Oxford: Oxford University Press, 2001).

Blair, Rt. Hon. Tony, 'Doctrine of the International Community', 22 Apr. 1999, Hilton Hotel, Chicago, Illinois, www.number10.gov.uk/Page1297.

Blix, Hans, *Disarming Iraq* (London: Bloomsbury, 2004).

Bobbitt, Philip, 'A Reemphasis More than a Reply', in David Fisher and Brian Wicker (eds.), *Just War on Terror? A Christian and Muslim Response* (Aldershot: Ashgate, 2010).

Bobbitt, Philip, *Terror and Consent: The Wars for the Twenty-First Century* (London and New York: Allen Lane, 2008; paperback edn., New York: Anchor Books, 2009).

Bradbury, Steven, memorandum to John Rizzo, Acting General Counsel, CIA, 30 May 2005, www.aclu.org/safefree/general/olc_memos.html.

Brockes, Emma, 'What Happens in War Happens', an interview with Lynddie England, *Guardian*, 3 Jan. 2009.

Brodie, Bernard, 'The Atomic Bomb and American Security', Memorandum no. 18, Yale Institute of International Studies, 1945, repr. in Brodie (ed.), *The Absolute Weapon* (New York: Harcourt, Brace, 1946).

Browning, Christopher R., *Ordinary Men: Reserve Police Battalion 101 and the Final Solution* (New York: HarperCollins, 1992).

Bull, Hedley, *The Anarchical Society* (Houndsmill: Palgrave, 2002).

Bull, Hedley (ed.), *Intervention in World Politics* (Oxford: Oxford University Press, 1984).

Bush, George W., *The National Security Strategy of the United States of America*, 17 Sept. 2002, www.whitehouse.gov/nsc/nss.pdf.

Butler Report, *The Review of Intelligence on Weapons of Mass Destruction*, Report of a Committee of Privy Counsellors, chaired by Lord Butler of Brockenwell (House of Commons 898, 14 July 2004).

Calder, Angus, *The People's War: Britain 1939–1945* (London: Cape, 1969).

Cavanaugh, T. A., *Double-Effect Reasoning: Doing Good and Avoiding Evil* (Oxford and New York: Oxford University Press, 2006).

Chandler, David, *From Kosovo to Kabul: Human Rights and International Intervention* (London: Pluto Press, 2002).

Church of England, General Synod, Board for Social Responsibility, *Iraq: Would Military Action Be Justified? The Church's Contribution to the Debate*, GS Report 1475 (London: Church House, 2002).

Clark, G., and Sohn, L., *World Peace through World Law* (Cambridge, MA: Harvard University Press, 1960).

Coates, A. J., *The Ethics of War* (Manchester and London: Manchester University Press, 1997).

Cornford, F. M., *Thucydides Mythistoricus* (London: Edward Arnold, 1907).

Countering International Terrorism: The United Kingdom's Strategy, July 2006, Cm. 6888 (Norwich: HMSO, 2006). The strategy was updated in *The United Kingdom's Strategy for Countering International Terrorism, March 2009*, Cm. 7547 (Norwich: The Stationery Office).

Crisp, Roger (ed.), *How Should One Live? Essays on the Virtues* (Oxford: Oxford University Press, 2003).

Crisp, Roger, and Slote, Michael (eds.), *Virtue Ethics* (Oxford: Oxford University Press, 1997).

Daalder, Ivo H., and O'Hanlon, Michael E., *Winning Ugly: NATO's War to Save Kosovo* (Washington: Brookings Institution, 2000).

Dannatt, General Sir Richard, 'Foreword', in Charles Reed and David Ryall (eds.), *The Price of Peace: Just War in the Twenty-First Century* (Cambridge: Cambridge University Press, 2007).

Dawkins, Richard, *The Selfish Gene* (Oxford: Oxford University Press, 1976).

Dent, N. J. H., *The Moral Psychology of the Virtues* (Cambridge: Cambridge University Press, 1984).

Dershowitz, Alan M., 'Tortured Reasoning', in Sanford Levinson (ed.), *Torture: A Collection* (Oxford: Oxford University Press, 2004).

Dershowitz, Alan M., 'Want to Torture? Get a Warrant', *San Francisco Chronicle*, 22 Jan. 2002.

Dershowitz, Alan M., *Why Terrorism Works* (New Haven and London: Yale University Press, 2002).

Devlin, Lord, *The Enforcement of Morals* (Oxford: Oxford University Press, 1959).

Dostoyevsky, Feodor, *The Brothers Karamazov*, trans. David Magarshack (London: Penguin Books, 1982).

Dover, Kenneth, *The Greeks* (Oxford: Oxford University Press, 1982).

Draper, Theodore, 'Nuclear Temptations', *New York Review of Books*, 30/21–2 (Jan. 1984).

Dunne, Tim, and Wheeler, Nicholas J. (eds.), *Human Rights in Global Politics* (Cambridge: Cambridge University Press, 1999).

Elshtain, Jean Bethke, *Just War against Terror* (New York: Basic Books, 2005).

Elshtain, Jean Bethke, 'Reflection on the Problem of "Dirty Hands"', in Sanford Levinson (ed.), *Torture: A Collection* (Oxford: Oxford University Press, 2004).

Faulkner, Robert, *The Case for Greatness* (New Haven and London: Yale University Press, 2007).

Finer, S. E., *The Man on Horseback: The Role of the Military in Politics* (1962; London: Pinter Publishers, 1988).

Finnis, John, *Fundamentals of Ethics* (Oxford: Clarendon Press, 1983).

Fisher, David, 'Terror and Pre-emption: Can Military Pre-emption ever be Just?', in David Fisher and Brian Wicker (eds.), *Just War on Terror? A Christian and Muslim Response* (Aldershot: Ashgate, 2010), 79–91.

Fisher, David, 'Humanitarian Intervention', in Charles Reed and David Ryall (eds.), *The Price of Peace: Just War in the Twenty-First Century* (Cambridge: Cambridge University Press, 2007), 111–17.

Fisher, David, 'Can Deterrence Be Just in the Twenty-First Century?', in Brian Wicker and Hugh Beach (eds.), *Britain's Bomb: What Next?* (London: SCM Press, 2006), 45–56.

Fisher, David, 'Some Corner of a Foreign Field' and 'The Ethics of Intervention and Former Yugoslavia', in Roger Williamson (ed.), *Some Corner of a Foreign Field: Intervention and World Order* (Basingstoke: Macmillan; New York: St Martin's Press, 1998), 28–38, 166–74.

Fisher, David, 'The Ethics of Intervention', *Survival: The IISS Quarterly*, 36/1 (Spring 1994), 51–60.

Fisher, David, *Morality and the Bomb* (London: Croom Helm; New York: St Martin's Press, 1985).

Fisher, David, 'Why should I Be Just?' *Proceedings of the Aristotelian Society*, 77 (1976), 43–61.

Fisher, David, and Wicker, Brian (eds.), *Just War on Terror? A Christian and Muslim Response* (Aldershot: Ashgate, 2010).

Foot, Philippa, *Natural Goodness* (Oxford: Clarendon Press, 2001).

Foot, Philippa, *Virtues and Vices* (Oxford: Basil Blackwell, 1978).

Foot, Philippa, 'Morality as a System of Hypothetical Imperatives', *Philosophical Review*, 81/3 (1952), repr. in Foot, *Virtues and Vices* (Oxford: Basil Blackwell, 1978), 157–73.

Ford, John C. F., 'Morality of Obliteration Bombing', *Theological Studies*, 5 (1944); repr. in Richard Wasserstrom, *War and Morality* (Belmont, CA: Wadsworth, 1970).

Freedman, Lawrence, and Karsh, Efraim, *The Gulf Conflict 1990–1991* (London: Faber and Faber, 1993).

French, Shannon E., 'An American Ethicist's Perspective', in Charles Reed and David Ryall (eds.), *The Price of Peace: Just War in the Twenty-First Century* (Cambridge: Cambridge University Press, 2007).

French, Shannon E., *The Code of the Warrior: Exploring Warrior Values Past and Present* (Lanham, MD: Rowman & Littlefield, 2003).

Fukuyama, Francis, *The End of History and the Last Man* (New York: Avon Books, 1992).

Garrett, Stephen A., 'Airpower and Non-Combatant Immunity: The Road to Dresden', in Igor Primoratz (ed.), *Civilian Immunity in War* (Oxford: Oxford University Press, 2007).

Geach, Peter, *The Virtues* (Cambridge: Cambridge University Press, 1977).

Gevers, J. K. M., 'Legal Developments concerning Active Euthanasia on Request in the Netherlands', *Bioethics*, 1 (1987), 156–62.

Glover, Jonathan, *Causing Death and Saving Lives* (London: Allen Lane, 1977).

Goldstone Report, *Report of the United Nations Fact-Finding Mission on the Gaza Conflict,* report by Justice Richard Goldstone, 29 Sept. 2009, www2.ohchr.org/english/bodies/hrcouncil/docs/1.

The Governance of Britain: Constitutional Renewal, Cm. 7342-1, presented to Parliament 25 Mar. 2008 (Norwich: HMSO, 2008).

Grotius, Hugo, *On the Law of War and Peace*, in Gregory Reichberg, Henrik Syse, and Endre Begby (eds.), *The Ethics of War: Classic and Contemporary Readings* (Oxford: Basil Blackwell, 2006).

Grotius, Hugo, *De jure et pacis*, trans. F. W.Kelsey, *The Classics of International Law*, no. 3, vol. 2 (Oxford: Clarendon Press, 1925).

Guthrie, Charles, and Quinlan, Michael, *Just War* (London: Bloomsbury, 2007).

Hackett, Sir John Winthrop, 'Society and the Soldier: 1914–18', in Malham M. Wakin (ed.), *War, Morality, and the Military Profession* (Boulder, CO: Westview Press, 1979).

Haleem, Harfiyah Abdel, Ramsbotham, Oliver, Risaluddin, Saba, and Wicker, Brian (eds.), *The Crescent and the Cross: Muslim and Christian Approaches to War and Peace* (Houndmills and London: Macmillan, 1998).

Hamilton, Nigel, *Monty: Master of the Battlefield 1942–1944* (London: Hamish Hamilton, 1983).

Hampshire, Stuart, 'Public and Private Morality', in Hampshire (ed.), *Public and Private Morality* (Cambridge: Cambridge University Press, 1978).

Hampshire, Stuart (ed.), *Public and Private Morality* (Cambridge: Cambridge University Press, 1978).

Hare, R. M., *The Language of Morals* (Oxford: Oxford University Press, 1952).

Harman, Gilbert, 'Moral Relativism', in Gilbert Harman and Judith Jarvis Thomson, *Moral Relativism and Moral Objectivity* (Oxford: Blackwell, 1996).

Harman, Gilbert, and Thomson, Judith Jarvis, *Moral Relativism and Moral Objectivity* (Oxford: Blackwell, 1996).

Hart, B. H., *Sherman: Soldier, Realist, American* (New York: Da Capo Press, 1993).

Hart, H. L. A., *Punishment and Responsibility* (Oxford: Oxford University Press, 1968).

Hart, H. L. A., *Law, Liberty and Morality* (London: Oxford University Press, 1963).

Hart, H. L. A., *The Morality of the Criminal Law* (London: Oxford University Press, 1963).

Hobbes, Thomas, *Leviathan* (1651; London: Dent, Everyman Library, 1953).

Howard, Michael, 'Philip Bobbitt's *Terror and Consent*: A Brief Critique', in David Fisher and Brian Wicker (eds.), *Just War on Terror? A Christian and Muslim Response* (Aldershot: Ashgate, 2010), 55–63.

Howard, Michael, 'Are we at War?', *Survival*, 50/4 (Aug.–Sept. 2008), 247–56.

Howard, Michael, *War and the Liberal Conscience* (1978; London: Hurst & Co., 2008).

Human Rights Watch, 'Civilian Deaths in the NATO Air Campaign: The Crisis in Kosovo', report (2000), www.hrw.org/reports/2000/nato/Natbm20001.htm.

Human Rights Watch, 'Rain of Fire: Israel's Unlawful Use of White Phosphorus in Gaza', report, 25 Mar. 2009, www.hrw.org/en/report/2009/03/25rain-fire.

Hume, David, *A Treatise of Human Nature*, ed. L. A. Selby Biggs and P. H. Nidditch (Oxford: Oxford University Press, 1978).

Huntington, Samuel P., *The Soldier and the State* (Cambridge, MA, and London: Harvard University Press, 1957; repr. 2000).

Hursthouse, Rosalind, *On Virtue Ethics* (Oxford: Oxford University Press, 1999).

Hursthouse, Rosalind, Lawrance, Gavin, and Quinn, Warren (eds.), *Virtues and Reasons: Essays in Honour of Philippa Foot* (Oxford: Clarendon Press, 1995).

International Commission on Intervention and State Sovereignty, *The Responsibility to Protect* (Ottawa: International Development Research Centre, Dec. 2001).

IISS (International Institute of Strategic Studies), 'Iraq's Weapons of Mass Destruction: A Net Assessment', strategic dossier, 9 Sept. 2002.

Iraq Survey Group Final Report, 30 Sept. 2004, www.globalsecurity.org/wmd/library/report/2004/isg-final-report.

James, William, *The Principles of Psychology* (London: Dover Publications, 1950; repr. from the original 1890 publication by Henry Holt & Co.).

Jenkins, Brian M., 'Combating Global War on Terrorism', in Peter Katona, Michael B. Intriligator, and John P. Sullivan (eds.), *Countering Terrorism and WMD: Creating a Global Counter-Terrorist Network* (Abingdon and New York: Routledge, 2006).

Johnson, James Turner, *Just War Tradition and the Restraint of War* (Princeton: Princeton University Press, 1981).

Johnson, James Turner, *Ideology, Reason and the Limitation of War* (Princeton: Princeton University Press, 1975).

Jones, David Martin, and Smith, M. L. R., 'Language and Atrocity in Cool Britannia', *International Affairs*, 82/6 (Nov. 2006), 1077–1100.

Kaldor, Mary, *New and Old Wars: Organised Violence in a Global Era* (1999; repr. with a new afterword, Cambridge: Polity Press, 2001).

Kant, I., *Perpetual Peace: A Philosophical Sketch*, in *Kant's Political Writings*, ed. Hans Reiss (Cambridge: Cambridge University Press, 1970).

Katona, Peter, Intriligator, Michael B., and Sullivan John P. (eds.), *Countering Terrorism and WMD: Creating a Global Counter-Terrorist Network* (Abingdon and New York: Routledge, 2006).

Keegan, John, *The Iraq War* (London: Pimlico, 2005).

Keegan, John, *War and our World: The Reith Lectures 1998* (London: Pimlico, 1999).

Kelsey, John, 'Arguments concerning Resistance in Contemporary Islam', in Richard Sorabji and David Rodin (eds.), *The Ethics of War: Shared Problems in Different Traditions* (Aldershot: Ashgate, 2006).

Kennan, George, *American Diplomacy 1900–1950* (London: Secker & Warburg, 1952).

Kenny, Anthony, 'Philippa Foot on Double Effect', in Rosalind Hursthouse, Gavin Lawrance, and Warren Quinn (eds.), *Virtues and Reasons: Essays in Honour of Philippa Foot* (Oxford: Clarendon Press, 1995).

Kenny, Anthony, *The Logic of Deterrence* (London: Firethorn Press, 1985).

Kershaw, Ian, *Fateful Choices: Ten Decisions that Changed the World, 1940–41* (London: Allen Lane, 2007).

Khan, Kamran, and Moore, Molly, 'Nuclear Experts Briefed Bin Laden, Pakistanis Say', *Washington Post*, 12 Dec. 2001.

Lawrence, Bruce (ed.), *Messages to the World: The Statements of Osama bin Laden* (New York: Verso, 2005).

Layard, Richard, an interview with Stuart Jeffries, 'Will this Man Make you Happy?', *Guardian*, G2, 24 June 2008.

Layard, Richard, *Happiness: Lessons from a New Science* (London: Allen Lane, Penguin Books, 2005).

Levinson, Sanford (ed.), *Torture: A Collection* (Oxford: Oxford University Press, 2004).

Lewin, Ronald, *Rommel as Military Commander* (London: B. T. Batsford, 1968).

Lewis, C. S., *Voyage to Venus* (London: Pan Books, 1953).

Maas, Peter, 'A Bulletproof Mind', *New York Times Magazine*, 10 Nov. 2002.

McCabe, Herbert, *The Good Life* (London: Continuum, 2005).

Machiavelli, Niccoló, *The Prince*, trans. George Bull (London: Penguin Books, 2003).

MacIntyre, Alasdair, *Dependent Rational Animals* (Chicago and La Salle, IL: Open Court, 1999).

MacIntyre, Alasdair, *Three Rival Versions of Moral Enquiry* (London: Duckworth, 1990).

MacIntyre, Alasdair, *Whose Justice? Which Rationality?* (London: Duckworth, 1988).

MacIntyre, Alasdair, *After Virtue: A Study in Moral Theory* (London: Duckworth, 1985).

McMahan, Jeff, 'Preventive War and the Killing of the Innocent', in Richard Sorabji and David Rodin (eds.), *The Ethics of War: Shared Problems in Different Traditions* (Aldershot: Ashgate, 2006).

McMahan, Jeff, 'Just Cause for War', *Ethics and International Affairs*, 19/3 (2005), 1–21.

McMahan, Jeff, 'War as Self-Defence', *Ethics and International Affairs*, 18/1 (2004), 75–80.

Mahan, A. T., 'The Military Rule of Obedience', *Retrospect and Prospect* (London: Sampson Low, Marston, 1902).

Mann, Thomas, *Nietzsche's Philosophy in the Light of Recent Events* (Washington: Library of Congress, 1947).

Mearsheimer, John J., *The Tragedy of Great Power Politics* (New York: W. W. Norton, 2001).

Meyer, Christopher, *Getting our Way: 500 Years of Adventure and Intrigue: The Inside Story of British Diplomacy* (London: Weidenfeld & Nicolson, 2009).

Midgely, Mary, 'Towards an Ethic of Global Responsibility', in Tim Dunne and Nicholas J. Wheeler (eds.), *Human Rights in Global Politics* (Cambridge: Cambridge University Press, 1999).

Mill, J. S., *On Liberty* (1859), in Stefan Collini (ed.), *J. S. Mill, On Liberty and Other Writings* (Cambridge: Cambridge University Press, 2000), ch. 3.

Mill, J. S., *Utilitarianism* (1863), in Alan Ryan (ed.), *John Stuart Mill and Jeremy Bentham: Utilitarianism and Other Essays* (London: Penguin Books, 1987).

Modernising Defence Training: Report of the Defence Training Review (London: UK Ministry of Defence, 2001).

Moore, G. E., *Principia Ethica* (Cambridge: Cambridge University Press, 1903; repr. 1971).

Morgenthau, Hans J., *Politics among Nations* (New York: Alfred A Knopf, 1973).

Morgenthau, Hans J., *Scientific Man* (Chicago: Chicago University Press, 1946).

Murnion, Philip J. (ed.), *Catholics and Nuclear War* (London: Geoffrey Chapman, 1983).

Nagel, Thomas, 'Ruthlessness in Public Life', in Stuart Hampshire (ed.), *Public and Private Morality* (Cambridge: Cambridge University Press, 1978).

Nagl, John A., *Learning to Eat Soup with a Knife: Counterinsurgency Lessons from Malaya and Vietnam* (Chicago: University of Chicago Press, 2005).

National Conference of US Catholic Bishops, 'The Harvest of Justice is Sown in Peace', Pastoral Letter, 17 Nov. 1993, www.usccb.org/sdwp/harvest.shtml.

National Conference of US Catholic Bishops, 'The Challenge of Peace: God's Promise and our Response', Pastoral Letter on War and Peace, 3 May 1983, in Philip J. Murnion (ed.), *Catholics and Nuclear War* (London: Geoffrey Chapman, 1983).

Nussbaum, Martha C., *Frontiers of Justice* (Cambridge, MA, and London: Harvard University Press, 2007).

Nussbaum, Martha C., 'Aristotle, Nature and Ethics', in J. E. J. Altham and R. Harrison (eds.), *World, Mind and Ethics* (Cambridge: Cambridge University Press, 1995).

Nussbaum, Martha C., 'Non-Relative Virtues: An Aristotelian Approach', in Martha Nussbaum and Amartya Sen (eds.), *The Quality of Life* (Oxford: Clarendon Press, 1993).

Obama, Barack, *National Security Strategy*, May 2010, www.whitehouse.gov/sites/default/files/rss_viewer/national_security_strategy.pdf.

O'Donovan, Oliver, *The Just War Revisited* (Cambridge: Cambridge University Press, 2003).

Orend, Brian, *The Morality of War* (Toronto: Broadview Press, 2006).

Osiel, Mark, *Obeying Orders: Atrocity, Military Discipline and the Law of War* (New Brunswick: Transaction Publishers, 1999).

Parekh, B. (ed.), *Jeremy Bentham: Ten Critical Essays* (London: Frank Cass, 1974).

Parker Report, *Report of the Committee of Privy Counsellors Appointed to Consider Authorised Procedures for the Interrogation of Persons Suspected of Terrorism*, Chairman: Lord Parker of Waddington, Cmnd. 4901 (London: HMSO, Mar. 1972).

Paskins, Barrie, 'Realism and the Just War,' *Journal of Military Ethics*, 6/2 (2007), 117–30.

Paskins, Barrie, and Dockrill, Michael, *The Ethics of War* (London: Duckworth, 1977).

Petraeus, General David H., Commander, Multi-National Force–Iraq, 'Report to Congress on the Situation in Iraq, 8–9 April 2008'.

Petraeus, General David H., 'Foreword', in *US Army and Marine Corps Counterinsurgency Field Manual* (2006; repr. Chicago: Chicago University Press, 2007).

Pisan, Christine de, *The Book of Fayttes of Armes and of Chivalry*, trans. William Caxton, ed. A. T. P. Byles (London: Oxford University Press, 1932).

Plato, *The Republic*, trans. H. P. D. Lee (Harmondsworth: Penguin Books, 1965).

Porter, Jean, 'Basic Goods and the Human Good in Recent Catholic Moral Theology', *Thomist*, 57/1 (Jan. 1993).

Pouncey, Peter R., *The Necessities of War: A Study of Thucydides' Pessimism* (New York: Columbia University Press, 1980).

Power, Samantha, *A Problem from Hell: America and the Age of Genocide* (New York: Basic Books, 2002).

Primoratz, Igor (ed.), *Civilian Immunity in War* (Oxford: Oxford University Press, 2007).

Pritchard, Tim, *Ambush Alley* (New York: Ballantine Books, 2005).

Prosner, Richard A., 'Torture, Terrorism and Interrogation', in Sanford Levinson (ed.), *Torture: A Collection* (Oxford: Oxford University Press, 2004).

Ramsey, Paul, *The Just War: Force and Political Responsibility* (New York: Scribner, 1968).

Ramsey, Paul, *War and the Christian Conscience* (Durham, NC: Duke University Press, 1961).

Rawls, John, *Political Liberalism* (New York: Columbia University Press, 1996).

Rawls, John, *A Theory of Justice* (London, Oxford, and New York: Oxford University Press, 1973).

Reed, Charles, and Ryall, David (eds.), *The Price of Peace: Just War in the Twenty-First Century* (Cambridge: Cambridge University Press, 2007).

Reichberg, Gregory, Syse, Henrik, and Begby, Endre (eds.), *The Ethics of War: Classic and Contemporary Readings* (Oxford: Basil Blackwell, 2006).

Rengger, Nicholas, 'The Just War Tradition in the Twenty-First Century', *International Affairs*, 78/2 (Apr. 2002), 353–63.

Ricks, Thomas E., *The Gamble, General Petraeus and the Untold Story of the American Surge in Iraq, 2006–8* (London and New York: Allen Lane, 2009).

Ricks, Thomas E., *Fiasco: The American Military Adventure in Iraq* (London and New York: Allen Lane, 2006).

Ridley, Matt, *The Origins of Virtue* (Harmondsworth: Penguin Books, 1997).

Robbins, Lionel, *On the Nature and Significance of Economic Science* (London: Macmillan, 1932).

Rodin, David, *War and Self-Defence* (Oxford: Clarendon Press, 2002).

Rodin, David, 'War and Self-Defence', *Ethics and International Affairs*, 18/1 (2004), 63–8.

Rorty, Richard, *Achieving our Country: Leftist Thought in Twentieth-Century America* (Cambridge, MA: Harvard University Press, 1998).

Rorty, Richard, *Contingency, Irony and Solidarity* (Cambridge: Cambridge University Press, 1989).

Ross, Sir W. David, *Foundations of Ethics: Gifford Lectures, 1935/6* (Oxford: Clarendon Press, 1939).

Russell, F. H., *The Just War in the Middle Ages* (Cambridge: Cambridge University Press, 1975).

Saint-Pierre, Abbé de, *Projet pour rendre la paix perpetuelle en Europe*, ed. Simone Goyard-Fabre (Paris: Fayard, 1986).

Sandel, Michael J., *Justice: What's the Right Thing to Do?* (London and New York: Allen Lane, 2009).

Sandel, Michael J., *Reith Lectures 2009: A New Citizenship*, www.bbc.co.uk/radio4/reith.

Sandel, Michael J., *Liberalism and the Limits of Justice* (1982; 2nd edn., New York and Cambridge: Cambridge University Press, 1998).

Sands, Philippe, *Torture Team: Deception, Cruelty and the Compromise of Law* (London: Allen Lane, 2008).

Scruton, Roger, *The West and the Rest* (London and New York: Continuum, 2002).

Sewall, Sarah, 'Introduction', in *US Army and Marine Corps Counterinsurgency Field Manual* (Chicago: University of Chicago Press, 2007).

Shawcross, William, *Deliver Us from Evil* (London: Bloomsbury Publishing, 2000).

Sherman, Nancy, *Stoic Warriors: The Ancient Philosophy behind the Military Mind* (Oxford and New York: Oxford University Press, 2005).

Sherman, William Tecumseh, *Memoirs of General W. T. Sherman* (New York: Literary Classics of the United States, 1990).

Shue, Henry, and Rodin, David (eds.), *Preemption: Military Action and Moral Justification* (Oxford: Oxford University Press, 2007).

Sifry, Micah L., and Cerf, Christopher (eds.), *The Iraq War Reader: History, Documents, Opinions* (New York and London: Simon Schuster International, 2003).

Slim, Hugo, *Killing Civilians* (London: Hurst & Co., 2007).

Smart, J. J. C., and Williams, Bernard, *Utilitarianism for and Against* (Cambridge: Cambridge University Press, 1973).

Smith, General Sir Rupert, *The Utility of Force: The Art of War in the Modern World* (London and New York: Allen Lane, 2005).

Sorabji, Richard, and Rodin, David (eds.), *The Ethics of War: Shared Problems in Different Traditions* (Aldershot: Ashgate, 2006).

Steele, Jonathan, *Defeat: Why They Lost Iraq* (London and New York: I. B. Tauris, 2008).

Stevenson, C. L., *Ethics and Language* (New Haven: Yale University Press, 1945).

Strawson, P. F., 'Freedom and Resentment', in Strawson (ed.), *Studies in the Philosophy of Thought and Action* (Oxford: Oxford University Press, 1968).

Suarez, Francisco, *Disputation XIII: On War*, in Gregory Reichberg, Henrik Syse, and Endre Begby (eds.), *The Ethics of War: Classic and Contemporary Readings* (Oxford: Basil Blackwell, 2006).

Synnott, Hilary, *Bad Days in Basra* (London and New York: I. B. Tauris, 2008).

Thucydides, *The Peloponnesian War*, trans. Rex Warner (Harmondsworth: Penguin Books, 1977).

Thucydides, *Thucydides*, trans. Benjamin Jowett (Oxford: Clarendon Press, 1900).

Trials of War Criminals before the Nuremberg Military Tribunals (Washington: US Government Printing Office, 1950–1), xi.

UN General Assembly 2005, *World Summit Outcome*, 15 Sept. 2005.

UN Secretary General's High Level Panel on Threats, Challenges, and Change, *A More Secure World: Our Shared Responsibility*, report (New York: United Nations, 2004).

US Army and Marine Corps Counterinsurgency Field Manual (2006; Chicago: Chicago University Press, 2007).

Vitoria, Francisco de, *On the American Indians* and *On the Law of War*, in *Vitoria: Political Writings*, ed. Anthony Pagden and Jeremy Lawrance (Cambridge: Cambridge University Press, 1991).

Von Wright, Georg Henrik, *The Varieties of Goodness* (London: Routledge & Kegan Paul, 1963).

Waltz, Kenneth N., *Man, the State and War* (New York: Columbia University Press, 2001).

Waltz, Kenneth N., 'The Origins of War in Neorealist Theory', in Robert I. Rotberg and Theodore K. Rabb (eds.), *The Origin and Prevention of Major Wars* (Cambridge: Cambridge University Press, 1989).

Walzer, Michael, *Arguing about War* (New Haven and London: Yale University Press, 2004).

Walzer, Michael, *Thick and Thin: Moral Arguments at Home and Abroad* (Notre Dame, IN: University of Notre Dame, 1994).

Walzer, Michael, *Spheres of Justice: A Defence of Pluralism and Equality* (Oxford: Basil Blackwell, 1985).

Walzer, Michael, *Just and Unjust Wars: A Moral Argument with Historical Illustrations* (London: Allen Lane, 1978).

Walzer, Michael, 'Political Action: The Problem of Dirty Hands', *Philosophy and Public Affairs* (1973), repr. in Sanford Levinson (ed.), *Torture: A Collection* (Oxford: Oxford University Press, 2004).

Wasserstrom, Richard (ed.), *War and Morality* (Belmont, CA: Wadsworth, 1970).

Wheeler, Nicholas J., *Saving Strangers* (Oxford: Oxford University Press, 2002).

Wiggins, David, *Ethics: Twelve Lectures in Moral Philosophy* (London: Penguin Books, 2006).

Williams, Bernard, 'Replies', in J. E. J. Altham and R. Harrison (eds.), *World, Mind and Ethics* (Cambridge: Cambridge University Press, 1995).

Williams, Bernard, *Ethics and the Limits of Philosophy* (London: Fontana Press, 1985).

Williams, Bernard, 'Politics and Moral Character', in Stuart Hampshire (ed.), *Public and Private Morality* (Cambridge: Cambridge University Press, 1978).

Williams, Bernard, and Smart, J. J. C., *Utilitarianism for and Against* (Cambridge: Cambridge University Press, 1973).

Williamson, Roger, *Just War in the Gulf?* (Uppsala: Life and Peace Institute, 1991).

Wohlforth, William C., 'Realism and the End of the Cold War', *International Security*, 19/3 (1994), 91–129.

Woodward, Bob, *State of Denial* (New York: Simon and Schuster, 2006).

Index